1st PRINT	APRIL 1993	10 000
2nd PRINT	MAY 1993	10 000
3rd PRINT	JULY 1993	10 000
	(BY THE IQRAA CHARITABLE SOCIETY)	
4th PRINT	AUGUST 1993	10 000
	(STATE OF BAHRAIN SUNNI WAQF COUNCIL)	
5th PRINT	SEPTEMBER 1993	30 000
	(FAHIL KHAIR – SAUDI ARABIA)	
	AABF	
6TH PRINT	OCTOBER 1993	10 000
	IPCA – SA – HABIB BANK A/c	

AHMED DEEDAT
49 TREVENNEN ROAD
VERULAM 4340
REPUBLIC OF SOUTH AFRICA

The CHOICE

ISLAM AND CHRISTIANITY

VOLUME ONE

BY AHMED DEEDAT

In the Name of Allah, Most Gracious, Most Merciful

**King Faisal International Award
for Service to Islam**

Certificate of King Faisal International Award for Service to Islam

The Committee of King Faisal International Award, after perusing the Regulations of King Faisal International Award as approved by the Board of Trustees of the King Faisal Charity Foundation by Resolution No. 11-68-98 dated on 10-8-1398 Hijri, and the Minutes of the Selection Committee of King Faisal International Award for Services to Islam, in its ninth session on 30th Rabi'ul Awwal, 1406 Hijri, corresponding to 12th December, 1985, decided hereby to grant:

Ustaz Ahmed Hoosen Deedat

King Faisal International Award for Service to Islam jointly of this year, 1406 Hijri, in appreciation to his continuous and serious efforts exerted in propagating Islam for around thirty five years, on the local, regional, international and global levels, particularly as regards the following:

- **His serious participation in numerous Islamic conferences.**
- **Giving numerous lectures in a number of Islamic countries.**
- **His argumentation against the opponents of Islam, and debating with them in open meetings.**
- **His founding of "As-Salaam" — an institution — for raising up students and propagators, and training them to take up the task of Islamic propagation.**
- **His writing of a number of pamphlets and books published for the cause of the propagation and combating missionary activities, in addition to enlightening the Muslims on the principles of their illustrious belief and the rules of their religion.**

Verily the Committee of the Award, while presenting this to him supplicates Allah to grant him success, and increase the number of men like him.

Allah is the Grantor of Success

**Chairman
of the Award Committee**

**Issued at Riyadh, under No. 33
date 28/6/1406 H
corresponding to 9/3/1986 C.E.**

رئيس هيئة الجائزة

خالد الفيصل بن عبد العزيز

Khalid Al-Faisal bin Abdul Aziz

صدرت في الرياض برقم ٣٣
وتاريخ ١٤٠٦/٦/٢٨ هـ الموافق ١٩٨٦/٣/٩م

TRANSLATED FROM THE ORIGINAL

AHMED DEEDAT

ABOUT THE AUTHOR

Born in the Surat district of India in 1918, Ahmed Hoosen Deedat had no recollection of his father until 1926. His father a tailor by profession had emigrated to South Africa shortly after the birth of Ahmed Deedat.

With no formal education and fighting off the extreme pangs of poverty, he went to South Africa in 1927 to be with his father. His farewell to his mother in India in 1927 was the last time he saw her alive for she passed away a few months later.

In a foreign land, a boy of nine with no formal schooling and command of the English language began preparing for the role he was to play decades later without realizing it.

Applying himself with diligence to his studies, the little boy not only was able to overcome the language barrier but excelled in school. His avid passion for reading helped him gain promotions until he completed standard 6. Lack of finance interrupted his schooling and at the early age of about 16 he took on the first of many jobs in retailing.

The most significant of these was in 1936 where he worked at a Muslim owned store near a Christian seminary on the Natal South Coast. The incessant insults of the trainee missionaries hurled against Islam during their brief visits to the store infused a stubborn flame of desire within the young man to counteract their false propaganda.

As fate would have it, Ahmed Deedat discovered by pure chance a book entitled **Izharul-Haq**, meaning the Truth revealed. This book recorded the techniques and enormous success of the efforts of Muslims in India in turning the tables against Chrisitan missionary harassment during the British subjugation and rule of India. In particular the idea of holding debates had a profound effect on Ahmed Deedat.

Armed with this new found zeal, Ahmed Deedat purchased his first Bible and began holding debates and discussions with the trainee missionaries. When they beat a hasty retreat in the face of his incisive counter arguments, he personally called on their teachers and even priests in the surrounding areas.

These successes spurred Ahmed Deedat in the direction of Da'wah. Not even his marriage, birth of children and a 3 year sojourn to Pakistan after its independence dampened his enthusiasm or dulled his desire to defend Islam from the deceitful distortions of the Christian missionaries.

With missionary zeal to project the Truth and beauty of Islam, Ahmed Deedat immersed himself into a host of activities over the next three decades. He conducted classes on Bible studies and gave numerous lectures. He established the As-Salaam, an institute to train propagators of Islam. He, together with his family, almost single-handedly erected the buildings including the masjid which is still a landmark today.

He was a founder member of the Islamic Propagation Centre International (IPCI) and became its President, a position he still holds today. He has published over 20 books and distributed millions of copies free of charge. He has delivered thousands of lectures all over the world and successfully engaged Christian Evangelists in public debates. Several thousand people have come into the fold of Islam as a result of these efforts.

In a fitting tribute to this monumental achievement, he was awarded the King Faisal International award in 1986, a prestigious recognition of enormous value in the world of Islam.

No number of awards and honours can truly capture the man's essence and zeal for Islam. This anthology of books is no exception. It demonstrates Sheikh Deedat's analytical compilations drawn from personal encounters and experiences against Christian distortions.

May Allah (SWT) bless him for this book, the ones to follow and all his efforts for Islam, Insha-Allah!

EBI LOCKHAT
20 SHAWWAL 1413 / APRIL 13, 1993
DURBAN, SOUTH AFRICA

CONTENTS

PART ONE

What the
BIBLE
says about
MUHUMMED
(Peace be upon Him)

by Ahmed Deedat

CHAPTER ONE

My First Major Encounter

> SAY: "DO YOU SEE? WHETHER THIS MESSAGE BE
> FROM ALLAH (God Almighty), AND YET YOU REJECT IT,
> AND A WITNESS FROM AMONG THE CHILDREN OF
> ISRAEL[1] BORE WITNESS OF ONE LIKE HIM . . . . . ."
>
> *(SÚRA AHQÁF)* Holy Qur'an 46:10

Mr. Chairman, Ladies and Gentlemen,

The subject of this evening's talk[*] — **"What the BIBLE says
about MUHUMMED (Peace be upon him)"** — will no doubt
come as a surprise to many of you because the speaker is a
Muslim. How does it come about that a Muslim happens to be
expounding prophecies from the Jewish and Christian Scriptures?

As a young man, about 30 years ago, I attended a series of
religious lectures by a Christian theologian, a certain Rev. Hiten,
at the "Theatre Royal", Durban.

[*] This is the text of a lecture delivered by the author in the early seventies.

POPE OR KISSINGER?

This Reverend gentleman was expounding Biblical prophecies. He
went on to prove that the Christian Bible foretold the rise of
Soviet Russia, and the Last Days. At one stage he went to the
extent of proving that his Holy Book did not leave the Pope out
of its predictions. He expatiated vigorously in order to convince
his audience that the **"Beast 666"** mentioned in the Book of
Revelation — the last book of the New Testament — was the

---

1. This refers to Moses. See Yusuf Ali's commentaries Nos. 4783/4 to this verse. His
translation with text and commentary available from the I.P.C.I., 124 QUEEN STREET,
DURBAN 4001, R.S.A.

POPE, who was the Vicar of Christ on earth. It is not befitting for us Muslims to enter into this controversy between the Roman Catholics and the Protestants. By the way, the latest Christian exposition of the **"Beast 666"** of the Christian Bible is Dr. Henry Kissinger.[1] Christian scholars are ingenious and indefatigable in their efforts to prove their case.

Rev. Hiten's lectures led me to ask that if the Bible foretold so many things — not even excluding the "Pope" and "Israel", — then surely it must have something to say about the greatest benefactor of mankind[2] — the Holy Prophet Muhummed (may the peace of Allah be with him).

As a youngster I set out to search for an answer. I met priest after priest, attended lectures, and read everything that I could lay my hands relating to the field of Bible prophecies. Tonight I am going to narrate to you one of these interviews with a dominee[3] of the Dutch Reformed Church.

LUCKY THIRTEEN

I was invited to the Transvaal[4] to deliver a talk on the occasion of the Birthday celebration of the Holy Prophet Muhummed. Knowing that in that Province of the Republic of South Africa, the Afrikaans language is widely spoken, even by my own people, I felt that I ought to acquire a smattering of this language so as to feel a little more "at home" with the people. I opened the telephone directory and began phoning the Afrikaans-

---

1. Christian exegetists give progressive numerical values by sixes, to the English alphabet and add up to get the total 666 i.e. A = 6, B = 12, C = 18, D = 24 and so on. Progression by 6's because the number of the Beast in the Bible is "666". Try it for Dr. Kissinger.

2. The writer has just delivered another talk in the City Hall, Durban on the 10th December, 1975 on the subject — **"Muhummed the Greatest"**, booklet on that topic now available **FREE** from the Centre.

3. "Dominee" is the Afrikaans equivalent of priest, parson and predikant.

4. One of the Provinces of the Republic of South Africa.

speaking churches. I indicated my purpose to the priests that I was interested in having a dialogue with them, but they all refused my request with "plausible" excuses. No. 13 was my lucky number. The thirteenth call brought me pleasure and relief. A dominee Van Heerden agreed to meet me at his home on the Saturday afternoon that I was to leave for the Transvaal.

He received me on his verandah with a friendly welcome. He said if I did not mind, he would like his father-in-law from the Free State (a 70-year-old man) to join us in the discussion. I did not mind. The three of us settled down in the dominee's library.

WHY NOTHING?

I posed the question: "What does the Bible say about Muhummed?" Without hesitation he answered, "Nothing!" I asked: "Why nothing? According to your interpretation the Bible have so many things to say about the rise of Soviet Russia and about the Last Days and even about the Pope of the Roman Catholics?" He said, "Yes, but there was nothing about Muhummed!" I asked again, "Why nothing? Surely this man Muhummed who had been responsible for the bringing into being a world-wide community of millions of Believers who, on his authority, believe in —

(1)   the miraculous birth of Jesus,
(2)   that Jesus is the Messiah,[1]
(3)   that he gave life to the dead by God's permission, and that he healed those born blind and the lepers by God's permission.

---

1. The word "Messiah" comes from the Arabic and Hebrew word **masaha** which means to rub, to massage, to anoint. The religious significance is **"the one who is anointed'** — priests and kings were anointed in consecration to their offices. Messiah translated Christ does not mean God. Even **the heathen** Cyrus is called "Christ" in the Bible, (Isaiah 45:1).

Surely this book (the Bible) must have something to say about this great Leader of men who spoke so well of Jesus and his mother Mary?" (Peace be upon them both).

The old man from the Free State replied. "My son,* I have been reading the Bible for the past 50 years, and if there was any mention of him, I would have known it."

* I was much younger and clean shaven then.

NOT ONE BY NAME!

I enquired: "According to you, are there not hundreds of prophecies regarding the coming of Jesus in the Old Testament." The dominee interjected: "Not hundreds, but thousands!" I said, "I am not going to dispute the 'thousand and one' prophecies in the Old Testament regarding the coming of Jesus Christ, because the whole Muslim-world has already accepted him without the testimony of any Biblical prophecy. We Muslims have accepted the **de facto** Jesus on the authority of Muhummed alone, and there are in the world today no less than 900,000,000[1] followers of Muhummed who love, respect and revere this great Messenger of God — **JESUS CHRIST** — without having the Christians to convince them by means of their Biblical dialectics. Out of the 'thousands' of prophecies referred to, can you please give me just **ONE** single prophecy where Jesus is mentioned by name? The term 'Messiah', translated as 'Christ', is not a name but a title. Is there a single prophecy where it says that the name of the Messiah will be **JESUS,** and that his mother's name will be **MARY,** that his supposed father will be **JOSEPH THE CARPENTER;** that he will be born in the reign of **HEROD THE KING,** etc. etc.? No! There are no such details! Then how can you conclude that those 'thousand' prophecies refer to Jesus?"

---

1. This was first written in 1976.

WHAT IS PROPHECY?

The dominee replied: "You see, prophecies are word-pictures of something that is going to happen in the future. When that thing actually comes to pass, we see vividly in these prophecies the fulfilment of what had been predicted in the past." I said: "What you actually do is that you deduce, you reason, you put two and two together." He said: "Yes." I said: **"If this is what you have to do with a 'thousand' prophecies to justify your claim with regards to the genuineness of Jesus, why should we not adopt the very same system for Muhummed?"**[1] The dominee agreed that it was a fair proposition, a reasonable way of dealing with the problem.

I asked him to open up Deuteronomy, chapter 18, verse 18 (the fifth Book of the Christian and Jewish Bibles), which he did. I read from memory the verse in Afrikaans, because this was my purpose in having a little practice with the language of the ruling race in South Africa.[2]

> *'N PROFEET SAL EK VIR HULLE*
> *VERWEK UIT DIE MIDDE VAN HULLE BROERS,*
> *SOOS JY IS,*
> *EN EK SAL MY WOORDE IN SY MOND LÊ,*
> *EN HY SY SAL AAN HULLE SE*
> *ALLES WAT EK HOM BEVEEL.*   *Deut. 18:18.*

The English translation reads as follows:—

> ***I will raise them up a Prophet***
> ***from among their brethren,***

---

1. Muhummed is mentioned by name in the Song of Solomon 5:16. The Hebrew word used there is **Mahammudim.** The end letters **IM** is a plural of respect, majesty and grandeur. Minus **"im"** the name would be **Mahammud** translated as "altogether lovely" in the Authorised Version of the Bible or **'The Praised One'** — 'the one worthy of praise' i.e. **MUHUMMED!** (P.B.U.H.)

2. If this booklet is translated into any language, please change the Afrikaans words into the local dialect; and do not try a free hand translation of the Biblical quotations. Obtain a Bible in the language in which translation is being made and transcribe exactly as the words occur in that Bible.

like unto thee,
and I will put my words in his mouth;
and he shall speak unto them
all that I shall command him.
(HOLY BIBLE)   Deuteronomy 18:18

PROPHET LIKE MOSES

Having recited the verse in Afrikaans, I apologised for my uncertain pronunciation. The dominee assured me that I was doing fine. I enquired: "To whom does this prophecy refer?" Without the slightest hesitation he answered: **"JESUS!"** I asked: **"Why Jesus — his name is not mentioned here?"** The dominee replied: "Since prophecies are word-pictures of something that is going to happen in the future, we find that the wordings of this verse adequately describe him. You see the most important words of this prophecy are 'SOOS JY IS' **(like unto thee)**, — LIKE YOU — like Moses, and Jesus is like Moses. I questioned: "In which way is Jesus like Moses?" The answer was: "In the first place Moses was a **JEW** and Jesus was also a **JEW**; secondly, Moses was a **PROPHET** and Jesus was also a **PROPHET** — therefore Jesus is like Moses and that is exactly what God had foretold Moses — **"SOOS JY IS"**. "Can you think of any other similarities between Moses and Jesus?" I asked. The dominee said that he could not think of any. I replied: "If these are the only two criteria for discovering a candidate for this prophecy of Deuteronomy 18:18, then in that case this criteria could fit any one of the following Biblical personages after Moses: — Solomon, Isaiah, Ezekiel, Daniel, Hosea, Joel, Malachi, John the Baptist, etc., because they were also **ALL** "Jews" as well as "Prophets." Why should we not apply this prophecy to any one of these prophets, and why only to Jesus? Why should we make fish of one and fowl of another?" The dominee had no reply. I continued: "You see, my conclusions are that Jesus is most unlike Moses, and if I am wrong I would like you to correct me."

THREE UNLIKES

So saying, I reasoned with him:

In the **FIRST** place Jesus is not like Moses, because, according to **YOU** — 'JESUS IS A GOD', but Moses is not God, Is this true?" He said: "Yes." I said: **"Therefore Jesus is not like Moses!**

"SECONDLY, according to **YOU** — 'JESUS DIED FOR THE SINS OF THE WORLD', but Moses did not have to die for the sins of the world. Is this true?" He again said: "Yes." I said: **"Therefore Jesus is not like Moses!"**

"THIRDLY, according to **YOU** —'JESUS WENT TO HELL FOR THREE DAYS', but Moses did not have to go there. Is this true?" He answered meekly: "Y-e-s." I concluded: **"Therefore Jesus is not like Moses!"**

"But dominee," I continued: "these are not hard facts, solid facts, tangible facts; they are mere matters of belief over which the little ones can stumble and fall. Let us discuss something very simple, very easy that if your little ones are called in to hear the discussion, they would have no difficulty in following it, shall we?" The dominee was quiet happy at the suggestion.

CHAPTER TWO

Eight Irrefutable Arguments

FATHER AND MOTHER

(1) "Moses had a father and a mother. Muhummed also had a father and a mother. But Jesus had only a mother, and no human father. Is this true?" He said: "Yes." I said: DAAROM IS JESUS NIE SOOS MOSES NIE, MAAR MUHUMMED IS SOOS MOSES!" Meaning: **"THEREFORE JESUS IS NOT LIKE MOSES, BUT MUHUMMED IS LIKE MOSES!"** (By now the reader will realise that I was using the Afrikaans language only for practice purposes. I shall discontinue its use in this narration).

MIRACULOUS BIRTH

(2) "Moses and Muhummed were born in the normal, natural course, i.e. the physical association of man and woman; but Jesus was created by a special miracle. You will recall that we are told in the Gospel of St. Matthew 1:18 *"... **BEFORE THEY CAME TOGETHER,** (Joseph the Carpenter and Mary) **SHE WAS FOUND WITH CHILD BY THE HOLY GHOST.**"* And St. Luke tells us that when the good news of the birth of a holy son was announced to her, Mary reasoned: *"... HOW SHALL THIS BE, SEEING I KNOW NOT A MAN? AND THE ANGEL ANSWERED AND SAID UNTO HER, THE HOLY GHOST SHALL COME UPON THEE, AND THE POWER OF THE HIGHEST SHALL OVERSHADOW THEE ..."* (Luke 1:35). The Holy Qur'an confirms the miraculous birth of Jesus, in nobler and sublimer terms. In answer to her logical question: **'O my Lord! How shall I have a son when no man hath**

touched me?' the angel says in reply: **'Even so: Allah createth what He willeth: when he hath decreed a Plan, He but saith to it "BE" and it is!'**[1] (Holy Qur'an 3:47). It is not necessary for God to plant a seed in man or animal. He merely wills it and it comes into being. This is the Muslim conception of the birth of Jesus. (When I compared the Qur'anic and the Biblical versions of the birth of Jesus to Rev. Dunkers the head of the Bible Society in our largest city, and when I enquired: "Which version would you prefer to give your daughter, the **QUR'ANIC** version or the **BIBLICAL** version?" The man bowed his head and answered: "The Qur'anic.") In short, I said to the dominee: "Is it true that Jesus was born miraculously as against the natural birth of Moses and Muhummed?" He replied proudly: "YES!" I said: **"THEREFORE JESUS IS NOT LIKE MOSES, BUT MUHUMMED IS LIKE MOSES.** And God says to Moses in the Book of Deuteronomy 18:18 *"LIKE UNTO THEE"* (Like You, Like Moses) **and Muhummed is like Moses."**

MARRIAGE TIES

(3) "Moses and Muhummed married and begot children, but Jesus remained a bachelor all his life. Is this true?" The dominee said: "Yes." I said: **THEREFORE JESUS IS NOT LIKE MOSES, BUT MUHUMMED IS LIKE MOSES."**

JESUS REJECTED BY HIS PEOPLE

(4) "Moses and Muhummed were accepted as prophets by their people in their very lifetime. No doubt the Jews gave endless

---

1. Please open the Holy Qur'an 3:42 and 19:16 where the birth of Jesus is spoken about; read it with the commentary, and draw the attention of your Christian friends to the high position which Jesus and his mother occupy in Islam.

trouble to Moses and they murmured in the wilderness, but as a nation, as a whole, they acknowledged that Moses was a Messenger of God sent to them. The Arabs too made Muhummed's life impossible. He suffered very badly at their hands. After 13 years of preaching in Mecca, he had to emigrate from the city of his birth. But before his demise, the Arab nation as a whole accepted him as the Messenger of Allah. But according to the Bible — *'HE (Jesus) CAME UNTO HIS OWN, BUT HIS OWN RECEIVED HIM NOT.' (John 1:11).* **And even today, after two thousand years, his people — the Jews, as a whole, have rejected him.** Is this true?" The dominee said: "Yes." I said: **"THEREFORE JESUS IS NOT LIKE MOSES, BUT MUHUMMED IS LIKE MOSES."**

"OTHER-WORLDLY" KINGDOM

(5) "Moses and Muhummed were prophets as well as kings. By prophet I mean a man who receives Divine Revelation for the Guidance of Man and this Guidance he conveys to God's creatures as received without any addition or deletion. A king is a person who has the power of life and death over his people. It is immaterial whether the person wears a crown or not, or whether he was ever addressed as king or monarch: if the man has the prerogative of inflicting capital punishment — **HE IS A KING.** Moses possessed such a power. Do you remember the Israelite who was found picking up firewood on the Sabbath Day, and Moses had him stoned to death? (Numbers 15:36). There are other crimes also mentioned in the Bible for which capital punishment was inflicted on the Jews at the behest of Moses. Muhummed too, had the power of life and death over his people.

There are instances in the Bible of persons who were given gift of **prophecy only,** but they were not in a position to implement their directives. Some of these holy men of God who were helpless in the face of stubborn rejection of their message were the prophets Lot, Jonah, Daniel, Ezra and John the Baptist. They could only deliver the message, but could not enforce the Law. The Holy Prophet Jesus unfortunately also belonged to this category. The Christian Gospel clearly confirms this: when Jesus was dragged before the Roman Governor, Pontius Pilate, charged for sedition, Jesus made a convincing point in his defence to refute the false charge: *JESUS ANSWERED,* **'MY KINGDOM IS NOT OF THIS WORLD':** *IF MY KINGDOM WERE OF THIS WORLD, THEN WOULD MY SERVANTS FIGHT, THAT I SHOULD NOT BE DELIVERED TO THE JEWS; BUT NOW IS MY KINGDOM NOT FROM HENCE" (John 18:36).* This convinced Pilate (A Pagan) that though Jesus might not be in full possession of his mental faculty, he did not strike him as being a danger to his rule. Jesus claimed **a spiritual kingdom only;** in other words he only claimed to be a prophet. Is this true?" The dominee answered: "Yes." I said: **"THEREFORE JESUS IS NOT LIKE MOSES BUT MUHUMMED IS LIKE MOSES."**

NO NEW LAWS

(6) "Moses and Muhummed brought new laws and new regulations for their people. Moses not only gave the Ten Commandments to the Israelites, but a very comprehensive ceremonial law for the guidance of his people. Muhummed comes to a people steeped in barbarism and ignorance. They married their stepmothers; they buried their daughters alive; drunkenness, adultery, idolatry and gambling where the order of the day. Gibbon describes the Arabs before Islam in his **"Decline and Fall of the Roman Empire",** 'THE HUMAN BRUTE, ALMOST WITHOUT SENSE, IS POORLY DISTINGUISHED FROM THE REST OF THE ANIMAL

CREATION.' There was hardly anything to distinguish between the "man" and the "animal" of the time; they were animals in human form.

From this abject barbarism, Muhummed elevated them, in the words of Thomas Carlysle, **'into torch-bearers of light and learning.'** **'TO THE ARAB NATION IT WAS AS A BIRTH FROM DARKNESS INTO LIGHT. ARABIA FIRST BECAME ALIVE BY MEANS OF IT. A POOR SHEP-HERD PEOPLE, ROAMING UNNOTICED IN ITS DE-SERTS SINCE THE CREATION OF THE WORLD. SEE, THE UNNOTICED BECOMES WORLD NOTABLE, THE SMALL HAS GROWN WORLD-GREAT. WITHIN ONE CENTURY AFTERWARDS ARABIA WAS AT GRANADA ON ONE HAND AND AT DELHI ON THE OTHER. GLANCING IN VALOUR AND SPLENDOUR, AND THE LIGHT OF GENIUS, ARABIA SHINES OVER A GREAT SECTION OF THE WORLD ...'** The fact is that Muhummed gave his people a Law and Order they never had before.

As regards Jesus, when the Jews felt suspicious of him that he might be an imposter with designs to pervert their teachings, Jesus took pains to assure them that he had not come with a new religion — **no new laws and no new regulations.** I quote his own words: *'THINK NOT THAT I AM COME TO DESTROY THE LAW, OR THE PROPHETS: I AM NOT COME TO DESTROY, BUT TO FULFIL. FOR VERILY I SAY UNTO YOU, TILL HEAVEN AND EARTH PASS, ONE JOT OR ONE TITTLE SHALL IN NO WISE PASS FROM THE LAW, TILL ALL BE FULFILLED.' (Matthew 5:17-18).*

In other words he had not come with any new laws or regulations; he came only to fulfil the old law. This is what he gave the Jews to understand — unless he was speaking with the tongue in his cheek trying to bluff the Jews into accepting him as a man of God and by subterfuge trying to ram a new religion down their throats. No! This Messenger of God would never resort to such foul means to subvert the Religion of God. He himself fulfilled the laws. He observed the commandments of Moses, and he respected the Sabbath. At no time did a single Jew point a finger at him to say, **'why don't you fast'** or **'why don't you wash your hands before you break bread'**, which charges they always levied against his disciples, but never against Jesus. This is because as a good Jew he honoured the laws of the prophets who preceded him. In short, he had created no new religion and had brought no new law like Moses and Muhummed. Is this true?" I asked the dominee, and he answered: "Yes." I said: **"THEREFORE JESUS IS NOT LIKE MOSES BUT MUHUMMED IS LIKE MOSES."**

HOW THEY DEPARTED

(7) "Both Moses and Muhummed died natural deaths, but according to Christianity, Jesus was violently killed on the cross.[1] Is this true?" The dominee said: "Yes." I averred: **"THEREFORE JESUS IS NOT LIKE MOSES BUT MUHUMMED IS LIKE MOSES."**

HEAVENLY ABODE

(8) "Moses and Muhummed both lie buried in earth, but according to you, Jesus rests in heaven. Is this true? The dominee agreed. I said: **"THEREFORE JESUS IS NOT LIKE MOSES BUT MUHUMMED IS LIKE MOSES."**

---

1. For full exposition of this topic see Vol. II under **"CRUCIFIXION OR CRUCI-FICTION?**

CHAPTER THREE

Further Proofs

ISHMAEL THE FIRST BORN

Since the dominee was helplessly agreeing with every point, I said, "Dominee, so far what I have done is to prove only one point out of the whole prophecy — that is proving the phrase **'LIKE UNTO THEE'** — 'like you' — 'like Moses.' The prophecy is much more than this single phrase which reads as follows: *"I WILL RAISE THEM UP A PROPHET **FROM AMONG THEIR BRETHREN** LIKE UNTO THEE ..."* The emphasis is on the words — **"From among their brethren.'** Moses and his people, the Jews, are here addressed as a racial entity, and as such their **'brethren'** undoubtedly be the Arabs. You see, the Holy Bible speaks of Abraham as the "Friend of God". Abraham had two wives — Sarah and Hagar. Hagar bore Abraham a son — HIS FIRST-BORN — **'... And Abram[1] called HIS SON'S name, which Hagar bare, Ishmael.'** *(Genesis 16:15).* **'And Abraham took Ishmael HIS SON ..."** *(Genesis 17:23).* **'And Ishmael HIS SON was thirteen years old, when he was circumcised in the flesh of his foreskin.'** *(Genesis 17:25).* Up to the age of THIRTEEN Ishmael was the ONLY **son** and **seed** of Abraham, when the covenant was ratified between God and Abraham. God grants Abraham another son through Sarah, named Isaac, who was very much the junior to his brother Ishmael.

ARABS AND JEWS

If Ishmael and Isaac are the sons of the same father Abraham, then they are brothers. **And so the children of the one are**

---

1. According to the Bible Abraham's name was **Abram** before it was changed by God to **Abraham**.

the **BRETHREN of the children of the other.** The children of
Isaac are the Jews and the children of Ishmael are the Arabs —
so they are **BRETHREN** to one another. The Bible affirms, *'AND
HE (ISHMAEL) SHALL DWELL IN THE PRESENCE OF **ALL HIS
BRETHREN.'** (Genesis 16:12).* *'AND HE (ISHMAEL) DIED IN
THE PRESENCE OF **ALL HIS BRETHREN.'** (Genesis 25:18).*
The children of Isaac are the brethren of the Ishmaelites. In like
manner Muhummed is from among the brethren of the Israelites
because he was a descendant of Ishmael the son of Abraham.
This is exactly as the prophecy has it — *'FROM AMONG THEIR
BRETHREN'. (Deut. 18:18).* There the prophecy distinctly men-
tions that the coming prophet who would be like Moses, must
arise NOT from the **'children of Israel'** or from **'among
themselves',** but from among their brethren. MUHUMMED
THEREFORE WAS FROM AMONG THEIR BRETHREN!

WORDS IN THE MOUTH

The prophecy proceeds further: *'... AND I WILL PUT MY WORDS
INTO HIS MOUTH ...'* What does it mean when it is said **'I will
put my words in your mouth'?** You see, when I asked you
(the dominee) to open Deuteronomy, chapter 18, verse 18, at the
beginning, and if I had asked you to read, and if you had read:
would I be putting my words into your mouth? The dominee
answered: "No." But, I continued: "If I were to teach you a
language like Arabic about which you have no knowledge, and if
I asked you to read or repeat after me what I utter i.e.

$$\text{قُلْ هُوَ اللّٰهُ اَحَدٌ ۞}$$

SAY: HE IS ALLAH THE ONE AND ONLY;

$$\text{اَللّٰهُ الصَّمَدُ ۞}$$

ALLAH, THE ETERNAL ABSOLUTE;

$$\text{لَمْ يَلِدْ ۄ وَلَمْ يُوْلَدْ ۞}$$

HE BEGETTETH NOT, NOR IS HE BEGOTTEN:

$$وَلَمْ يَكُن لَّهُ كُفُوًا اَحَدٌ$$

AND THERE IS NONE LIKE UNTO HIM.

(SÚRA IKHLÁS) Holy Qur'an 112:1-4

Would I not be putting these unheard words of a foreign tongue which you utter, **into** your **mouth?"** The dominee agreed that it was indeed so. In an identical manner, I said, the words of the Holy Qur'an, the Revelation vouchsafed by the Almighty God to Muhummed were revealed.

History tells us that Muhummed was forty years of age. He was in a cave some three miles north of the City of Mecca. It was the 27th night of the Muslim month of Ramadaan. In the cave the Archangel Gabriel commands him in his mother tongue: اِقْرَأْ which means **READ!** or **PROCLAIM!** or **RECITE!** Muhummed is terrified and in his bewilderment replies: مَا اَنَا بِقَارِءٍ which means: **I AM NOT LEARNED!** The angel commands him a second time with the same result. For the third time the angel continues:

$$اِقْرَأْ بِاسْمِ رَبِّكَ الَّذِى خَلَقَ$$

Now, Muhummed, grasps, that what was required of him was to **repeat!** to **rehearse!** And he repeats the words as they were put into his mouth:

$$اِقْرَأْ بِاسْمِ رَبِّكَ الَّذِى خَلَقَ$$

"READ! IN THE NAME OF THY LORD AND CHERISHER, WHO CREATED —

$$خَلَقَ الْاِنْسَانَ مِنْ عَلَقٍ$$

CREATED MAN, FROM A (MERE) CLOT OF CONGEALED BLOOD:

$$اِقْرَأْ وَرَبُّكَ الْاَكْرَمُ$$

READ! AND THY LORD IS MOST BOUNTIFUL, —

الَّذِىْ عَلَّمَ بِالْقَلَمِ ۙ

HE WHO TAUGHT (THE USE OF) THE PEN, —

عَلَّمَ الْاِنْسَانَ مَا لَمْ يَعْلَمْ ۗ

TAUGHT MAN THAT WHICH HE KNEW NOT."

(SÚRA 'ALAQ)   *Holy Qur'an 96:1-5*

These are the first five verses which were revealed to Muhummed which now occupy the beginning of the 96th chapter of the Holy Qur'an.

THE FAITHFUL WITNESS

Immediately the angel had departed, Muhummed rushed to his home. Terrified and sweating all over he asked his beloved wife Khadija to 'cover him up!' He lay down, and she watched by him. When he had regained his composure, he explained to her what he had seen and heard. She assured him of her faith in him and that Allah would not allow such a terrible thing to happen to him. Are these the confessions of an imposter? Would imposters confess that when an angel of the Lord confronts them with a Message from on High, they get fear-stricken, terrified, and sweating all over, run home to their wives? Any critic can see that his reactions and confessions are that of an honest, sincere man, the man of Truth — **'AL-AMIN'** — THE Honest, the Upright, the Truthful.

During the next twenty-three years of his prophetic life, words were **'put into his mouth',** and he uttered them. They made an indelible impression on his heart and mind: and as the volume of the Sacred Scripture (Holy Qur'an) grew, they were recorded on palm-leaf fibre, on skins and on the shoulder-blades of animals; and in the hearts of his devoted disciples. Before his demise these words were arranged in the order in which we find them today in the Holy Qur'an.

The words (revelation) were actually **put into his mouth,** exactly as foretold in the prophecy under discussion: *'AND I WILL PUT MY WORDS IN HIS MOUTH.' (HOLY BIBLE)* Deut. 18:18.

UNLETTERED PROPHET

Muhummed's experience in the cave of Hira, later to be known as Jabal-un-Noor — **The Mountain of Light,** and his response to that first Revelation is the exact fulfilment of another Biblical prophecy. In the Book of Isaiah, chapter 29, verse 12, we read: *"AND THE BOOK"* (**al-Kitaab, al-Qur'an** — the 'Reading', the 'Recitation') *"IS DELIVERED TO HIM THAT IS NOT LEARNED,"* النَّبِيِّ الأُمِّيِّ the unlettered Prophet, Holy Qur'an 7:158) *"SAYING, READ THIS, I PRAY THEE:"* (the words **'I pray thee",** are not in the Hebrew manuscripts, compare with the Roman Catholics' "Douay Version" and also with the "Revised Standard Versions") *"AND HE SAITH, I AM NOT LEARNED."* (**"I am not learned."** is the exact translation of the words مَا أَنَا بِقَارِءٍ which words Muhummed uttered twice to the Holy Ghost — the **Archangel Gabriel,** when he was commanded إِقْرَأ "READ!").

Let me quote the verse in full without a break as found in the "King James Version," or the "Authorised Version" as it is more popularly known: *"AND THE BOOK IS DELIVERED TO HIM THAT IS NOT LEARNED, SAYING, READ THIS, I PRAY THEE: AND HE SAITH, I AM NOT LEARNED." (HOLY BIBLE)* Isaiah 29:12.

It may be noted that there were no Arabic Bibles[1] in existence in the 6th Century of the Christian Era when Muhummed lived and preached! Besides, he was absolutely unlettered and unlearned. No human had ever taught him a word. His teacher was his Creator —

---

1. There are today Arabic Bibles in fifteen different scripts and dialects for the Arabs alone. See **"The Gospels in many tongues",** a reproduction, in Book 1 of Vol. II under the heading **"A MUSLIM DICTIONARY OF THE BIBLE."** Alternative title — **"COMBAT KIT" AGAINST BIBLE THUMPERS.**

$$\text{وَمَا يَنْطِقُ عَنِ الْهَوَىٰ}$$

"HE DOES NOT SPEAK (AUGHT), OF (HIS OWN) DESIRE

$$\text{إِنْ هُوَ إِلَّا وَحْيٌ يُوحَىٰ}$$

IT IS NO LESS THAN INSPIRATION SENT DOWN TO HIM:

$$\text{عَلَّمَهُ شَدِيدُ الْقُوَىٰ}$$

HE WAS TAUGHT BY ONE MIGHTY IN POWER,"

(SÚRA NAJM) Holy Qur'an 53:3-5

Without any human learning, **'he put to shame the wisdom of the learned'."**

GRAVE WARNING

"See!" I told the dominee, "how the prophecies fit Muhummed like a glove. We do not have to stretch prophecies to justify their fulfilment in Muhummed."

The dominee replied, "All your expositions sound very well, but they are of no real consequence, because we Christians have Jesus Christ the "incarnate" God, who has redeemed us from the Bondage of Sin!"

I asked, "Not important?" God didn't think so! He went to a great deal of trouble to have His warnings recorded. God knew that there would be people like you who will flippantly, light-heartedly discount his words, so he followed up Deuteronomy 18:18 with a dire warning: the very next verse, *"AND IT SHALL COME TO PASS,"* (it is going to happen) *"THAT WHOSO-EVER WILL NOT HEARKEN UNTO **MY WORDS** WHICH HE SHALL SPEAK **IN MY NAME**, I WILL REQUIRE IT OF HIM."* (in the Catholic Bible the ending words are — **"I will be the revenger"**, — I will take vengeance from him — I will take revenge!) "Does not this terrify you? **God Almighty is threatening revenge!** We shake in our pants if some hoodlums threaten us, yet you have no fear of God's warning?"

"Miracle of miracles! in the verse 19 of Deuteronomy chapter 18, we have a further fulfilment of the prophecy in Muhummed! Note the words — '... **MY WORDS** WHICH HE SHALL SPEAK **IN MY NAME**," In whose name is Muhummed speaking?" I opened the Holy Qur'an — Allama Yusuf Ali's translation, at chapter 114 — **'Súra Nás'**, or 'Mankind' — the last chapter, and showed him the formula at the head of the chapter:

بِسْمِ اللهِ الرَّحْمٰنِ الرَّحِيْمِ

and the meaning: "IN THE NAME OF GOD, MOST GRACIOUS, MOST MERCIFUL." And the heading of chapter 113:

بِسْمِ اللهِ الرَّحْمٰنِ الرَّحِيْمِ

and the meaning: "IN THE NAME OF GOD, MOST GRACIOUS, MOST MERCIFUL". And every chapter downwards 112, 111, 110 ... was the same formula and the same meaning on every page, because the end **SÚRAS** (chapters) are short and take about a page each.

"And what did the prophecy demand? '... WHICH HE SHALL SPEAK **IN MY NAME**,' and in whose name does Muhummed speak? **'IN THE NAME OF GOD,** MOST GRACIOUS, MOST MERCIFUL.' The Prophecy is being fulfilled in Muhummed to the letter!

"Every chapter of the Holy Qur'an except the 9th begin with the formula بِسْمِ اللهِ الرَّحْمٰنِ الرَّحِيْمِ IN THE NAME OF GOD, MOST GRACIOUS, MOST MERCIFUL.' The Muslim begins his every lawful act with the Holy formula. But the Christian begins: **"In the name of the Father, son and holy ghost."**"[1]

Concerning Deuteronomy chapter eighteen, I have given you more than 15 reasons as to how this prophecy refers to Muhummed and **NOT** to Jesus.

---

1. The Christian theologians are ignorant of even the "name of God. Because **"God"** is not a name, and **"Father"** is also not a name. Write for **"WHAT'S HIS NAME?"** from the I.P.C.I.

CHAPTER FOUR

New Testament Also Confirms

BAPTIST CONTRADICTS JESUS

In New Testament times, we find that the Jews were still expecting the fulfilment of the prophecy of 'ONE LIKE MOSES'; refer John 1:19-25. When Jesus claimed to be the Messiah of the Jews, the Jews began to enquire as to where was Elias? The Jews had a parallel prophecy that before the coming of the Messiah, Elias must come first in his second coming. Jesus confirms this Jewish belief:

*"... ELIAS TRULY SHALL FIRST COME, AND RESTORE ALL THINGS. BUT I SAY UNTO YOU, THAT ELIAS IS COME ALREADY, AND THEY KNEW HIM NOT, ... THEN THE DIS- CIPLES UNDERSTOOD THAT **HE SPAKE UNTO THEM OF JOHN THE BAPTIST."** (HOLY BIBLE)* Matthew 17:11-13.

According to the New Testament the Jews were not the ones to swallow the words of any would-be Messiah. In their investigations they underwent intense difficulties in order to find their true Messiah. And this the Gospel of John confirms: *"AND THIS IS THE RECORD OF JOHN,"* (the Baptist) *"WHEN THE JEWS SENT PRIESTS AND LEVITES FROM JERUSALEM TO ASK HIM, WHO ART THOU? AND HE CONFESSED AND DENIED NOT; BUT CONFESSED, I AM NOT THE CHRIST."* (This was only natural because there can't be two Messiahs[1] at the same time. If Jesus was the Christ then John couldn't be the Christ!)" *"AND THEY ASKED HIM, WHAT THEN? ART THOU ELIAS? AND HE SAITH, I AM NOT."* (Here **John the Baptist** contradicts Jesus! Jesus says that John is "Elias" and John denies that he is what Jesus ascribes him to be. One of the **TWO** (Jesus or John), God

---

1. The Jews were expecting a single Messiah not two.

forbid! is definitely not speaking the **TRUTH!** On the testimony of Jesus himself, **John the Baptist** was the greatest of the Israelite prophets: *"VERILY I SAY UNTO YOU, AMONG THEM THAT ARE BORN OF WOMEN THERE HAS NOT RISEN A GREATER THAN JOHN THE BAPTIST: ... "* **(HOLY BIBLE)** Matthew 11:11.

We Muslims know John the Baptist as Hazrut **YAHYAA** Alai-his-salaam (peace be upon him). We revere him as a true prophet of Allah. The Holy Prophet Jesus known to us as Hazrut **ISAA** Alai-his-salaam (peace be upon him), is also esteemed as one of the mightiest messengers of the Almighty. How can we Muslims impute lies to either of them? We leave this problem between Jesus and John for the Christians to solve, for their "sacred scriptures" abound in discrepancies which they have been glossing over as the **"dark sayings of Jesus"**.[1] We Muslims are really interested in the last question posed to **John the Baptist** by the Jewish elite — *"ART THOU **THAT PROPHET?** AND HE ANSWERED, NO."* **(HOLY BIBLE)** John 1:21.

THREE QUESTIONS!

Please note that three different and distinct questions were posed to **John the Baptist** and to which he gave three emphatic **"NO's"** as answers. To recapitulate:—

(1) Art thou the Christ?
(2) Art thou Elias?
(3) Art thou that prophet?

But the learned men of Christendom somehow only see two questions implied here. To make doubly clear that the Jews definitely had T-H-R-E-E separate prophecies in their minds when they were interrogating **John the Baptist,** let us read the remonstrance of the Jews in the verses following —

---

1. See the **"TIMES"** Magazine December 30th, 1974, article **"How true is the Bible?"** And write for your free copy of "50,000 Errors in the Bible?" — a reproduction from the Christian Magazine **"AWAKE!"** September 8, 1957.

"AND THEY ASKED HIM, AND SAID UNTO HIM, WHY BAPTI-ZEST THOU THEN, IF THOU BE

(a) *NOT THAT CHRIST,*
(b) *NOR ELIAS,*
(c) *NEITHER THAT PROPHET?"*

(HOLY BIBLE) John 1:25

The Jews were waiting for the fulfilment of **THREE** distinct prophecies: **One,** the coming of CHRIST. **Two,** the coming of ELIAS, and **Three,** the coming of THAT PROPHET.

"THAT PROPHET"

If we look up any Bible which has a concordance or cross-references, then we will find in the marginal note where the words **"the prophet"**, or **"that prophet"** occur in John 1:25, that these words refer to the prophecy of Deuteronomy 18:15 and 18. And that **'that prophet'** — **'the prophet like Moses'** — "LIKE UNTO THEE", we have proved through overwhelming evidence that he was MUHUMMED and **NOT** Jesus!

We Muslims are not denying that Jesus was the "Messiah", which word is translated as "Christ".[1] We are not contesting the "thousand and one prophecies" which the Christians claim abound in the Old Testament foretelling the coming of the Messiah. What we say is that Deuteronomy 18:18 does **NOT** refer to Jesus Christ but it is an explicit prophecy about the Holy Prophet **MUHUMMED!"**

The dominee, very politely parted with me by saying that it was a very interesting discussion and he would like me very much to come one day and address his congregation on the subject. A decade and half has passed since then but I am still awaiting that privilege.

---

1. How the word Messiah was transmuted to Christ? Refer Part 2 following.

I believe the dominee was sincere when he made the offer, but prejudices die hard and who would like to lose his sheep?

THE ACID TEST

To the lambs of Christ I say, why not apply that acid test which the Master himself wanted you to apply to any would be claimant to prophethood? He had said: ***"BY THEIR FRUITS YE SHALL KNOW THEM.** DO MEN GATHER GRAPES FROM THE THORNS, OR FIGS FROM THE THISTLES? EVERY GOOD TREE WILL BEAR GOOD FRUIT AND EVERY EVIL TREE WILL BEAR EVIL FRUIT ... **BY THEIR FRUITS YE SHALL KNOW THEM.***
(HOLY BIBLE) Matthew 7:16-20.

Why are you afraid to apply this test to the teachings of Muhummed? You will find in the **Last** Testament of God — **the Holy Qur'an** — the true fulfilment of the teachings of Moses and Jesus which will bring to the world the much-needed peace and happiness. "IF A MAN LIKE MOHAMED WERE TO ASSUME THE DICTATORSHIP OF THE MODERN WORLD, HE WOULD SUCCEED IN SOLVING ITS PROBLEMS THAT WOULD BRING IT THE MUCH NEEDED PEACE AND HAPPINESS."
(George Bernard Shaw)

THE GREATEST!

The Weekly News magazine "TIME" dated July 15, 1974, carried a selection of opinions by various historians, writers, military men, businessmen and others on the subject: **"Who Were History's Great Leaders?"** Some said that it was Hitler; others said — Gandhi, Buddha, Lincoln and the like. But Jules Masserman, a United States psychoanalyst put the standards straight by giving the correct criteria wherewith to judge. He said:

"LEADERS MUST FULFIL THREE FUNCTIONS:—

(1) Provide for the well-being of the led,
(2) Provide a social organization in which people feel relatively secure, and
(3) Provide them with one set of beliefs."

With the above three criteria he searches history and analyses — Hitler, Pasteur, Caesar, Moses, Confucius and the lot, and ultimately concludes:—

"PEOPLE LIKE PASTEUR AND SALK ARE LEADERS IN THE FIRST SENSE. PEOPLE LIKE GANDHI AND CONFUCIUS, ON ONE HAND, AND ALEXANDER, CAESAR AND HITLER ON THE OTHER, ARE LEADERS IN THE SECOND AND PERHAPS THE THIRD SENSE. JESUS AND BUDDHA BELONG IN THE THIRD CATEGORY ALONE. **PERHAPS THE GREATEST LEADER OF ALL TIMES WAS MOHAMMED, WHO COMBINED ALL THREE FUNCTIONS.** To a lesser degree, **MOSES DID THE SAME.**"

According to the objective standards set by the Professor of the Chicago University, whom I believe to be Jewish, — JESUS and BUDDHA are nowhere in the picture of the **"Great Leaders of Mankind"**, but by a queer coincidence **groups** Moses and Muhummed **together** thus adding further weight to the argument that JESUS is not like MOSES, but MUHUMMED is like MOSES: *Deut. 18:18 "LIKE UNTO THEE"* — *Like Moses!*

Reverend James L. Dow in **Collins Dictionary of the Bible** gives further proof, that JESUS is not like MOSES, but MUHUMMED is like MOSES: "AS A STATESMAN AND LAWGIVER MOSES IS THE CREATOR OF THE JEWISH PEOPLE. HE FOUND A LOOSE CONGLOMERATION OF SEMITIC PEOPLE, NONE OF . . . . . .

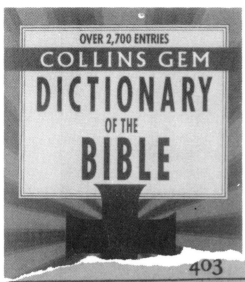

OVER 2,700 ENTRIES

COLLINS GEM

DICTIONARY

OF THE

BIBLE

". . . . . . THE ONLY MAN OF HISTORY WHO CAN BE COM- PARED EVEN RE- MOTELY TO HIM IS MAHOMET."
(Rev. James L. Dow)

403

and whose ideas of religion were ~~complete~~ con- fusion. He led them out and he h~~ad formed~~ them into a nation, with a law and a ~~n~~ ~~pride~~, and a compelling sense of being chosen by a particular God who was supreme. The only man of hist. who can be compared even remotely to him is Mahomet. The Scripture account tends to elaborate for the sake of impression, but behind all the elaborations stands a man of tremendous worth and achievement, whose mark upon the life of the world is as important as it is incalculable. The word so translated means somethin~~g~~

In conclusion, I end with a quotation of a Christian Reverend the commentator of the Bible, followed by that of his Master:

"THE ULTIMATE CRITERION OF A TRUE PROPHET IS THE MORAL CHARACTER OF HIS TEACHINGS."

(Prof. Dummelow.)

"BY THEIR FRUITS YE SHALL KNOW THEM."

(Jesus Christ)

COME LET US REASON TOGETHER!

SAY: "O PEOPLE OF THE BOOK!
COME TO COMMON TERMS AS BETWEEN US AND YOU:
THAT WE WORSHIP NONE BUT GOD;
THAT WE ASSOCIATE NO PARTNERS WITH HIM;
THAT WE ERECT NOT, FROM AMONG OURSELVES,
LORDS AND PATRONS OTHER THAN GOD."
IF THEN THEY TURN BACK,
SAY: "BEAR WITNESS THAT WE (AT LEAST)
ARE MUSLIMS (BOWING TO GOD'S WILL)."

(SÚRA ÁL-I-'IMRÁN) Holy Qur'an 3:64

"PEOPLE OF THE BOOK" is the respectful title given to the Jews and the Christians in the Holy Qur'an. The Muslim is here commanded to invite — **"O People of the Book!"** — O Learned People! O People who claim to be the recipients of Divine Revelation, of a Holy Scripture; let us gather together onto a common platform — **"that we worship none but God"**, because none but God is worthy of worship, not because *"THE LORD THY GOD IS A JEALOUS GOD VISITING THE INQUITY OF THE FATHERS UPON THE CHILDREN UNTO THE THIRD AND FOURTH GENERATION OF THEM THAT HATE ME."* (Exodus 20:5). But because He is our Lord and Cherisher, our Sustainer and Evolver, worthy of all praise, prayer and devotion.

In the abstract the Jews and the Christians would agree to all the three propositions contained in this Qur'anic verse. In practice they fail. Apart from doctrinal lapses from the unity of the One True God, **(ALLAH subhanahu wa ta-ala)** there is the question of a consecrated Priesthood (among the Jews it was hereditary also), as if a mere human being — **Cohen,** or **Pope,** or **Priest,** or **Brahman,** — could claim superiority apart from his learning and the purity of his life, or could stand between man and God in some special sense. **ISLAM DOES NOT RECOGNISE PRIESTHOOD!**

The Creed of Islam is given to us here in a nutshell:

> **Say ye: "We believe in Allah,**
> **And the revelation given to us,**
> **And to Abraham, Isma'il, Isaac,**
> **Jacob, and the Tribes,**
> **And that given to Moses and Jesus**
> **And that given to (all)**
> **Prophets from their Lord:**
> **We make no difference**
> **Between one and another of them:**
> **And we bow to Allah (in Islam)."**
>
> *(SÚRA BAQARA)*   Holy Qur'an 2:136.

The Muslim position is clear. The Muslim does not claim to have a religion peculiar to himself. Islam is not a sect or an ethnic religion. In its view all religions are one, for the Truth is one. IT WAS THE SAME RELIGION PREACHED BY ALL THE EARLIER PROPHETS. (Holy Qur'an 42:13). It was the truth taught by all the inspired Books. In essence it amounts to a consciousness of the Will and Plan of God and a joyful submission to that Will and Plan. **IF ANYONE WANTS A RELIGION OTHER THAN THAT, HE IS FALSE TO HIS OWN NATURE, AS HE IS FALSE TO GOD'S WILL AND PLAN.** Such a one cannot expect guidance, for he has deliberately renounced guidance.

Establish the "KINGDOM OF GOD" on earth
as prayed for by Jesus (peace be upon him)

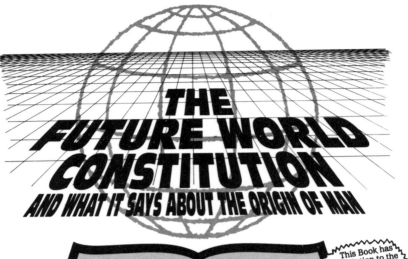

This Book has a solution to the problems of mankind. It will "Guide you into all truth" — *Jesus Christ*

This Book has over six thousand explanatory notes alone!

> O mankind!
> We created you
> From a single (pair)
> Of a male and a female,
> And made you into
> Nations and tribes,
> That ye may recognise
> one another
>
> (Not that ye may
> Despise each other).
> Verily, the most
> Honoured of you
> In the sight of God
> Is (he who is) the
> Best in conduct.
>
> Holy Quran 49 : 13

You can now own this Encyclopedia of Islam "The Future World Constitution" consisting of 1824 pages for only £6 UK, $10 USA, R10 RSA and $12 Middle East.

ISLAMIC PROPAGATION CENTRE INTERNATIONAL

124 Queen Street, Durban, 4001, RSA
Telephone (027-31) 306-0026. Telex (095) 6-21815 IPCI SA
Telefax (027-31) 304-0326

PART TWO

Muhummed

(PEACE BE UPON HIM)

THE NATURAL SUCCESSOR TO

Christ

(PEACE BE UPON HIM)

BY AHMED DEEDAT

CHAPTER ONE

The Final Messenger

"... AND GIVING GLAD TIDINGS
OF A MESSENGER

TO COME AFTER ME,

WHOSE NAME SHALL BE AHMED."

وَمُبَشِّرًا بِرَسُولٍ يَأْتِي

مِنْ بَعْدِيَ

اسْمُهُ أَحْمَدُ

(SÚRA ṢAFF) Holy Qur'an 61:6[1]

MULTI-FACETED SUCCESSION

Successions are of many kinds like the birthright of the **"first-born"** as in Jewish law. Or the ascending of the eldest son or daughter to the kingly throne. Or by election, to select a candidate by the vote of the majority. Or Theologically, an appointment by Divine Decree of God's chosen Messengers. Like the call of Abraham, Moses, Jesus or Muhummed (May the Peace and Blessings of God be upon them all) who were appointed or **"anointed"**[2] in consecration to their office.

Muhummed's (pbuh) succession to Jesus Christ (pbuh) is multi-faceted.

1. Chronologically, in history as a sequence of event in time.

2. By being Chosen[3] by God.

3. In the fulfilment of the prophecies of his predecessors, and last but not least ...

---

1. In this book as well as in my other publications, I quote extensively from the Arabic Qur'an not only for blessings or adornment. It presents a golden opportunity for my learned brethren to memorize these quotations with their meanings and to share their knowledge with others.

2. **"ANOINTED:"** or appointed; Hebrew word *"Messiah."* See my book -**"Christ in Islam,"** for fuller explanation.

3. **"CHOSEN:"** Arabic — **Mustafa.** A title of the Prophet of Islam.

4. By bringing the Guidance of God to perfection -
    "For he will Guide you into all Truth."   said, Jesus Christ

HISTORICALLY

The Holy Prophet Moses preceded Jesus Christ (pbuh) by some 1300 years and Muhummed (pbuh) succeeded to that high office vacated by Jesus some six centuries later.

It was the 12 of **Rabi I.**, in the year of the Elephant, or the 29th of August 570 of the Christian Era[1] that Muhummed the Praiseworthy, to whom all praise is due, was born in the sacred city of Makkah in pagan Arabia. His people the Quraish remembered the year of his birth as the **"Era of the Elephant"**, because just two months before the birth of the child Abraha al-Ashram, the Abyssinian viceroy of Yemen had attacked the sacred sanctuary at Makkah at the head of his troops riding a huge African elephant. A terrifying sight never to be erased from their memory and a still more shocking end to the invasion — the miraculous destruction of Abraha and his army as recorded in *Súra Fíl* or the Elephant —

> **Seest thou not how thy Lord dealt
> with the Companions of the
> Elephant?**
>
> **Did He not make their treacherous
> plan go astray?**
>
> **And He sent against them
> flights of Birds,**
>
> **Striking them with stones
> of baked clay.**
>
> **Then did He make them like an
> empty field of stalks and straw,
> (of which the corn) has been
> eaten up.**
>
> *(SÚRA FÍL)*   *Holy Qur'an 105:1-5*[2]

---

1. Always use A.C. (After Christ) or C.E. (Christian Era) and not A.D. as Muslims often do unthinkingly.
2. Consult Yusuf Ali's commentary on these verses. We will help you to own this encyclopaedia. See inside back cover for a most tempting offer.

GOD'S OWN STANDARDS

God Almighty chooses His Own Messengers. He uses His Own Standards although we may not always understand the wisdom of it. Paul cries the anomaly -

> *For the Jews require a sign*
> (miracles to convince) *and the*
> *Greeks seek after wisdom:*
>
> *(HOLY BIBLE)*   1 Corinthians 1: 22

But worldly-wise as Paul was, he found that his wisdom was **"a stumbling-block"** to the Jews and **"foolishness"** to the Greeks.

God chose Moses (pbuh) a man who was a fugitive from justice and a stutterer. The Holy Bible calls him a man with **"uncircumcised lips."** (Exodus 6: 12).

Despite his difficulties when commissioned to confront Pharaoh, the greatest tyrant of the age, Moses (pbuh) cries out to the God of Mercy —

> **(Moses) said: "O my Lord!**
> **expand for me my breast;"** [1]
>
> **Make my task easy for me;**
>
> **"And remove the impediment from**
> **my speech,**
>
> **"So that they may understand what**
> **I have to say:**
>
> **"And give me a Minister from**
> **my family,**
>
> **"Aaron, my brother;**
>
> **"Add to my strength through him,**
>
> **"And make him share my task:**
>
> **"That we may celebrate Thy praise**
> **without stint,**

---

1. Meaning - give me courage, make me bold.

"And remember Thee without stint:

"For Thou art He that (ever) regardeth us.
(God) said: "Granted is thy
prayer, O Moses!"

(SÚRA TÁ-HÁ)   Holy Qur'an 20: 25-36

WHY "SUPPOSED"?

Then comes Jesus (pbuh) who was chosen by God. According to Christian teachings, he was a carpenter and the son of a carpenter, with a dubious genealogy as recorded in the Gospels —

*And Jesus himself began to be
about thirty years of age, being
(as was supposed)[1] the son of
Joseph ...*

(HOLY BIBLE)   Luke 3: 23

Acknowledged today by a thousand million Muslims that Jesus Christ (pbuh) was born miraculously — without any male intervention; the followers of Christ created two separate genealogies for a man who had no genealogy. Between the Gospels of Matthew and Luke they give this mighty Messenger of God sixty-six fathers and grandfathers. And of these two separate lists only one name is common to these two lists and that is of Joseph the Carpenter, who does not fit in anywhere because, as Luke records above, he was only the **"SUPPOSED"** father of Jesus.[2]

EVEN BISHOPS DOUBT

In a "SHOCK SURVEY OF ANGLICAN BISHOPS" in June 1984 it was revealed that 31 of their 39 Bishops thought that **"Christ's miracles, the virgin birth and the resurrection might not have happened exactly as described in the Bible."**

---

1. The words you see here in brackets are the exact replica from the King James and the Roman Catholic Versions of the phrase - **"(as was supposed)"** brackets and all.

2. Consult — **"Is the Bible God's Word?"** VOL. II PART 2 for a fuller explanation of these anomalies.

In deference to the Bishops of the Church of England (the "Anglicans") the Church of Scotland most respectfully omitted any reference to the **"Virgin Birth"** from its most recent publication **"A STATEMENT OF FAITH."** The topic of the miraculous conception of Jesus (pbuh) is getting increasingly hotter for Western Christianity to handle as you see here:

The Daily News

DURBAN, TUESDAY, MAY 22, 1990

Virgin Birth omitted by Church of Scotland

LONDON: Direct reference to the Virgin Birth has been omitted from the Church of Scotland's new publication, A Statement of Faith, to "avoid potential division among the church's members".

The Rev David Beckett, secretary of the special working party that produced the publication, said the omission would move the Church of Scotland away from traditional Anglo-Catholic theology and towards the more liberal faction of the Church of England championed by the Bishop of Durham, David Jenkins.

The new document was debated by the Church of Scotland's annual General Assembly in Edinburgh. Designed to express the Westminster Confession, written in the 1640s, in a more up-to-date language, the church's Panel on Doctrine also took the opportunity to tailor the text on the Virgin Birth.

Said Mr Beckett: "We wanted to come up with a statement that was inclusive rather than divisive. One that would be welcomed by the whole church, not just those who accept the Virgin Birth as a historical fact, but also by those who regard it as mainly pictorial theology."

Leading churchmen claim the Westminster Confession has not been replaced, merely summarised and updated.
— Foreign service

AND GOD CHOSE JESUS (PBUH)

Jesus Christ (pbuh) though spiritually rich in wisdom, light and truth; philosophised light-heartedly about the beggars of the world, when he said:

> **There came unto him** (Jesus) **a
> woman having an albaster box
> of very precious ointment, and
> poured it on his head ...**
>
> **But when his disciples saw it, they
> had indignation, saying, To what
> purpose is this waste?**
>
> **For this ointment might have been
> sold for much, and given to the
> poor.**
>
> **... he** (Jesus) **said unto them ...
> For ye have the poor always with
> you, but** (poor) **me ye have not
> always.**
>
> **(HOLY BIBLE)**   Matthew 26: 7-11

But when destitution stared him in the face, when poverty, penury and need touched his own dear self; he cried pathetically:

> **And Jesus saith unto him,
> The foxes have holes, and the
> birds of the air have nests; but
> the son of man** (referring to himself)
> **hath not where to lay his head.**
>
> **(HOLY BIBLE)**   Matthew 8: 20 also repeated in Luke 9: 58

And yet God chose him (Jesus pbuh): Unique and inscrutable are Thy ways O Lord!

M-U-S-T-A-F-A THE CHOSEN ONE

It is He Who sent amongst the
unlettered a messenger from
among themselves, to rehearse to
them His Signs, to sanctify
them, and to instruct them in
Scripture and Wisdom, —
although they had been, before,
in manifest error;-

(SÚRA JUMÚA)   *Holy Qur'an 62: 2*

Amazing as it may seem, I am not amazed anymore! For this is His way — He chooses an **Ummi**[1] non-literate Prophet for an **Ummi** illiterate nation.

"A POOR SHEPHERD PEOPLE, ROAMING UNNOTICED IN ITS DESERTS SINCE THE CREATION OF THE WORLD: A HERO-PROPHET WAS SENT DOWN TO THEM WITH A WORD THEY COULD BELIEVE: SEE, THE UNNOTICED BECOMES WORLD-NOTABLE, THE SMALL HAS GROWN WORLD-GREAT; WITHIN ONE CENTURY AFTERWARDS, ARABIA IS AT GRENADA (Spain) ON THIS HAND, AT DELHI (India) ON THAT; — GLANCING IN VALOUR AND SPLENDOUR AND THE LIGHT OF GENIUS, ARABIA SHINES THROUGH LONG AGES OVER A GREAT SECTION OF THE WORLD. BELIEF IS GREAT, LIFE-GIVING. THE HISTORY OF A NATION BECOMES FRUITFUL, SOUL ELEVATING, GREAT, SO SOON AS IT BELIEVES. THESE ARABS, THE MAN MAHOMET, AND THAT ONE CENTURY, — IS IT NOT AS IF A SPARK HAD FALLEN, ONE SPARK, ON A WORLD OF WHAT SEEMED BLACK UNNOTICEABLE SAND; BUT LO, THE SAND PROVES EXPLOSIVE POWDER, BLAZES HEAVEN HIGH FROM DELHI TO GRENADA! I SAID, THE

---

1. **UMMI** : "Unlettered." **"One other circumstance we must not forget: that he had no school-learning; of the thing we call school-learning; none at all."** *Thomas Carlyle* in his **"HEROES AND HERO-WORSHIP"**

GREAT MAN WAS ALWAYS AS LIGHTNING OUT OF HEAVEN;
THE REST OF MEN WAITED FOR HIM LIKE FUEL, AND THEN
THEY TOO WOULD FLAME."

Thus concluded the speech of Thomas Carlyle, one of the
greatest thinkers of the past century. It was Friday, the 8th of
May 1840. His theme — **"The Hero as Prophet."** His
audience: were Anglicans — English Christians.

THE CHOSEN PEOPLE

God chooses His Messengers and God chooses His People. In the
realm of the Spirit no nation was as favoured as the Jews and
yet Moses (pbuh) is made to bewail against his own people —

> **Ye have been rebellious against the
> Lord from the day I knew you.**
>
> **(HOLY BIBLE)**   Deutronomy 9: 24

In this last will and testament of Moses (pbuh) the Israelites
frustrate their "meek and gentle" Messenger who is forced to rail
against their continual stubborn resistance and arrogant attitudes
to God's guidance —

> **For I knew thy rebellion, and thy
> stiff neck: behold, while I am yet
> alive with you this day, ye have
> been rebellious against the lord;
> and how much more after my death?**
>
> **(HOLY BIBLE)**   Deutronomy 31: 27

Alas how true! I am not going to philosophise on God's choice.
But in the very next chapter the fire of God's anger is
kindled to a blaze and He decries the Jews -

> **They have moved me to jealousy
> with that which is not God; they**
> (the Jews) **have provoked me to
> anger with their vanities:
> and I will move them to jealousy**

with those which are <u>Not A</u>
<u>People</u>; I will provoke them to
anger with a <u>Foolish Nation.</u> [1]

(HOLY BIBLE)   Deutronomy 32: 21

JEWS SUBSTITUTED

Anyone with a modicum of Scriptural knowledge will be able to guess who in the eyes of these arrogant, racist Jews is **"not-a-people"** — a nonentity and **'a foolish nation"** if not their Ishmaelite cousins — the Arabs who in the words of Thomas Carlyle have been **"ROAMING UNNOTICED IN ITS DESERTS SINCE THE CREATION OF THE WORLD."!?**

THE ARABS. Alexander the Great passed them by; the Persians passed them by; the Egyptians passed them by; and the Romans passed them by. It would have been an absolute liability for any nation to conquer and colonise them. But the Creator did not pass them by. He picked them up from the depths of darkness and transformed them into torchbearers of light and learning to the world. **"I will move them** (the Jews) **to jealousy."** [2] This jealousy is a cultivated sickness. Remember, Sarah and Hagar the two wives of Abraham (pbuh) — the Friend of God. The jealousy of Sarah was bequeathed to her children and on to nations and tribes yet unborn.

Not so long ago I read a book on the discovery of medicine written by a Jewish medical man. I can unfortunately not remember the name of the author and failed to retrace the book. However, the wordings of the tribute paid by this Jewish author to his Semitic (Arab) cousins have made an indelible impression on my mind. And I quote from memory:

---

1. Emphasis are mine.
2. If the Romans or the Greeks had displaced the Jews as the "Chosen of God" then the envy would not have been as acute or as intolerable to the Jews.

"GOATHERDS AND CAMEL DRIVERS SITTING ON THE THRONE OF THE CAESARS."

Full of spite, venom and sarcasm, but how true! This is what God did and always does. He honours whom He wills. This is what He does to show His Mighty Hand (Power)!

IF YE TURN BACK (FROM THE PATH), وَإِن تَتَوَلَّوْا

HE WILL SUBSTITUTE IN YOUR STEAD, ANOTHER PEOPLE; يَسْتَبْدِلْ قَوْمًا غَيْرَكُمْ

THEN THEY WOULD NOT BE LIKE YOU! ثُمَّ لَا يَكُونُوٓا أَمْثَالَكُم

(SÚRA MUHAMMAD) *Holy Qur'an 47: 38* [1]

IT IS SURELY ONE OF THE GREATEST MIRACLES OF HISTORY THAT FROM THE BACKWATER OF ARABIA THERE SHOULD HAVE EXPLODED A GROUP OF MEN, COMPANIONS OF A PROPHET, WHO WITHIN THE SPACE OF A FEW BRIEF DECADES WERE ABLE TO CREATE A MAGNIFICENT CIVILISATION EXTENDING FROM THE PYRENEES TO THE GATES OF CHINA
Abdul Wadod Shalabi in *"Islam Religion of Life."*

THE LAST WARNING

The foregoing is the exact fulfilment of Jesus Christ's (pbuh), (the last of the great Jewish prophets) own prediction of the displacement of the Jewish race in the spiritual guidance of man. In the words of the Master himself —

> *Therefore I say unto you* (Jews),
> *The kingdom of God* [2] *shall be*
> *taken away from you* (Jews), *and*
> *shall be given to a nation bringing*
> *forth the fruits thereof.*

(HOLY BIBLE) *Matthew 21: 43*

---

1. With this book still in your hands, please memorize the Arabic words with their meaning phrase by phrase: For its commentary obtain your own volume of the Holy Qur'an, obtainable from the I.P.C.I.

2. **"Kingdom of God:"** The honour, the privilege of being God's chosen people to guide mankind - **"Ye** (Jews) **shall be unto me** (God Almighty) **a kingdom of priests, and a holy nation."** (Exodus 19: 6). This grand commission ended with Jesus (pbuh).

CHAPTER TWO

In The Words Of The Master

JUST ONE FULL PROPHECY[1]

AND REMEMBER, JESUS,
THE SON OF MARY, SAID:

وَاِذْ قَالَ عِيْسَى ابْنُ مَرْيَمَ

"O CHILDREN OF ISRAEL!
I AM THE MESSENGER OF
GOD (SENT) TO YOU,

يٰبَنِيۤ اِسْرَآءِيْلَ اِنِّيْ رَسُوْلُ
اللهِ اِلَيْكُمْ

CONFIRMING THE LAW
(WHICH CAME) BEFORE ME,

مُصَدِّقًا لِّمَا بَيْنَ يَدَيَّ مِنَ التَّوْرٰۤةِ

AND GIVING GLAD TIDINGS OF
A MESSENGER
TO COME AFTER ME,

وَمُبَشِّرًۢا بِرَسُوْلٍ يَّأْتِيْ مِنْۢ بَعْدِيۤ

WHOSE NAME SHALL BE AHMED."

اسْمُهٗۤ اَحْمَدُ ط

(SÚRA ṢAFF) *Holy Qur'an 61: 6*

A COMMON TRAIT

Just a cursory glance, a rapid reading, a hurried look at the previous verse will satisfy the Muslim that Jesus Christ (pbuh) did indeed prophesy the advent of Muhummed (pbuh), the Messenger of God. The Muslim is puzzled at the stubbornness, vanity and tunnel vision of the Christian which prevents him from seeing his own inner light and listening to his conscience so as not to recognise the obvious.

The Christian in turn is puzzled at the hardhearted obstinacy of the Jews, a nation endowed with such creative genius, which,

---

1. This section only expounds a single prophecy from the New Testament. Refer to Part 1 of this volume — **"What the Bible says about Muhummed (pbuh)"** for prophecies from the Old Testament.

despite a thousand and one prophecies in their own Bible (the Old Testament) regarding the coming of the **"Messiah,"** are totally incapable of recognising their lord and **"saviour."** Are they both somewhat blind?

No! Neither the Jews nor the Christians are necessarily impervious to truth. The trouble is that we **all** pick up our prejudices from childhood. The Americans call it being **"programmed."**

Simply reading the verses or listening to lectures and getting that smug satisfaction of being in the know will not help spreading the truth. This is the age of the "EVERYMAN."[1] The age of the professionals is over. It is the duty of every Muslim — man, woman or child to get involved. Each according to his or her capacity. Memorize the above verse with its meaning as well as the quotations preceding and those that follow so that you may feel equipped to share our **Deen** with non-Muslims. There are no short cuts to **Da'wah** (propagation)!

PRODUCE YOUR PROOF!

Perhaps this is not the first time you are reading or might have heard about the prophecies in the Jewish and Christian Scriptures regarding the advent of the last and final Messenger of God — Muhummed (pbuh) the Mercy unto all mankind. And perhaps you have at times made some half-hearted and skimpy efforts at suggesting that our **Nabi-e-Kareem** was prophesied in the Holy Bible. But when proof was demanded, you simply not able to, because you had not done any homework. Remember, there is no substitute for hard work. I believe what I say and I practise what I preach. **Insha-Allah!**

---

1. **"EVERYMAN:"** is a new series of books to equip every man or woman to learn an art or trade such as - plumbing, pottery, woodwork, etc by studying at home.

I have personally memorized various selections from the Bible in a dozen different languages, including Arabic and Hebrew. Not for show but because of the openings these snippets of religion create for me in propagating our faith to various language groups. Languages are the keys to people's hearts.

IN THE LAND OF THE PHARAOHS

Notwithstanding many assurances, I got stranded in Cairo for lack of an entry visa.[1] A kind gentleman from the Al-Azhar, who was trying to help us obtain the relevant documents, got frustrated with the delay and in order to attend to his Friday prayers, handed me and my son Yousuf to a young Egyptian lady, well-groomed in Western attire.

After much effort and time she returned to us with the good news. "Forty dollars," she said. I asked, "For what?" "The visas," she answered. Twenty dollars for me and twenty for my son. "But I am a guest of the Government," I insisted. She said that she knew nothing about it, so I smiled and paid.

From the lady's speech and deportment, I had sensed that she was well-educated and a lady of culture, so undauntedly I asked her again what her name was in my broken Arabic. However, her name was too novel for me to remember. I asked her further: "Are you a Muslim?" She said, "No, I am an Egyptian Christian." This was the opening I was waiting for. I began, "Do you know that before Jesus Christ departed from this world, he told his disciples," and I started to quote, now in meticulous Arabic, a verse from the Arabic Bible, (see next page), which I had memorized for opportunities just like this particular one.

---

1. The Muslims of South Africa have a very rough time in all the O.A.U. and Arab countries. The poor ignorant customs officers do not know the difference between the oppressors and the oppressed of my country.

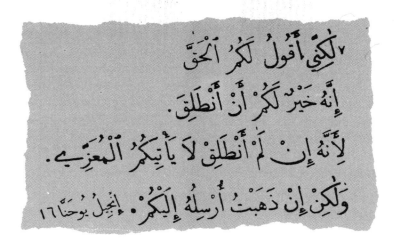

THE TRANSLATION

I had no need to translate the above Arabic to her, because as an Arab she understood the verse perfectly. But for the benefit of those who do not know Arabic I give you its exact equivalent from the English Bible, which I had also taken the trouble to memorize in my spare time. You can create that spare time also if you have true love for Allah's **Deen** and wish to share it with others.

> **Nevertheless, I tell you the truth;**
> **it is expedient for you that I go**
> **away: for if I go not away, the**
> **Comforter will not come unto**
> **you; but if I depart, I will send**
> **him unto you.**

(HOLY BIBLE) *John 16: 7*

"AL-MOOUZZI" THE COMFORTER

I implore my bretheren who can read the Arabic quotation to memorize it together with the English translation above and create opportunities for using it. Learn the verses in conjunction with other languages that you know. There will be a definite all-round improvement in your fluency, and proficiency in preaching Islam to other people.

The word **"Comforter"** above is ٱلْمُعَزِّي "al-Moouzzi" in Arabic. I asked the lady, "Who is the ٱلْمُعَزِّي "al-Moouzzi" of this prophecy?" She said, "I do not know." She was honest. She did not beat around the bush. So I said that we are told in the Holy Qur'an that Jesus Christ (pbuh) had told his disciples —

"... AND GIVING GLAD TIDINGS
OF A MESSENGER

TO COME AFTER ME,
WHOSE NAME SHALL BE AHMED."

وَمُبَشِّرًا بِرَسُولٍ يَأْتِي مِنْ بَعْدِي اسْمُهُ أَحْمَدُ ط

(SÚRA ṢAFF)   Holy Qur'an 61: 6

I continued that, "This **Ahmed** is another name for **Muhummed**, and **Muhummed** is *Moouzzi!"* "Very funny," she exclaimed, "these Egyptians" (meaning the Muslim Egyptians) "take us to the cinema, they take us" (meaning Christian women) "to the dance, but no one ever tells us anything about this **Moouzzi!"** Through her Allah *soobha-nahoo-wa-ta-aalaa,* armed me with a fourteen-pound sledgehammer before leaving Cairo Airport. *Alhumdo-lillah!* And, did I use that sledgehammer!!

An integrated explanation of Comforter/Moouzzi of John 16: 7 and Ahmed/Muhummed of The Holy Qur'an 61: 6 will be slotted in place when explaining the *Áyat* (the verse) heading this chapter.

BIBLICAL CONFIRMATION

Remember, that in the sixth century of the Christian Era, when Muhummed (pbuh) was chanting God's words which was systematically **"put into his mouth,"**[1] the Arabic Bible had not

---

1. Muhummed (pbuh) fulfils yet another prophecy, see page 16 of Part 1 **"What the Bible says about Muhummed** (pbuh)" for this aspect.

yet been translated. He could never have known that he was fulfilling and confirming the utterances of his predecessor (Jesus pbuh) to the letter.

ONLY FOR THE ISRAELITES

1. ***AND REMEMBER, JESUS THE SON OF MARY, SAID:***

    وَاِذْ قَالَ عِيْسَى ابْنُ مَرْيَمَ

    "O CHILDREN OF ISRAEL!

    يٰبَنِىٓ اِسْرَآءِيْلَ

    I AM THE MESSENGER OF GOD (SENT) TO YOU" (the Jews)

    اِنِّىْ رَسُوْلُ اللهِ اِلَيْكُمْ

JESUS FOR JEWS ONLY

These twelve Jesus sent forth, and commanded them saying,

Go ye not into the way of the Gentiles,[1]

and into any city of the Samaritans enter ye not:

But go ye rather unto The Lost Sheep Of The House Of Israel.

(HOLY BIBLE)   Matthew 10: 5-6

NOT FOR DOGS

And behold a woman of Canaan[2] ***came ... and cried unto him saying, have mercy on me ... my daughter is seriously possessed with a devil.***

But he answered her not a word.

---

1. **Gentiles:** non-Jews.
2. Mark 7: 26 says that the woman was a **Greek.**

And his disciples came and begged him, saying, Send her away: for she crieth after us.

But he answered and said, <u>I am Not Sent But Unto The Lost Sheep Of The House Of Israel</u>.

But she came and knelt before him, saying, Lord, help me.

But he answered her and said, <u>It Is Not Fair To Take The Children's Bread And Cast It To The Dogs</u>.[1]

(HOLY BIBLE) *Matthew 15: 22-26*

It goes to the credit of this Jewish prophet, that he practised what he preached. In his lifetime he never converted a single Gentile (non-Jew). And of his hand-picked elect (his twelve disciples), he made sure that they belonged to his tribe so that his other prophecy might find fulfilment: **"when the son of man** (Jesus pbuh referring to himself) **shall sit on the throne of his glory, ye** (the disciples) **also shall sit upon twelve thrones, judging the twelve tribes of Israel"** (Matthew 19: 28).

NO NEW RELIGION

2. *"CONFIRMING THE LAW*[2] *(WHICH) CAME BEFORE ME,"*

مُصَدِّقًا لِّمَا بَيْنَ يَدَىَّ مِنَ التَّوْرَٰىةِ

The Messiah was no mealy-mouthed Messenger among the Jews. Like his predecessors Amos and Ezekiel or Isaiah and Jeremiah, he was trenchant in his condemnation of Jewish formalism and hypocrisies. His novel approach and militant preaching had

---

1. Meaning non-Jews.
2. **"LAW"**: The word in the Arabic text here is *"Taurat."* (Heb. *"Torah."*)

created certain misgivings amongst the religious hierarchy. The Scribes and the Pharisees came to him again and again to test him as to his **bona fides.**[1]

To allay their suspicions that he had brought no newfangled religion, and that his was the confirmation of all the teachings that had gone before him. He says —

> *Think not that I am come to*
> *destroy the law* (Hebrew - Torah), *or*
> *the prophets: I am come not to*
> *destroy, but to fulfil.*
>
> *For verily I say unto you, Till*
> *heaven and earth pass, one jot or*
> *one tittle shall in no wise pass*
> *from the law* (Torah), *till all be*
> *fulfilled.*
>
> *Whosoever therefore shall break*
> *one of these least commandments,*
> *and shall teach men so, he shall*
> *be called the least in the kingdom*
> *of heaven: but whosoever shall*
> *do and teach them, the same shall*
> *be called great in the kingdom of*
> *heaven.*

HOLY BIBLE   *Matthew 5: 17-19*

Compare this phrase "**CONFIRMING THE LAW (WHICH CAME) BEFORE ME,**" - these seven words at the beginning of this section on page 40 with the three verses of Matthew above, and you will not fail to note that there is no wordiness in the Qur'anic diction. It conveys God's Message concisely, with clarity and precision.

---

1. His Genuineness.

"THE FATHER[1] OF TRUTH CHOOSES HIS OWN PRO-PHETS, AND HE SPEAKS TO THEM IN A VOICE STRONGER THAN THE VOICE OF THUNDER."

Sayed Amir Ali in *"The Spirit of Islam."*

The Qur'an had come to **Confirm, Correct** and **Complete** Divine Revelation, or whatever was left of it in unworthy hands.

THIS QUR'AN IS NOT SUCH   وَمَا كَانَ هٰذَا الْقُرْاٰنُ

AS CAN BE PRODUCED
BY OTHER THAN ALLAH;   اَنْ يُّفْتَرٰى مِنْ دُوْنِ اللّٰهِ

ON THE CONTRARY IT IS A
CONFIRMATION OF (REVELATION)   وَلٰكِنْ تَصْدِيْقَ الَّذِيْ
THAT WENT BEFORE IT,   بَيْنَ يَدَيْهِ

AND A FULLER EXPLANATION   وَتَفْصِيْلَ الْكِتٰبِ
OF THE BOOK

WHEREIN THERE IS NO   لَا رَيْبَ فِيْهِ مِنْ رَّبِّ الْعٰلَمِيْنَ ۝
DOUBT FROM THE LORD OF THE WORLDS.

(SÚRA Y-ÚNUS)   Holy Qur'an 10: 37

THE GOOD NEWS

3. *"AND GIVING GLAD TIDINGS OF*   وَمُبَشِّرًۢا بِرَسُوْلٍ يَّأْتِيْ
   A MESSENGER
   TO COME AFTER ME,   مِنْ بَعْدِے

   WHOSE NAME SHALL BE AHMED."   اسْمُهٗٓ اَحْمَدُ ط

I will not apologise, nor am I called upon to apologise for reproducing here **verbatim** (a word for word) commentary on the word **"AHMED,"** from ABDULLAH YUSUF ALI'S English translation. But before I do that permit me to pay a fitting tribute to the **KING FAHD HOLY QUR'AN PRINTING COMPLEX** in

---

1. **FATHER:** The use of the word **"FATHER"** in relation to God was cut from Islamic terminology owing to the perversion of the idea among the Christians.

Al-Madinah Al-Munawwarah which is turning out millions of Holy Qur'ans in many different languages.

Their reason for using YUSUF ALI as a base for their reproduction is summed up in these words:

"A NUMBER OF INDIVIDUALS HAVE IN THE PAST VENTURED TO TRANSLATE THE QUR'AN, BUT THEIR WORKS HAVE GENERALLY BEEN PRIVATE ATTEMPTS, GREATLY INFLUENCED BY THEIR OWN PREJUDICES. IN ORDER TO PRODUCE A RELIABLE TRANSLATION FREE FROM PERSONAL BIAS, A ROYAL DECREE (No. 19888, DATED 16/8/1400 AH) WAS ISSUED BY THE CUSTODIAN OF THE TWO HOLY MOSQUES, KING FAHD IBN ABDUL AZIZ, AT THAT TIME THE DEPUTY PRIME MINISTER ... THE TRANSLATION OF THE LATE USTADH **ABDULLAH YUSUF ALI** WAS CONSEQUENTLY CHOSEN FOR ITS DISTINGUISHING CHARACTERISTICS, SUCH AS A HIGHLY ELEGANT STYLE, A CHOICE OF WORDS CLOSE TO THE MEANING OF THE ORIGINAL TEXT, ACCOMPANIED BY SCHOLARLY NOTES AND COMMENTARIES."

The Presidency of Islamic Researches, Ifta,
Call and Guidance

Out of over six thousand profound explanatory notes in Yusuf Ali's translation, the following is just one of three explaining the prophecy in the words of Jesus (pbuh) regarding the advent of Muhummed (pbuh) the Messenger of God.

Note No: 5438:

> *"Ahmed"*, or *"Muhummed"*, the Praised One, is almost a translation of the Greek word *Periclytos*. In the present Gospel of John 14:16, 15:26, and 16:7, the word "Comforter" in the English version for the Greek word *"Paracletos"*, which means "Advocate", "one called to the help of another, a kind friend", rather than "Comforter". Our doctors contend that Paracletos is a corrupt reading for
> *CONT. NEXT PAGE*

Periclytos, and that in the original saying of Jesus there was a prophecy of our holy Prophet **Ahmed** by name. Even if we read Paraclete, it would imply to the Holy Prophet, who is "a Mercy for all creatures" (H.Q. 21:107) and "most kind and merciful to the Believers" (H.Q. 9:128) See also note 416 to H.Q. 3:81.[1]

4.   *BUT WHEN HE CAME TO THEM WITH CLEAR SIGNS,*

فَلَمَّا جَاءَهُم بِالْبَيِّنَتِ

THEY SAID: "THIS IS EVIDENT SORCERY!"

قَالُوا هٰذَا سِحْرٌ مُّبِينٌ ۝

Thus concludes *(Ayat)* verse 6 of *(Súra)* chapter 61 under discussion. "The Prophet of Islam was foretold in many ways; and when he came he showed forth many Clear Signs, for his whole life from beginning to end was one vast miracle. He fought and won against odds. Without learning from men he taught the highest wisdom. He melted hearts that were hard, and he strengthened hearts that were tender and required support. In all his sayings and doings men of discernment could see the working of God's hand;" yet the sceptics called it *SORCERY* — jugglery — magic!

FORGER AND JUGGLER! NO, NO! THIS GREAT FIERY HEART, SEETHING, SIMMERING LIKE A GREAT FURNACE OF THOUGHTS, WAS NOT A JUGGLER'S.

Thomas Carlyle, page 88 in his book -
"Heroes and Hero-worship"

And they called his miraculous fulfilment of prophecy magic, jugglery, enchantment — that which became the most solid fact of human history — **Islam!**

---

1. Obtain your own volume of the translation. Contact the I.P.C.I.

CHAPTER THREE

Muhummed (pbuh) Is The "Paraclete"

To the sincere seekers of Truth it is obvious that Muhummed (pbuh) is the promised **Paraclete** or Comforter, alternatively called Helper, Advocate, Counsellor, etc of the prophecies of Jesus (pbuh) in the Gospel of St. John. There are millions of Christians — men and women like our good lady at the Cairo Airport (see page 42) who are hungry for this simple straightforward Message. But alas, we can only weep with Jesus (pbuh) for our utter ineptitude —

> **The harvest truly is plenteous, but**
> **the workers are few.**
>
> **(HOLY BIBLE)**   Matthew 9: 37

LANGUAGE OF JESUS (PBUH)

In the Holy Qur'an God Almighty puts the name **"Ahmed'** which is another name for Muhummed (pbuh) in the mouth of Jesus (pbuh). The Christian controversialist, Bible-thumper, Hot-Gospeller flippantly scoffs at the suggestion. The Christian missionary does not deny that Jesus (pbuh) did make a prophecy about someone coming after him. But "Ahmed" to him seems too far-fetched.

The most commonly accepted name by Christendom is **"Comforter."** It does not really matter. Comforter or any other equivalent term will do. We will settle for Comforter as used in the most popular Bible Translation the **"King James Version."**

Ask your adversary, your disputant whether Jesus (pbuh) spoke the English language? "Most definitely not!" any Christian will say. If you are sharing this with an Arab Christian then you can ask him whether his "lord" used the word "MOOUZZI?" Surely

---

1.   I take it that you have already memorized John 16:7 in Arabic from page 43.

not, because Arabic was not his language. Did Jesus (pbuh) prophesy **"uMthokozisi?"** (Comforter in Zulu) or **"Trooster"** from the Afrikaans Bible? The answer again is a definite NO!"

The Christians are rightfully boasting that they now have translated the complete .Bible into hundreds of different languages, and the New Testament (in which this prophecy abounds) into more than two thousand different languages and dialects. So the Christian genius has invented more than 2000 different names in 2000 different languages for this one candidate — Comforter!

PNEUMA: GHOST OR SPIRIT?

The Church fathers had developed a sickness by translating names of people, for which they had no right to do. For example like **Esau** to Jesus, **Messiah** to Christ, **Cephas** to Peter[1] and so on.

The closest one can ever get to the original utterance of Jesus (pbuh) in the Christian Scriptures is the Greek word **"Paracletos,"** which also has to be rejected because the Master did not speak Greek! But let's not be difficult for the purpose of this discussion and accept the Greek word Paracletos and its English equivalent Comforter.

Ask any learned Christian man as to who the Comforter is? You will unmistakingly hear - **"The Comforter is the HOLY GHOST!"** from John 14: 26. This sentence is only part of verse twenty six. We will deal with the verse fully in due course. But first we must educate the Christian mind with regards to this misnomer — **"Holy Ghost."** "Pneuma," is the Greek root word for SPIRIT. There is no separate word for GHOST in the Greek manuscripts of the New Testament, and the Christians now boast 24,000 different manuscripts in their possession of which no two are identical!

---

1. Get your **FREE** copy of **"What is His Name?"** for a better clarification on this point.

The editors of the KJV *(The King James Version)* alternatively called AV *(The Authorised Version)* and the DOUAY *(The Roman Catholic Version)* of the Bibles gave preference to the word **"GHOST"** instead of the word SPIRIT when translating **"pneuma."**

The revisers of the RSV *(Revised Standard Version),*[1] the most up-to-date version of the Bible, are going back, as claimed, to the Most Ancient manuscripts. These revisers, described as **"thirty-two scholars of the highest eminence, backed by fifty co-operating denominations,"** who courageously replaced the shady word "ghost" with the word "spirit." Hence from now on you will read in all modern translations — **"The Comforter which is the Holy SPIRIT"**! However, the Christian crusaders and the televangelists stubbornly cling to the spooky **("ghost"**-ly) past. They will not opt for the Newer Versions. It's better fishing with the old bait - the KJV and the RCV *(Roman Catholic Version).*

With the new change in spirit, the verse under scrutiny will read:

> *But the Comforter, <u>Which Is The Holy Spirit,</u> whom the Father will send in my name,*
>
> *he shall teach you all things, and bring all things to your rememberance, whatsoever I have said unto you.* (Emphasis added).
>
> **(HOLY BIBLE)** *John 14: 26*

You do not have to be a Bible scholar of any calibre to sense that the expression **"which is the Holy Spirit"** is actually an interpolation. It ought to be in parenthesis, in brackets, like my words which have been interpolated in the quotation, i.e.

---

1. For greater detail on the RSV see **"Is the Bible God's Word?"** obtainable **FREE** from the IPCI.

"**(emphasis added)**." Although the editors of the RSV have expunged dozens of interpolations from their boasted Revised Standard Version, they have retained this jarring phrase which contradicts other explicit predictions of Jesus (pbuh) on the subject of the Comforter itself.

"HOLY SPIRIT" IS HOLY PROPHET

(i) It may be noted that no Biblical scholar of any standing has ever equated the **"paracletos"** of John in the original Greek with the Holy Ghost. Now we can say with one breath that if the Comforter is the "Holy Spirit" then that Holy Spirit is the **Holy Prophet!**

As Muslims we acknowledge that every true prophet of God is Holy and without sin. But whenever the expression "The Holy Prophet" is used among Muslims it is universally accepted as referring to the Holy Prophet Muhummed (pbuh). So even if we accept the above incongruous saying — **"the Comforter which is the Holy Spirit,"** as Gospel truth, even then this prophecy will fit Muhummed (pbuh) like a glove, without any stretching of its meaning.

The same John, who is supposed to have authored the Gospel bearing his name, also penned three more Epistles which are also part of the Christian Bible. Amazingly he has used the same terminology of "Holy **Spirit**" for "Holy **Prophet**."

> *Beloved, believe not every Spirit,*
> *but try the Spirits whether they*
> *are of God; because many false*
> *Prophets are gone out into the*
> *world.*   **(HOLY BIBLE)**   1 John 4: 1

You can observe that the word spirit is used here synonymously with a prophet. A true spirit is a true prophet, and a false spirit is a false prophet. But for the so-called "born-again" Christians who see only with eyes of emotion, I recommend that they lay their hands on C.I. Scofield's Authorized King James Version of the Bible who with an Editorial Committee of 9 D.D.'s adding their notes and comments. When they come to the first word **"spirit"** in the above verse they should give a notation to compare it with Matthew 7: 15 which confirms that false prophets are false spirits. So according to St. John the Holy **Spirit** is the Holy **Prophet,** and the Holy Prophet is Muhummed (pbuh) the Messenger of God.

A VALID TEST

But St. John does not leave us in the air, guessing the true from the false. He gives us an acid test for recognising the true Prophet, he says —

> ***Hereby know ye the Spirit[1] of***
> ***God: Every Spirit that con-***
> ***fesseth that Jesus Christ is come***
> ***in the flesh is of God.***
>
> **(HOLY BIBLE)**   1 John 4: 2

According to John's own interpretation in verse one above the word "spirit" is synonymous with the word prophet. So verse two **"Spirit of God"** would mean Prophet of God and **"Every spirit"** would stand for every Prophet. You have a right to know as to what the Holy Prophet Muhummed (pbuh) says about **"Jesus Christ."**[2]

Jesus Christ (peace be upon him) is spoken by name no less than 25 times in the Holy Qur'an. He is honoured as —

Isa ibn Maryam   **(Jesus, the son of Mary)**

---

1. For **SPIRIT**, read **PROPHET**.
2. See Vol. III Part 1 — **"Christ in Islam"** for detailed information of the high position that Jesus (pbuh) occupies in the house of Islam.

As-saaliheen	**(The Righteous)**
Kalimatu-Llah	**(Word of God)**
Ruhu-Llah	**(Spirit of God)**
Masih-uLlah	**(Christ of God)**

Behold the angels said:
"O Mary! God giveth thee
Glad tidings of a Word from
Him: his name will be Christ
Jesus, the son of Mary, held
In honour in this world and
The Hereafter and of (the
Company of) those nearest to God.

(SÚRA ÁL-i-'IMRÁN) *Holy Qur'an 3: 45*[1]

MUHUMMED (PBUH) IS THE "OTHER"

(ii) The Comforter in John 14: 26 can never be the "Holy **Ghost"** because Jesus (pbuh) had already explained —

And I will pray the Father, and he
shall give you Another Com-
forter, that he may abide with
you for ever.

(HOLY BIBLE) *John 14: 16*

The emphasis here is on the word **"ANOTHER"** an other, a different one, an additional one, but of the same kind, yet distinctly different from the first. Who is then the first Comforter? The Christian world is unanimous that in this case the speaker himself — Jesus Christ (pbuh) is the **first** Comforter; **then the other,** the one to follow must be of like nature, subject to the same conditions of hunger, thirst, fatigue, sorrow and death.

---

1. You can do **no** better than get your Christian friends to read this verse with its commentary directly from the Holy Qur'an. See inside back cover for offer.

But this promised Comforter was to **"abide with you for EVER!"** No one lives for ever. Jesus (pbuh) was mortal so must the coming Comforter also be mortal. No son of man can ever be immortal!

> **Every soul shall have a taste of death.**
>
> *(SÚRA ÁL-i-'IMRÁN)*   *Holy Qur'an 3: 185*

ALIVE IN THEIR TEACHINGS

The soul does not really die, but when it separates from the body at the time of the death of the body, the soul will get a taste of death. But our Comforter was to **"ABIDE,"** continue, endure for ever. All Comforters abide with us for ever. Moses is here with us today in his **teachings.** Jesus is here with us today in his **teachings** and Muhummed also is here with us in his **teachings** today. (May the peace and blessings of God be upon them all). This is not my novel idea trying to justify the preposterous. I say this with conviction and on the authority of Jesus Christ (pbuh) himself.

In Luke, chapter sixteen, Jesus (pbuh) tells us the story of the **"Rich Man, Poor Man."** At death both find themselves at opposite ends — one in Heaven and the other in Hell. The rich man (Dives) simmering in Hell cries to Father Abraham to send the beggar (Lazarus) to assuage his thirst. But when every plea fails, he, as a last favour, requests that Father Abraham send the beggar back to earth to warn his living brothers against their impending doom if they heeded not the warnings of God.

> *But Abraham said, "If they* (those still alive on earth) *won't listen to Moses and the prophets, they won't listen even though someone rises from the dead."* (to warn them)
>
> *(HOLY BIBLE)* *Luke 16: 31*

Jesus (pbuh) uttered the above fact centuries after the demise of the prophets of Israel like Jeremiah, Hosea, Zechariah, etc and over thirteen hundred years after Moses (pbuh). The Pharisees at the time of Jesus (pbuh) and we today can still listen to **"MOSES AND THE PROPHETS,"** for they are still alive, and with us here today in their **teachings.**

'YOU' OF THE TIME

If it is said that the Comforter was promised to the immediate disciples of Jesus (pbuh) and not to a people six hundred years later:

> *and he* (God) *shall give You another*
> *Comforter, that he may abide*
> *with You for ever.*
>
> *(HOLY BIBLE)* John 14: 16

Surprisingly, the Christian sees no difficulty in justifying the fulfilment of prophecies **"since the world began,"**[1] and after over a millennium[2] when Peter in his second sermon to the Jews, reminds them:

> *For Moses truly said unto the*
> *fathers, A prophet shall the Lord*
> *Your God raise up unto You of*
> *Your brethren, like unto me; him*
> *shall ye hear in all things what-*
> *soever he shall say unto You.*
>
> *(HOLY BIBLE)* Acts 3: 22

All these **"YE, YOU** and **YOURS"** are from the Book of Deuteronomy, chapter 18,[3] when Moses (pbuh) addressed his

---

1. Acts 3: 21

2. **Millennium:** A thousand years.

3. This prophecy also refers to the Holy Prophet. Obtain **FREE** copy of the book — **"WHAT THE BIBLE SAYS ABOUT MUHUMMED (PBUH)"** from IPCI.

people and not the Jews at the time of Peter, thirteen hundred years later. The Gospel writers have put the same compromising words in the mouth of their Master which are begging for fulfilment for two thousand years. I think just one example will suffice:

> *But when they persecute You in*
> *this city, flee Ye into another:*
> *for verily* (most assuredly) *I* (Jesus)
> *say unto You, Ye shall not have*
> *gone over the cities of Israel till*
> *the son of man* (Jesus) *be come.*
>
> *(HOLY BIBLE)*   Matthew 10: 23

SCANNING THE CLOUDS

These early followers of the Messiah, forever ran, forlornly fleeing persecution. They ran from one city to another in Israel, scanning every dark cloud for the descent of Jesus (pbuh) in his second coming. The missionaries see no anomaly in their millennium of unfulfilled prophecies. God Almighty did not keep them waiting for even a quarter of the time for the advent of the **"paracletos,"** — the Comforter or **Ahmed** which is another name for the Praised One. Let them show gratitude to God by accepting this Last and Final Messenger of God — **Muhummed (pbuh)!**

ADVENT OF COMFORTER CONDITIONAL

(iii)   The Comforter is definitely not the **"Holy Ghost"** because the coming of the Comforter was conditional whereas that of the Holy Ghost was not as we observe in the prophecy —

> *Nevertheless, I tell you the truth:*
> *It is expedient for you that I go*
> *for If I Go Not Away, The*
> *Comforter Will Not Come unto*

you; but if I depart, I will send
him unto you.

(HOLY BIBLE)   John 16: 7

"If I don't go he won't come, but if I go, I will send him."
There are numerous instances in the Holy Bible about the
coming and going of the HOLY GHOST, before the birth and
departure of the Messiah. Do yourself a favour, please verify
these references in your Bible -

B.C. BEFORE CHRIST'S BIRTH:

1. *... and he* (John the Baptist) *shall be
    filled with the Holy Ghost,
    even from his mother's womb.*

    (HOLY BIBLE)   Luke 1: 15

2. *... and Elizabeth was filled
    with the Holy Ghost.*

    (HOLY BIBLE)   Luke 1: 41

3. *And his father Zacharias was
    filled with the Holy Ghost.*

    (HOLY BIBLE)   Luke 1: 67

A.C. AFTER CHRIST'S BIRTH:

4. *... and the Holy Ghost was
    upon him* (Simeon).

    (HOLY BIBLE)   Luke 2: 26

5. *And the Holy Ghost descended in
    a bodily shape like a dove upon
    him* (Jesus).

    (HOLY BIBLE)   Luke 3: 22

From the above quotations, before and after the birth of Jesus
(pbuh), one cannot help admiring St. Luke who appears to be a

specialist on the Holy Ghost. We may well ask the Christians, after the descent of the **"dove"**, with whose help did Jesus (pbuh) perform his many miracles if not with the help of the Holy Ghost? Let the Master himself tell us. When accused by his own people, the Jews, that he was working in league with Beelzebub (the chief of the devils) to work his miracles, Jesus (pbuh) rhetorically questions them, **"How can Satan cast out Satan?"** The Jews imputed that this spirit of holiness - the Spirit of God - which was helping him, was devilish. This was treason of the highest order. So he gives them a dire warning:

> *... but the blasphemy against the*
> *Holy Ghost, it shall never be*
> *forgiven ...*
>> **(HOLY BIBLE)** Matthew 12: 31

This "Holy Ghost" is none other than what Matthew himself has described in three verses before quoting the Master:

> *But if I* (Jesus) *cast out devils by*
> *the Spirit Of God, then the*
> *kingdom of God is come upon*
> *you.*
>> **(HOLY BIBLE)** Matthew 12: 28

Compare the same statement by another Gospel writer[1]

> *But if I* (Jesus) *by the Finger Of*
> *God cast out devils, no doubt the*
> *kingdom of God is come upon*
> *you.*
>> **(HOLY BIBLE)** Luke 11: 20

You do not have to be a Bible scholar to understand that the expressions (a) **"Finger of God"** (b) **"Spirit of God"** and (c) **"Holy Ghost"** are all synonymous phrases. So the Holy Ghost

---

1. Give a second glance at the two verses, top and bottom and you cannot help concluding that they are almost identical. Why? The answer is in **"Is the Bible God's Word?"** See Vol. II Part 2.

was helping Jesus (pbuh) in his ministry. The Holy Ghost was also helping his disciples on their missions of preaching and healing. If there is still any doubt in your minds about the workings of the Holy Ghost then please read:

EMPTY PROMISE

... as my Father hath sent me, even so I send you (the disciples of Jesus),

And when he had said this, he breathed on them, and saith unto them, <u>Receive Ye The Holy Ghost</u>

(HOLY BIBLE) *John 20: 21-22*

This was surely no empty promise. The disciples must have received the gift of the Holy Ghost. So if the **"Holy Ghost"** was with (1) John the Baptist, (2) Elizabeth, (3) Zacharias, (4) Simeon, (5) Jesus and (6) the Disciples of Jesus; then all this makes nonsense of the saying that **"if I go not away, the Comforter will not come unto you."** Therefore the Comforter is not the Holy **Ghost!**

The verse under discussion is John 16: 7. I remember the thrill and joy I got out of it when quoting it in Arabic to the Coptic Christian lady in the land of the Pharaohs (Page 42). The pleasure is immense when expounding Biblical verses in the standard native language of a country or locality. I have done it in a dozen different vernaculars. Won't you master the above verse in a language or two of your choice for the good of Islam?

AFRIKAANS A UNIQUE LANGUAGE

Of all the languages in which I have mastered the verse in question, I have derived the greatest excitement and benefit from Afrikaans. It is a language of the ruling race in South Africa. It is the youngest of the world's languages. The language is unique. In fact every language is unique. But Afrikaans is in a class of its own. It also happens to be the mother tongue of half the Muslim population of South Africa who were brought here as prisoners of war and enslaved by the Christians; that is simply by force of circumstances. For **their** immediate benefit and for your information I reproduce the verse here:

> *Maar ek sê julle die waarheid: dit is*
> *vir julle voordelig dat ek weggaan;*
> *want as ek Nie weggaan Nie, sal*
> *die Trooster[1] Nie na julle kom*
> *Nie; maar as ek weggaan, sal ek*
> *hom na julle stuur.*
>
> *Johanness 16: 7*

Believe it or not! It is the genius of this language that it uses four negatives **NIE, NIE, NIE, NIE,** to prove a positive! The departure of Jesus is an absolute imperative for the coming of the **"Trooster,"** the Comforter to come! This verse in this language has opened many doors for me, other than religious, and it locks the door against the idea of the **"Comforter which is the Holy Ghost"** (John 14: 26).

DISCIPLES NOT FIT

We now come to the four most comprehensive and decisive verses in John, chapter sixteen to solve the enigma of the Successor to Christ. For Jesus (pbuh) did truly say:

> *I have yet Many Things to say*
> *unto you, but Ye Cannot Bear*
> *Them Now.*
>
> **(HOLY BIBLE)** *John 16: 12*

---

1. **Trooster:** Now changed to **"VOORSPRAAK!"** See page 80

We will later tie up the phrase **"many things"** from the above verse with **"guide you into all truth"** from the verse that follows, when discussing it.[1] For now, let us discuss the phrase — **"YE CANNOT BEAR THEM NOW"**

The truth of this statement **"ye cannot bear them now"** is repeated monotonously throughout the pages of the New Testament:

* **And he** (Jesus) **saith unto them** (the disciples), **Why are ye fearful,**
  <u>**O Ye Of Little Faith?**</u>

  (HOLY BIBLE)   *Matthew 8: 26*

* And (Jesus) **said unto him** (Peter)
  <u>**O Thou Of Little Faith ...**</u>

  (HOLY BIBLE)   *Matthew 14: 31*

* ... **he** (Jesus) **said unto them** (the disciples), <u>**O Ye Of Little Faith,**</u>
  why reason among yourselves ...

  (HOLY BIBLE)   *Matthew 16: 8*

* **And he** (Jesus) **said unto them** (his disciples), <u>**Where Is Your Faith?**</u>

  (HOLY BIBLE)   *Luke 8: 25*

We must bear in mind that this is not the indictment of Jesus (pbuh) on the indecivisiveness of the Jews, but on his very own elect. He stoops down to the level of little children to make things plain to his disciples but he is compelled to burst out in frustration —

* **And Jesus said,**
  <u>**Are Ye Even Yet Without**</u>
  <u>**Understanding?**</u>

  (HOLY BIBLE)   *Matthew 15: 16*

---

1. Discussed on page 68

And when he was provoked to breaking point, he rails against his chosen ones —

* *... O Faithless And Perverse*
Generation, how long shall I
be with you, how long shall I
bear with you?

(HOLY BIBLE)   Luke 9: 41

OWN FAMILY THOUGHT HIM MAD

If Jesus (pbuh) would have been a Japanese instead of a Jew, he would happily have committed that honourable **"harakiri"** (suicide). Sadly, he was the most unfortunate of God's Messengers. His family disbelieved him **For neither did his** (Jesus') **brethren believe in him** (John 7: 5). In fact they went to the extent of wanting to apprehend him, believing that he was mad.

And when his relatives heard of it,
they went out to lay hold on him
(Jesus); *for they said, he is beside*
himself.

(HOLY BIBLE)   Mark 3: 21

Who were these friends and relatives of Jesus (pbuh) which had concern for his sanity? Let Rev. J.R. Dummelow, M.A. in his One Volume Bible Commentary tell us. On page 726 he says —

"FROM V.31" (just 10 verses following the above quotation) "THEY APPEAR TO HAVE BEEN HIS MOTHER AND BRETHREN ... HIS FAMILY SAID **'HE IS BESIDE HIMSELF,'**" (meaning that he is not right in his head); "THE SCRIBES SAID, **'HE IS POSSESSED BY THE DEVIL HIMSELF.'** IT IS NOT, HOWEVER, IMPLIED AT ALL THAT HIS FAMILY WAS IN SYMPATHY WITH THE SCRIBES" (the learned men of the Jews),

---

* Emphasis in all the six quotations are mine.

"THEIR APPREHENSION BEING SIMPLY THAT HIS MIND WAS UNSETTLED, AND THAT HE NEEDED TO BE PUT UNDER RESTRAINT."

JESUS — REJECTED BY HIS NATION

That was the verdict of the close relations of Jesus (pbuh). What then was the response of his own nation, the Jews, after all his beautiful preachings and mighty miracle workings? His disciple puts it very mildly:

> **He came unto his own** (the Jews) **and**
> **his own received him** (Jesus) **not.**
>
> **(HOLY BIBLE)**   John 1: 11

Actually "his own" mocked him, scorned him and vehemently rejected him. To the extent of making an attempt to crucify him.[1] Despite two thousand years of Christian persecutions and pogroms, and now their overweening love and infatuation for them, so as to salve their own conscience, the Jews as a people and as a whole can never accept Jesus as their Saviour, their Deliverer, their God, simply because of their one sound judgement —

"THAT NO JEW CAN EVER ACCEPT ANOTHER JEW AS A GOD!"

It is only in Islam that the Jews, the Christians and the Muslims can find accommodation — all believing in Jesus Christ (pbuh) for what he really was — one of the mightiest Messengers of God; and not as **God** or **His son!**

DISCIPLES DESERTED HIM

What was the response of the chosen twelve; of his own **"mother and bretheren!"** (Mark 3: 34), as he called them? I will allow Professor Momerie to describe it in his own inimitable words —

---

1. **Get** your **FREE** copy of the book — **"Crucifixion or Cruci-fiction?** from the IPCI.

"HIS IMMEDIATE DISCIPLES, WERE ALWAYS MISUNDER-
STANDING HIM AND HIS WORK: WANTING HIM TO CALL DOWN
FIRE FROM HEAVEN; WANTING HIM TO DECLARE HIMSELF KING
OF THE JEWS; WANTING TO SIT ON HIS RIGHT HAND AND ON HIS
LEFT HAND IN HIS KINGDOM; WANTING HIM TO SHOW THEM THE
FATHER, TO MAKE GOD VISIBLE TO THEIR BODILY EYES;
WANTING HIM TO DO, AND WANTING TO DO THEMSELVES,
ANYTHING AND EVERYTHING THAT WAS INCOMPATIBLE WITH
HIS GREAT PLAN. THIS WAS HOW THEY TREATED HIM UNTIL THE
END. (and) WHEN THAT CAME, THEY ALL FORSOOK HIM, AND
FLED."

Quoted from Sayed Amir Ali in his *"The Spirit of Islam"* page 31.

It was most unfortunate that Jesus Christ (pbuh) had no real choice in
selecting his disciples. They let him down as no other group of
devotees had ever let down their prophet before. It was no fault of the
Master. He bewailed his plight: **"The spirit indeed is willing, but
the flesh** (clay) **is weak"** (Matthew 26: 41). Truly, this is not the clay
out of which a new Adam could be made. He passes on that
responsibility to his Successor, whom he calls here — **"The Spirit of
Truth,"** ie the Prophet of Truth, the Prophet of Righteousness!

"SPIRIT" AND "PROPHET" SYNONYMOUS

*Howbeit when he, the Spirit Of
Truth, is come, he will guide you
into all truth*   (HOLY BIBLE) John 16: 13

It has already been established that, Biblically, the word **"Spirit"** is
used synonymously for **"Prophet,"** by the same author in 1
John 4: 1 (see page 53).

Hence the "Spirit of Truth" would be the Prophet of Truth. A prophet in
whom **Truth** is personified. He had walked through life so honourably
and industriously that he had won for himself even from his pagan
fellow countrymen the noble designation of **as-Saadiq** (the Truthful
One) and **al-Amîn,** "the Honest," "the Upright," "the Trustworthy;" the
Man of Faith who never broke his word. His life, his personality, his
teachings are the veritable proof of Muhummed (pbuh) being the
embodiment of Truth (al-Amîn) — the Spirit of Truth!

CHAPTER FOUR

Total Guidance!

"MANY AND "ALL"

As promised on page 62, we will now combine, **"I have yet MANY things to say unto you"** from verse twelve, with **"he will guide you into ALL truth."** From John 16: 12 and 13.

If the Christian still persists that the Spirit of Truth of this prophecy is the Holy Ghost then ask him or her whether in their language does **"MANY"** means more than one? Also if **"ALL"** in the above verse means more than one? If you get a halting, wavering, hesistant **"y-e-s"** then close the book, it is not worth pursuing dialogues with opinionated fools. But if you get the answer "yes!" with alacrity then proceed ...

The one prophesied by Jesus (pbuh) was to unravel **many** things which he had left unsaid, as well as to guide humanity into **all** truth. There are many problems facing mankind today, for which we are fumbling for answers. Can you please give me one new thing that the alleged Holy Ghost gave to anybody in the past two thousand years, which Jesus Christ had not already given in so many different words? I don't want many, I am looking for **just one!**

NO SOLUTION FROM HOLY GHOST

Believe me, in my forty years of questioning, I have not come across a single Christian with a single "new Truth" inspired by the Holy Ghost, yet the promise **was** that the coming Comforter -**"he will guide you into all truth!"** If the Spirit of Truth of this prophecy is the Holy Ghost then every Church and denomination, and every **'born-again'** Christian is claiming the gift of the Holy Ghost. The Roman Catholics claim that they have the whole Truth because of the so-called "in-dwelling" of the Holy Ghost. The Anglicans make the same claim, and the Methodists, the Jehovah's Witnesses, the Seventh Day Adventists, the Baptists, the Christadelphians, etc, etc, not forgetting the **'born-agains'** who claim to be numbering over 70 million in the United States alone.

You have the right to demand solutions from them, on the authority of the Holy Ghost, for the problems listed below:

1. **Alcohol**
2. **Gambling**
3. **Fortune Telling**
4. **Idol Worship, Devil Worship**
5. **Racism**
6. **Problem of Surplus Women etc etc.**

PROBLEM OF ALCOHOL

The Republic of South Africa with a small "white"[1] population of 4 million among its total population of 30 million, has over 300,000 alcoholics. In neighbouring Zambia, Kenneth Kaunda calls such people "drunkards!" It is recorded that the **"coloureds"**[2] in South Africa have five times the amount of alcoholics as any other race in the country. For the Indians and the Africans no statistics are available for their respective drunkards.

Jimmy Swaggart the televangelist records in his book "ALCOHOL" that the United States has 11 million alcoholics[3] and 44 million "heavy drinkers!", and he, like a good Muslim, goes on to say that he sees no difference between the two. To him they are all **drunkards!** The rampant evil of drunkenness is universal. The Holy Ghost has not yet made its pronouncement on this evil through any Church. Christendom winks at drunkenness on three flimsy pretences based on the Holy Bible.

---

1. Of European extraction.
2. A mixture between the Black and White Races.
3. The Americans euphemistically call them **"Problem Drinkers."**

(a) *Give strong drink* (hard liquor) *to him who is perishing* (one who is dying) *And wine to those who are bitter of heart.*

Let him drink and forget his poverty, And remember his misery no more.
                                    (HOLY BIBLE) Proverbs 31: 6-7

A very good philosophy to keep the subject nations under subjugation, you will agree.

HIS VERY FIRST MIRACLE

(b) Jesus (pbuh) was no **"killjoy,"** the imbibers say, he turned water into wine in his very first recorded miracle in the Bible:

Jesus saith unto them, Fill the waterpots with water. And they filled them up to the brim.

And he saith unto them, Draw out now ...

When the ruler of the feast had tasted the water that was made wine ...

And saith ... (why) *thou hast kept the good wine until now.*
                                    (HOLY BIBLE) John 2: 7-10

Since this alleged miracle, wine continues to flow like water in Christendom.

SOBER ADVICE

(c) Saint Paul the thirteenth self-appointed disciple of Christ, the real founder of Christianity, advises his new convert protege —

Timothy, born of a Greek father and a Jewish mother:

**Drink no longer water, but use a
little wine for thy stomach's
sake and thine often infirmities.**

(HOLY BIBLE)   1 Timothy 5: 23

The Christians accept all the Bible quotations on stimulating and intoxicating drinks given above as the infallible word of God. They believe that the Holy Ghost inspired the authors to pen such dangerous advices. Rev. Dummelow (see page 62) seems to have some qualms about this verse. He says,

"IT TEACHES US THAT IF THE BODY NEEDS THE STIMULANT OF WINE, IT IS RIGHT TO TAKE IT IN MODERATION."

ABSTINENCE THE ONLY ANSWER

There are thousands of Christian priests who have been lured into alcoholism by sipping the so-called mild wine in the Church rite of the Holy Communion. Islam is the only religion on the face of the earth which prohibits intoxicants in toto. The Holy Prophet (Spirit) Muhummed (pbuh) had said, "WHATEVER INTOXICATES IN GREATER QUANTITY, IS FORBIDDEN EVEN IN SMALLER QUANTITY." There is no excuse in the house of Islam for a nip or a tot. The **Kitab-al-Haq,** the Book of Truth **(Haq)** one of the titles of the Holy Qur'an condemned in the strongest terms not only the evil of alcohol but also items 2, 3, and 4, namely "gambling," "fortune telling and "idol worship," with just a single stroke —

O YE WHO BELIEVE!   يَاۤيُّهَا الَّذِيۡنَ اٰمَنُوۡاۤ

*MOST CERTAINLY INTOXICANTS
AND GAMBLING,*   اِنَّمَا الۡخَمۡرُ وَالۡمَيۡسِرُ

(DEDICATION OF) STONES,   وَالۡاَنۡصَابُ

AND (DIVINATION) OF ARROWS,   وَالۡاَزۡلَامُ

ARE AN ABOMINATION, -
OF SATAN'S HANDIWORK

SHUN SUCH (ABOMINATION),
THAT YE MAY PROSPER.

رِجۡسٌ مِّنۡ عَمَلِ الشَّيۡطٰنِ
فَاجۡتَنِبُوۡهُ لَعَلَّكُمۡ تُفۡلِحُوۡنَ ۞

(SÚRA MÁIDA) *Holy Qur'an 5: 93*[1]

When this verse was revealed, wine barrels were emptied in the streets of Madinah, never to be refilled. This simple straight-forward directive has created of the Muslim **Ummah** (religious community) the biggest society of teetotallers[2] in the world.

U.S.A. FAILS WITH "PROHIBITION"

The question arises, how is it that this Spirit of Truth — the Holy Prophet Muhummed (pbuh) succeeded with one verse whereas mighty America with the brain power of the nation and the money power of the Government, supported by its powerful propaganda machinery failed with **"Prohibition,"** the law outlawing alcohol?

Who coerced the American nation to enact prohibition? Which Arab nation threatened this mighty power with if you do not prohibit alcohol in your country, we will not supply you with oil? Not the Arabs as there was no such thing as oil as a **"POLITICAL INSTRUMENT"**[3] in the hands of the Arabs during the twenties to egg the United States. It was an intellectual awareness among the American (founding) fathers, based on study and statistics which brought them to the conclusion that intoxicants must be banned. They failed, notwithstanding the fact that the overwhelming majority of the nation was Christian, and that it was they who had voted their Congressmen into power. It is rightly said that that which comes from the brain (intel-

---

1. See Yusuf Ali's commentary for further clarification. I hope you are heeding my plea to memorize these Qur'anic quotations with their meanings.

2. **Teetotaller:** A person who abstains completely from all alcoholic drinks.

3. From **"YAMANI — THE INSIDE STORY"** by Jeffrey Robinson.

lectually) tickles the brain, but that which comes from the heart and soul of a man, will move the heart. The verse just quoted above from the Holy Qur'an on prohibition, had and has the power for change; we will allow Thomas Carlyle to reveal the source of that power:

"IF A BOOK COME FROM THE HEART, IT WILL CONTRIVE TO REACH OTHER HEARTS; ALL ART AND AUTHORCRAFT ARE SMALL AMOUNT TO THAT. ONE WOULD SAY THE PRIMARY CHARACTER OF THE KORAN IS THIS OF ITS *GENUINENESS*, OF ITS BEING A *BONA FIDE* BOOK."

HIGH SPIRITUALITY — A SOURCE OF POWER

All the beautiful thoughts, words and expressions, never mind how artistically constructed, remain like ringing bells or clanking cymbals unless they are backed up by a powerful personality charged with high spirituality. And that type of super spirituality comes only as Jesus (pbuh) put it through ***"fasting and prayer"*** (Matthew 17: 21).

Muhummed (pbuh) practised what he preached. After his demise someone asked his dear wife Áyeshá Siddiqá about the life-style of her husband. She said, **"He was the Qur'an in action."** He was the walking Qur'an. He was the talking Qur'an. He was the living Qur'an.

"IF THESE MEN AND WOMEN, NOBLE, INTELLIGENT, AND CERTAINLY NOT LESS EDUCATED THAN THE FISHERMEN OF GALILEE, HAD PERCEIVED THE SLIGHTEST SIGN OF EARTH-LINESS, DECEPTION, OR WANT OF FAITH IN THE TEACHER HIMSELF, MOHAMMED'S HOPES OF MORAL REGENERATION AND SOCIAL REFORM WOULD ALL HAVE BEEN CRUMBLED TO DUST IN A MOMENT."

"Spirit of Islam" by Sayed Amir Ali, page 21

CRITIC'S HERO

If it is said that these are the words of a devoted Believer about his beloved, then let us hear what a sympathetic Christian critic had to say about HIS **"Hero Prophet!"**

"A POOR, HARD-TOILING, ILL-PROVIDED MAN; CARELESS OF WHAT VULGAR MEN TOIL FOR. NOT A BAD MAN, I SHOULD SAY; SOMETHING BETTER IN HIM THAN **HUNGER** OF ANY SORT, — OR THESE WILD ARAB MEN, FIGHTING AND JOSTLING THREE-AND-TWENTY YEARS AT HIS HAND, IN CLOSE CONTACT WITH HIM ALWAYS, WOULD NOT HAVE REVERENCED HIM SO!

"... THEY CALLED HIM PROPHET, YOU SAY? WHY, HE STOOD THERE FACE TO FACE WITH THEM; BARE. NOT ENSHRINED IN ANY MYSTERY; VISIBLY CLOUTING HIS OWN CLOAK, COBBLING HIS OWN SHOES; FIGHTING, COUNSELLING, ORDER-ING IN THE MIDST OF THEM: THEY MUST HAVE SEEN WHAT KIND OF A MAN HE **WAS,** LET HIM BE **CALLED** WHAT YOU LIKE! NO EMPEROR WITH HIS TIARAS WAS OBEYED AS THIS MAN IN A CLOAK OF HIS OWN CLOUTING. DURING THREE-AND-TWENTY YEARS OF ROUGH ACUTAL TRIAL. I FIND SOMETHING OF A VERITABLE **HERO** NECESSARY FOR THAT, OF ITSELF."

"Hero and Hero-worship" by Thomas Carlyle, page 93

PROBLEM OF RACISM

> *... For he* (the Spirit of Truth) *will guide you into all truth!*
>
> **(HOLY BIBLE)** *John 16: 13*

NOT WITHOUT A SYSTEM

It is very easy for the followers of any religion to talk glibly about "THE FATHERHOOD OF GOD AND THE BROTHERHOOD

OF MAN" but how is this beautiful idea to be implemented? How to devise a system to bring mankind into a single brotherhood? Five times a day, every Muslim is obligated to gather together at the local mosque to strengthen himself spiritually. The black and the white; the rich and the poor; people of different nationalities, of varying hues are made to rub shoulders in the daily *Salaat,* the Muslim at Prayer.[1] Once a week, that is on Fridays, he has to congregate at the cathedral Mosque *(the Jaame Musjid)* for a wider gathering from the surrounding districts. And twice a year during the two Eids at still a larger venue, preferably in the open air, for a vaster communion. A-n-d, at least once in a life-time at the *Kaaba,* the Central Mosque in Makkah, for an international gathering; where one can witness the blonde-haired Turk, the Ethiopian, the Chinese, the Indian, the American and the African, all get levelled-up in the same pilgrim's garb of two unsewn sheets. Where is there such a great leveller in the religious rites of other faiths?

The infallible precept as enunciated in the Book of God is that the only standard recognised by God is on the basis of one's conduct, one's behaviour towards one's fellow human beings and not because of one's race or riches. These are the only true bases on which the **"Kingdom of God"** can be established.[2] All this does not mean that the Muslim is immaculate, that he is altogether free from this sickness of racism, but you will find the Muslim the least racist of all the religious groupings strutting the world today.

---

1. Take your non-Muslim friends to the Mosque to watch "The Muslim at Prayer." If you are too shy then show him the video - **"CHRISTIAN GUESTS IN YOUR MOSQUE,"** V51 from the IPCI. You will not fail to learn a lot of easy entertaining ways of discussing Islam.

2. See inside back cover for this **"The Future World Constitution,"** obtain a volume for yourself and a copy for your non-Muslim friend. You can't give a better gift!

PROBLEM OF SURPLUS WOMEN

Nature seems to be at war with mankind. It appears that it wants to take revenge for his cleverness. Man will not listen to the healthy, practical solution to his problems, which a Beneficial, Benevolent Providence offers him. So it says, **"go simmer in your SOUP!"** (in a manner of speaking).

It is an accepted fact that at birth the ratio of male and female is about equal everywhere. But in child mortality more males die than females. Amazing! The **"weaker sex"?** At any given time there are more widows in the world than widowers. Every civilized nation has a surplus of women. Great Britain 4 million. Germany 5 million. Soviet Russia 7 million, etc. But a solution acceptable to the problem of the mighty United States of America, will be a solution acceptable to nations everywhere. The statistics of this most sophisticated nation on earth is more readily verifiable.

AMERICA, O AMERICA!

We learn that the U.S.A. has a surplus of 7,8 million women. It means that if every man in America got married, there would still be 7 800 000 women left over, women who would be unable to get their share of a husband. One thing we do know, and that is that every man will never get married for so many different reasons. Man gets cold feet and finds many excuses. A woman, even if frigid, would not mind getting married. She would marry, even if it is just for shelter and protection.

But the American problem of surplus women is compounded. Ninety-eight percent of its prison population is male. Then they have 25 million sodomites. Euphemistically they call them **"gays"** a once beautiful word meaning — **happy and joyous** — now perverted!

America does everything in a big way. She produces everything mighty. Mighty in promoting God and also mighty in promoting the Devil. Let us for once, join the mighty televangelist (now fallen) Jimmy Swaggart, in his prayer. In his well-researched book — **"HOMOSEXUALITY,"** he cries,

"AMERICA — GOD WILL JUDGE YOU (meaning that God will destroy you), **FOR IF HE DOES NOT JUDGE YOU** (destroy you), **HE** (God) **MIGHT HAVE TO APOLOGIZE TO SODOM AND GOMORRAH"** for their hasty, utter destruction because of their practice of homosexuality or their wanton gratification of unnatural lust.

NEW YORK AS AN EXAMPLE

The City of New York has one million more women than men. Even if the total male population in this city mustered enough courage to unite with the opposite sex in matrimony; there would still remain 1 000 000 women without husbands.

But to make things worse, it is reputed that one third of the male population in this city is **"gay"** (homosexuals/sodomites). The Jews, a very vociferous lot in every controversy, remain quiet as mice, for fear of being labelled backward Easterners. The Church, with their millions of **born again** votaries claiming to be the dwelling houses of the Holy Ghost, are also silent on this topic.

The founders of the Mormon Church, Joseph Smith and Brigham Young, claiming a new revelation in 1830 preached and practised unlimited polygamy to solve the problem of surplus women. The present day prophets of Mormonism[1] have abrogated the teaching of their Church fathers to placate American prejudice on the subject of polygamy. What is the poor American/Western/European surplus women to do? They have literally gone to the dogs.[2]

---

1. The Mormons believe in an unbroken chain of living prophets in their Church.
2. Consult **"The life of the American Female,"** by Dr. Alfred Kinsey and the latest on the subject by Masters and Johnson.

ONLY SOLUTION - RESTRICTED AND REGULATED POLYGAMY

Al-Amin, the Prophet of Truth, the Spirit of Truth, under inspiration of God supplies the solution to their unfortunate plight. God ordains —

> **... Marry women of your choice,**
> **two, or three, or four;**
> **But if you fear that you will**
> **not be able to deal justly (with them)**
> **Then (marry) only one ...**
>
> *(SÚRA NISÁA)* Holy Qur'an 4: 3

The Western world feigns tolerance towards the millions of sodomites and lesbians in their midst. It is a joking matter in the West for a man to keep a dozen mistresses, and beget a dozen bastard[1] children every year. Such lecherous creatures are proudly labelled as **"studs."**[2] **"Let him sow his wild oats, but don't hold him responsible!"** says the West.

Islam says: "make man responsible for his pleasures." There is a type of man who is prepared to take on extra responsibility, and there is a type of woman who is prepared to share a husband. Why place obstacles in their way? You mock at (polygamy), which was practised by the prophets of God as recorded in the Holy Bible, you forget that Solomon The Wise had a thousand wives and concubines as recorded in the Good Book (1 King 11: 3), a healthy solution to your momentous problem, and yet smugly wink at the gratification of unnatural lusts by sodomites and lesbians! What a perversion? Polygamy was practised by the Jews and the pagans in the time of Jesus (pbuh). He did not say a single word against it. Not his fault. The Jews gave him no peace to propound solutions. His was a natural cry, **"when he**

---

1. **Bastard:** is Biblical. The Holy Bible has used it **three** times: Deut. 23: 2, Zech. 9: 6 and Heb. 12: 8 .

2. **Stud:** a slang used for a man considered to be excessively virile. The term usually reserved for animal husbandry.

the Spirit of Truth is come, he will guide you into All truth" (John 16: 13).

COMFORTER TO BE A MAN

If I take the liberty of quoting the prophecy under discussion, with an emphasis on the pronouns, you will agree without any persuasion that the coming Comforter was to be a **man** and not a **ghost.**

> *Howbeit when He, the Spirit of*
> *Truth, is come, He will guide you*
> *into all truth:*
>
> *for He shall not speak of Himself;*
> *but whatsoever He shall hear,*
> *that shall He speak: and He will*
> *show you things to come.*
>
> **(HOLY BIBLE)**   *John 16: 13*

Please count the number of **HE's** in the above verse. There are **s-e-v-e-n!** Seven masculine pronouns in a single verse! There is not another verse in the 66 books of the Protestant Bible or in the 73 Books of the Catholic Bible with seven masculine pronouns, or seven feminine pronouns, or with seven neuter genders. You will agree that so many masculine pronouns in one verse ill befits a **Ghost,** holy or not!

NON-STOP INTERPOLATIONS

When this point of the seven masculine pronouns in a single verse of the Bible was mooted by the Muslims in India in their debates with the Christian missionaries, the Urdu version of the Bible had the pronouns presently changed to SHE, SHE, SHE! so that the Muslims could not claim that this prophecy referred to Muhummed (pbuh) — **a man!** This Christian chicanery; deception

I have seen in the Urdu Bible myself. This is a common trickery by the missionaries, more specially in the vernacular. The very latest ruse I have stumbled across is in the Afrikaans Bible, on the very verse under discussion; they have changed the word **"Trooster"** (Comforter), to **"Voorspraak"** (Mediator), and inter-polated the phrase — **"die Heilige Gees"** — meaning THE HOLY GHOST, which phrase no Bible Scholar has ever dared to interpolate into any of the multifarious English Versions. No, not even the Jehovah's Witnesses.[1] This is how the Christians manu-facture God's word![2]

NINE MASCULINE PRONOUNS

The only other place an author has unknowingly used so many masculine pronouns for this mighty Messenger Muhummed (pbuh) is given below:

"HIS GENTLE DISPOSITION, **HIS** AUSTERITY OF CONDUCT, THE SEVERE PURITY OF **HIS** LIFE, **HIS** SCRUPULOUS REFINE-MENT, **HIS** EVER-READY HELPFULNESS TOWARDS THE POOR AND THE WEAK, **HIS** NOBLE SENSE OF HONOUR, **HIS** UNFLINCHING FIDELITY, **HIS** STERN SENSE OF DUTY HAD WON **HIM,** AMONG **HIS** COMPATRIOTS, THE HIGH AND ENVIABLE DESIGNATION OF AL-AMÍN, THE TRUSTY."

"Spirit of Islam," by Sayed Amir Ali, page 14

"AL-AMÍN," the Faithful, the Trustworthy, **"even the Spirit of Truth"** (John 14: 17). This expression is a figurative way of saying that SPEAKING TRUTH would be so characteristic of him that people would regard him as TRUTH PERSONIFIED: exactly as Jesus (pbuh) said about himself, **"I am the way, the truth and the life . . ."** (John 14: 6), that these noble qualities are

---

1. **Jehovah's Witnesses:** an incorrigible Christian sect which has contrived its own Bible translation.
2. See Vol. II Part 2 - **"Is the Bible God's Word?"** and learn, how the Christian has been interpolating his own prejudices in a Book he claims to be from God.

personified in me. Follow me! But **'when he the Spirit of truth, is come, he will guide you into all truth''** (John 16: 13), then you must follow him! But prejudices die hard, therefore we must work harder. But believe me, with the laser truth that Allah has given us, we can change the world with only a fraction of the energy that the Christian is expending.

SOURCE OF REVELATION

Howbeit when he, the Spirit of truth, is come, he will guide you into all truth! For He Shall Not Speak From Himself But What- soever He Shall Hear, That Shall He Speak.

(HOLY BIBLE) John 16: 13

I have consistently been using the King James Version in my Biblical quotations, but for greater clarity, I give below, alternate rendering from some different versions of the above emphasised sentence:

1. *for he will not speak on his Own Authority, But will tell only what he hears.*

The New English Bible

2. *He will not speak On His Own; He will Speak Only What He Hears.*

New International Version

3. *for he will not be presenting His Own Ideas, But He Will Be Passing On To You What He Has Heard.*

The Living Bible

This **"Spirit of Truth,"** this Prophet of Truth, "Al-Amin," will not be speaking spiritual truths on his own impulse, but he will speak on the same basis as his previous Comforter — Jesus (pbuh) had spoken:

> *For I speak not from myself; but the Father that sent me, he hath given me the commandment, what I should say, and what I should speak.*
>
> *... even as the Father hath saith unto me, so I speak.*
>
> **(HOLY BIBLE)**   John 12: 49-50

In an **identical** manner God Almighty testifies His revelation to His Messenger Muhummed (pbuh).

> **Nor does He say (aught) of (His own) desire.**
>
> **It is no less than, inspiration sent down to Him.**
>
> **He was taught by one mighty in power.** [1]
>
> **(SÚRA NAJM)**   Holy Qur'an 53: 3-5

This is how God communicated with all His chosen Messengers, whether Abraham, Moses or Jesus. It would be absurd to think that this **"Spirit of Truth"** is the Holy Ghost, because we are told that *"he will not speak from himself, but what he hears,"* surely not from himself?

GOD — A TRINITY?

It is universally accepted in Christendom, all orthodox Christians who believe in what they call the Holy Trinity; that the Father is God, the son is God and the Holy Ghost is God, but they are not

---

1. All Quranic Commentators understand this to refer to the archangel Gabriel. Call him the "Holy Ghost" if you like.

three Gods but one God. (?) Let an erudite Christian theologian, like the Rev. Dummelow tell us of this indivisibility, indissolubility of the Christian's "triune" God. Commenting on *"We will come"* of John 14: 23 he says —

WHERE THE SON IS, THERE OF NECESSITY IS THE FATHER ALSO, AS WELL AS THE SPIRIT, FOR THE **THREE ARE ONE,** BEING DIFFERENT FORMS OF THE SUBSISTENCE AND MANIFESTATION OF THE SAME DIVINE BEING. THIS PASSAGE ILLUSTRATES THAT THE PERSONS OF THE HOLY TRINITY **ARE INSEPARABLE, AND CONTAIN ONE ANOTHER.**

Please don't worry. You are not really expected to understand the above verbiage. In short the Christian believes that the "THREE" (I beg your pardon, the Christian says, "ONE!"), all the **three** are supposed to be Omnipresent and Omniscient and as such lead us to an amusing and ridiculous conclusion. Jesus (pbuh) according to the Christians agonized on the cross at Calvary. Being **"inseparable,"** the Father and the Holy Ghost also must have agonized with the Son, and when he died, the other two died with him! Little wonder we hear the cry in the West — **"God is Dead!"** Don't laugh. All this imposes on us a more sombre responsibility of extricating our Christian brethren from the spiritual quagmire into which they are wallowing.

CHAPTER FIVE

Fulfilled Prophecies

And he will show you things to come.

(HOLY BIBLE) John 16: 13

REFUGEE: ONLY FOR A WHILE

The Christians put great weight on the fulfilment of prophecies. Muhummed (pbuh) fulfilled many prophecies of the Old[1] and the New Testaments. To them, the prediction of events is considered to be the function of true prophecy — true prophethood.

The Prophet of Islam uttered many prophecies which are recorded for posterity in the Holy Qur'an. Here are a few taken at random.

> 1. **Verily, He Who** (God Almighty)
>   **ordained the Qur'an for thee,** (He)
>   **will bring thee back to the Place**
>   **of Return ...**
>
> *(SÚRA QASAS)* Holy Qur'an 28: 85

"Place of Return," is a title of the Holy City of Makkah. During the **Hijrat** (Migration) when the Holy Prophet was fleeing from Makkah to Madinah. It was a hopeless situation. Most of his followers had already migrated to Madinah. Now it was his turn. Together with Abu Bakr **(as-Siddiq)** he had reached a place called Juhfa, when this assurance was given by God that once again he will return to his birthplace Makkah, and so he did.

He migrated as a refugee and God returns him as a conqueror, fulfilling yet another prophecy.[2]

---

1. You will find some of these prophecies expounded in Part 1 — **"What the Bible says about Muhummed (pbuh)"** in this volume.

2. For a detailed exposition of this prophecy read **"Muhummed** (pbuh) **in the Bible"** by Abdul-Ahad Dawud, former Bishop of Uramiah obtainable from the Centre.

And he (Moses) *said, the Lord came*
from Sinai, and rose from Seir
unto them; he shined forth from
mount Paran (that is in Arabia), *and*
he (Muhummed) *came with* Ten
Thousand Saints:*[1] from his right*
hand went a fiery law for them.

(HOLY BIBLE)   Deuteronomy 33: 2

SUPERPOWERS: IN CONFLICT

2.   **The Roman Empire has been defeated**

In a land close by;
But they, (even) after (this)
Defeat of theirs, will soon be
victorious —

Within a few years. With God is
the Decision,
In the Past and in the Future:
On that day shall the Believers
rejoice —

(SÚRA RÚM)   Holy Qur'an 30: 2-4

The above prophecy was revealed to the Holy Prophet Muhummed (pbuh) in the year 615/16 of the Christian era. The Christian Empire of Rome had lost Jerusalem to the Persians, and Christianity had been humbled in the dust. In this holocaust between two of the superpowers of the day, the **Mushriks** (polytheists) of Makkah derived vicarious pleasure in the discomfiture of the Romans by the pagan Persians.

"THE PAGAN ARABS NATURALLY SIDED WITH THE PERSIANS IN THEIR DESTRUCTIVE ZEAL, AND THOUGHT THAT THE

---

1. The Holy Prophet was accompanied by 10 000 **SAHABÁS** (companions — veritable saints) at the conquest of Makkah.

DESTRUCTION OF THE CHRISTIAN POWER OF ROME WOULD ALSO MEAN A SETBACK TO THE MESSAGE OF THE PROPHET, **THE TRUE SUCCESSOR TO CHRIST.**[1] ... WHILE THE WHOLE WORLD BELIEVED THAT THE ROMAN EMPIRE WAS BEING KILLED BY PERSIA, IT WAS REVEALED TO HIM THAT THE PERSIAN VICTORY WAS SHORT-LIVED AND THAT WITHIN A PERIOD OF A FEW YEARS THE ROMANS WOULD CONQUER AGAIN AND DEAL A DEADLY BLOW AT THE PERSIANS."

Abdullah Yusuf Ali

Within ten years of the revelation of this Divine prediction, the prophecy was fulfilled!

CHALLENGE OF THE QUR'AN

3. The Holy Prophet claimed that the Holy Qur'an was from God Almighty, and that it was revealed to him by inspiration. The proof of its Divine authorship is its own beauty and nature, and the circumstances in which it was promulgated. To prove the veracity of his claim, he has placed before you many Súras. Can the unbeliever produce one like it? This is a standing challenge! An eternal prophecy of mankind's inability to equal or excel, or to rival successfully any of its chapters.

Your plea, "I don't know Arabic," is useless. There are millions of Christian Arabs living today. The Christians boast that there are at least 10-15 million Coptic Christians in Egypt alone and these are not all **fellaheens.**[2] Here is the challenge of God in His Own words —

<blockquote>

(a) **This Qur'an is not such as can be produced by other than Allah.**[3]
</blockquote>

Holy Qur'an 10: 37

---

1. The emphasis is mine. Though I own Yusuf Ali's translation for over half-a-century, I have only very recently come across the above phrase for the first time.
2. **Fellaheen:** A peasant or agricultural labourer in Arab countries.
3. **Allah:** A proper noun for God Almighty in the Semitic languages. See Vol III, Part 3 — **"What is His name?"** which explains this word in detail.

(b) **Say: "If the whole of mankind
and Jinns were to gather
together to produce the like of
this Qur'an, they could not
produce the like thereof, even if
they backed up each other with
help and support."**

(SÚRA BANI ISRÁ-ÍL) Holy Qur'an 17: 88

(c) **Or do they say, "He forged it"?
Say: "Bring then a Súra like
unto it, and call** (to your aid)
**anyone you can, besides Allah,
if it be that ye speak the truth!"**

(SÚRA Y-ÚNUS) Holy Qur'an 10: 38

(d) **And if ye are in doubt as to what
We have revealed from time to
time to Our servant, then
produce a Súra like thereunto;**

And call your witnesses or helpers
(if there are any) **besides Allah. If
your** (doubts) **are true.**

**But if ye cannot —
And of a surety ye cannot —**

**Then fear the Fire whose fuel is
Men and Stones,— which is
prepared for those who reject Faith.**

(SÚRA BAQARA) Holy Qur'an 2: 23-24

It is now fourteen hundred years since the above challenges, but mankind has singularly failed to produce anything similar or something better. This is an **Eternal Testimony** of the **Divine Origin** of the Holy Qur'an.

CHRISTIAN ARABS HAD A TRY!

The Arab Christians in the Middle East, not to be outwitted, launched a sixteen-year project lately and produced selected portions of the New Testament in Arabic, with a wholesale borrowing[1] of words and phrases verbatim from the Arabic Qur'an. It is an ignoble attempt! In this unashamed plagiarism,[2] **every** chapter of this **new** Arabic New Testament of theirs begin with the first verse of the Holy Qur'an —

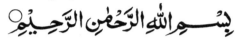

In the name of Allah, Most Gracious, Most Merciful.

(SÚRA FÁTIHA) Holy Qur'an 1: 1

Can you beat that?

There are many more challenges and prophecies in the Holy Qur'an and in the **Ahádith** (traditions of the Prophet) which can be expounded. It is a neglected field. Perhaps books can be written on the subject. I trust that Muslim scholars will take up the challenge. But let me end this theme of prophecy with one last reference from Allah's **Kalaam** (the book of God).

ISLAM TO PREVAIL

(e) **It is He who has sent His Messenger with Guidance and the Religion of Truth.**

That he may proclaim it over all religion.

Even though the associators may detest (it).

(SÚRA ṢAFF) Holy Qur'an 61: 9

---

1. "He who goes a borrowing, goes a sorrowing!"
2. **Plagiarism:** the act of stealing and using (the ideas or writings of another) as one's own. Stealing in literature.

Within decades the above promise became true. Islam prevailed. The two superpowers of the day, the Persian and the Roman Empires crumbled at the hands of the Muslims. And for centuries the power of Islam predominated — from the Atlantic to the Pacific.

Alas, the Muslims are in the doldrums today. But fear not, the world of Islam is arising. There is hope. Even non-Muslim Visionaries in the West have predicted its destiny to be in the skies.

"AFRICA IS A FAIR FIELD FOR ALL RELIGIONS, BUT THE RELIGION WHICH THE AFRICAN WILL ACCEPT, IS A RELIGION WHICH BEST SUITS HIS NEEDS: AND THAT RELIGION, EVERY-ONE WHO HAS A RIGHT TO SPEAK ON THE SUBJECT SAYS, IS ISLAM."

"The Shape of Things to Come" H.G. Wells

"IF ANY RELIGION HAS A CHANCE OF CONQUERING ENG-LAND, NAY EUROPE WITHIN THE NEXT HUNDRED YEARS, THAT RELIGION IS ISLAM."

George Bernard Shaw

Without any real effort on the part of the Muslims, we are told by the Westerners themselves that Islam is the fastest growing religion in the world today. I hope, this pleasant news does not lull us to sleep. The promise of God is true, the destiny is there, only a little exertion is required on our part. Allah can transform nations and peoples by His Own Will, but He has given us the privilege of serving His **Deen** by personal self-sacrifice. To be an effective soldier in this battle, arm yourself with John 16: 7 in one or more languages (see page 43), and watch how Allah fills you with more knowledge. It is our destiny to master, supercede and bulldoze every **ism,** never mind how much the unbeliever may be averse to the Message of Islam.

GLORIFYING JESUS (PBUH)

He (the Spirit of truth) *shall Glorify*
Me (Jesus): *for he shall receive of*
mine, and shall shew it unto you.

(HOLY BIBLE) *John 16: 13*

But when the Comforter is come,
whom I will send unto you
from the Father, even the Spirit
of truth, which proceedeth from
the Father, he shall Testify
of Me.

(HOLY BIBLE) *John 15: 26*

This promised Comforter, **even** the Spirit of Truth in whom Truth is personified, when he comes, will bear witness to the truthfulness of the Messiah and absolve him from the calumnies of his enemies.

This, Muhummed (pbuh), **Al-Amin,** the Prophet of Truth, eminently succeeded in doing. He made it possible that today, **a thousand million Muslims believe in Jesus Christ (pbuh) as one of the mightiest Messengers of God. They believe in his miraculous birth, which many modern-day Christians, even Bishops do not believe. And they also believe in his many miracles, including those of giving life to the dead by God's leave; and healing those born blind and the lepers by God's leave.** What a mighty testimony! Listen to the moving terms of the story of his Annunciation:

MIRACULOUS CONCEPTION

And mention in the Book, the
story of Mary, when she
withdrew from her people to a
place in the East.

And she placed a screen to screen
herself from them;
Then we sent unto her Our
Spirit, that appeared to her as
a man in all respects.

She said, "I take refuge in the
All-Merciful from you.
If you fear Allah ..."

He said, "I am but a messenger
come from your Lord, to
announce to you the gift of a
holy son."

She said, "How can I have a
son, seeing that no man has
touched me, and I am not
unchaste?"

He said, "Even so your Lord has
said:
'Easy is that for Me, and that
We may appoint him a sign unto
men and a mercy from Us; it is
a thing decreed'."

So she conceived him, and withdrew
with him to a distant place ...

(SÚRA MARYAM) Holy Qur'an 19: 16-22

At the present moment a billion Muslims throughout the world accept the Immaculate Conception of Jesus (pbuh) on the authority of Muhummed (pbuh) alone. Jesus (pbuh), his mother Mary and the whole Christian world can never thank **Al-Amin** — the Spirit of Truth, enough.

JEWISH RESPONSE TO JESUS

O Jerusalem, Jerusalem, thou
that killest the prophets, and
stonest them which are sent
unto thee, how often would I
(Jesus) *have gathered thy children*
together, even as a hen gathereth
her chickens under her wings,
but ye would not let me!

(HOLY BIBLE)   Matthew 23: 37

That mighty Messenger of God went after the Jews like a hen after her chickens, but they turned on him like vultures to tear him into pieces. Not satisfied with their relentless assaults and harassment and the eventual attempt on his life[1]; they charged his mother for having ill-begotten him in sin.

That they (the Jews) **rejected Faith;**
and they uttered against Mary a
grave false charge.

(SÚRA NISÁA)   Holy Qur'an 4: 156

What was that **"grave false charge"?** — The nearest to uttering the actual calumny, Muhummed (pbuh) the true **"Glorifier"** of Jesus (John 16: 13) is made to record.

"O sister of Aaron! thy father was
not a man of evil, nor thy
mother a woman unchaste!"

(SÚRA MARYAM)   Holy Qur'an 19: 28

WHAT SAY THE TALMUDISTS

The Jewish charge of the illegitimacy of Jesus (pbuh) and the adultery of Mary is referred to here as an insinuation of the Jews, questioning Mary's **chastity.** The Holy Qur'an does not

---

1. For a detailed record of how God foiled the Jewish plot on the life of the Messiah, consult Vol. II, Part 3 — **"Crucifixion or Cruci-fiction?**

stoop down to even reproducing the actual monstrous slander. Now compare this Qur'anic terminology with what the erudite and famous Rev. Dummelow, backed by no less than a team of sixteen Christian divines, all Reverends and D.D.s; as to **their** choice of words in recording the calumny of the enemies of Christ:

THE JEWISH TALMUDISTS SAID, 'THE SON OF THE **AD-ULTERESS'** (I.E. OF THE VIRGIN MARY) 'BROUGHT MAGIC OUT OF EGYPT, BY CUTTINGS WHICH HE HAD MADE IN HIS FLESH.' 'JESUS PRACTISED MAGIC AND DECEIVED, AND DROVE ISRAEL TO IDOLATRY.' **IT IS INTERESTING TO NOTICE THAT MAHOMET INDIGNANTLY REPUDIATED THESE JEWISH CALUMNIES."** (Emphasis added)

Dummelow's Bible Commentary page 668

EVANGELIST CORROBORATES JEWS

Josh Mc Dowell, described as a graduate of Wheaton College and magna cum laude graduate of Talbot Theological Seminary, and who is reputed to have spoken to more than five million students and faculty at over 550 universities in 53 countries, seems to have done more research than the whole galaxy of Biblical scholars, mentioned above, on the subject of the Jewish Talmud regarding the birth of his "Lord."

In his book — *"Evidence that Demands a Verdict,"* just to prove that Jesus (pbuh) was not a myth but a historical person, he quotes extensively from the **Jewish Talmud** without any inhibitions. I give you below a few brief excerpts from pages 85/86 of his book.

> *"Tol'doth Yeshu.* JESUS IS REFERRED TO AS 'BEN PANDERA.' "[1]

---

1. **"BEN PANDERA:"** means — son of Pandera. A Roman soldier alleged by the Jews to have raped Mary to produce her illigitimate offspring. (May God forbid!) May He forgive us for even reproducing such blasphemies.

Yeb. IV 3; 49a:

"R. SHIMEON BEN AZZAI SAID (CONCERNING JESUS): 'I FOUND A GENEALOGICAL ROLL IN JERUSALEM WHEREIN WAS RECORDED, SUCH-AN-ONE IS A BASTARD OF AN ADULTERESS.' "

Joseph Klausner adds to the above:

"CURRENT EDITIONS OF THE *Mishnah,* ADD: 'TO SUPPORT THE WORDS OF R. YEHOSHUA' (WHO IN THE SAME *Mishnah,* SAYS: WHAT IS A BASTARD? EVERYONE WHOSE PARENTS ARE LIABLE TO DEATH BY THE BETH DIN), THAT JESUS IS HERE REFERRED TO SEEMS TO BE BEYOND DOUBT ..."

5/35

MISSIONARY LOLLS HIS TONGUE

Josh McDowell, the great evangelist, **"born-again"** Christian; worshipper of Christ, filled with the Holy Ghost (?) lolls his tongue when quoting calumnies of the enemies against his Lord and God — Jesus! And the Christian world laps it up. His books are bestsellers in Christendom. A taste for filth and insults has been created in the votaries of Christ. I refuse to quote further from that filthy narration. If Jesus (pbuh) has such devoted friends (?), what need is there for him to have enemies.

Muhummed (pbuh) really was the true Friend, the Comforter, the Helper, the Advocate, the Glorifier, the Testifier of these prophecies in John chapters 14, 15 and 16. Let me repeat the ungrudging tribute of his enemies to this Benefactor of Jesus (pbuh), his mother Mary and humanity at large: **"It is interesting to notice that Mahomet[1] indignantly repudiated these Jewish calumnies."** (Rev. Dummelow and his associates).

---

1. **"Mahomet"**: It is a pity that scholars of Christianity of the highest eminence still misspell the name of the Holy Prophet, even at the end of the twentieth century.

CHAPTER SIX

Extremism Condemned

We will now allow the Spirit of Truth to lay the Ghost of Jewish and Christian extremism, and put the records straight regarding their controversies about the Messiah. The Jews said that Jesus (pbuh) was the illegitimate son of Mary because he could not point a finger to a father. The Christians for the same reason made him into a God and the **"begotten"** son of God. Just one verse to debunk this lie!

> **O People of the Book!**
>
> **Do not go to extremes in your religion: nor say of Allah anything but the truth.**
>
> **Verily, Christ[1] Jesus the son of Mary was no more than a messenger of Allah, and His Word which he bestowed upon Mary,**
>
> **And a Spirit proceeding from Him: so believe in Allah and his messengers.**
>
> **Say not "Trinity": desist: it will be better for you:**
>
> **For your Allah is One God: Glory be to Him:**

---

1. **Christ:** In the Arabic Text of the Holy Qur'an the word is **Masih,** which is the same as the Hebrew word Messiah.

**(Far Exalted is He) above having
a son. To Him belongs all
things in the heavens and the earth.**

And enough is Allah as a Disposer of affairs.

(SÚRA NISÁA)   *Holy Qur'an 4: 171*

Note 657/6 on the above verse

Just as a foolish servant may go wrong by excess of zeal for his master, so in religion people's excesses may lead them to blasphemy or a spirit the very opposite of religion.

The Jewish excesses in the direction of formalism, racialism, exclusiveness, and rejection of Christ Jesus have been denounced in many places in the Holy Qur'an.

Here the Christian attitude is condemned, which raises Jesus to an equality with God; in some cases venerates Mary almost to idolatry; attributes a physical son to God; and invents the doctrine of the Trinity, opposed to all reason, which according to the Athanasian Creed, unless a man believes, he is doomed to hell for ever."

The attributes of Christ are mentioned here:

1. That he was the son of a woman, Mary, and therefore a man.

2. But an apostle, a man with a mission from God, and therefore entitled to honour.

3. A Word bestowed on Mary, for he was created by God's word "Be" *(kun)* and he was. H.Q. 3: 59.

4. A spirit proceeding from God, but not God: his life and his mission were more limited than in the case of some other apostles, though we must pay equal honour to him as a man of God.

CONT. NEXT PAGE

> The doctrines of Trinity, equality with God, and sonship, are
> repudiated as blasphemies. God is independent of all needs
> and has no need of a son to manage His affairs."
> **Abdullah Yusuf Ali**[1]

NOTHING FROM SELF

You give this Spirit of Truth (Muhummed pbuh) too much credit,
when you allege that he wrote the preceding verses and further
authored more than six thousand other verses of the Noble
Qur'an.

He cries to us again and again in the Book of God, that this is
not my handiwork — **"IT IS NO LESS THAN AN INSPI-
RATION SENT DOWN TO HIM** (Muhummed)" (Holy Qur'an 53:
4). Exactly as it was prophesied by Jesus (pbuh) —

> *... for he shall not speak from
> himself; but whatsoever he shall
> hear, that shall he speak ...*
>
> **(HOLY BIBLE)** John 16: 13

CHRISTIAN "TRILEMMA"

All the testification and glorification by this **"another Comforter,"** does not placate the Christians. Because Muhummed
(pbuh) did not pander to their prejudices. To them glorification
meant to deify Jesus (pbuh) — to make him into a God. Instead
of solving their **dilemma**[2] whether Jesus (pbuh) "died" on the
cross as a man, or as a God? They have now invented a
trilemma. A word not to be found in any dictionary in the
world. Josh McDowell the Travelling Representative for Campus

---

1. The above consists of just two notes out of over six thousand explanatory notes from
   Yusuf Ali's translation. See inside back cover for an irresistible offer.
2. **Dilemma:** A situation that requires one to choose between two equally balanced and
   often equally unpleasant alternatives.

Crusade for Christ International, in his book — **"Evidence that Demands a Verdict,"** actually uses his new inspired (by the "Holy Ghost"?) conundrum[1] for his chapter 7 — **"TRILEMMA - Lord, Liar or Lunatic?"** You have now guessed it! The three L's! He wants his readers to answer whether Jesus Christ is your **LORD** (God), or was he a **LIAR,** or a **LUNATIC?** Very ingenious, you will agree! No Muslim could utter that Jesus Christ was a liar, or a lunatic: then what? It is more than any dilemma! It is actually blasphemy of the highest degree. But he is blinded by his preconceived notions. Roger Bacon, the philosopher who was born too soon, rightly said: "IT IS EASIER FOR A MAN TO BURN DOWN HIS OWN HOUSE THAN TO GET RID OF HIS PREJUDICES."

WISDOM OF THE CHILD

To say of any man that he is God, the **"begotten"** son of God, or that his father is God; is not an honour but an insult. A French peasant understood this distinction better than the millions of erudite Christian scholars walking the earth today.

It is reputed that Louis XV, King of France was a very lecherous person. No woman was safe from his debaucheries. After his death, when his son was well settled on the throne, a rumour spread around Paris that an exact duplicate of the young king was seen roaming about the capital. The King was naturally intrigued to see his double. It did not take the King's men long to have the rustic from the countryside presented before the King. The King was amused by the stark resemblance to himself and his late father. He was tickled to have a dig at the poor farmer. He politely asked, "Did your mother ever visit Paris during my father's reign?" **"No!"** the rustic replied, **"But my father did!"** This was a death-knell for the King, but he had asked for it!

---

1. **Conundrum:** A puzzling problem or question admitting of no satisfactory solution.

DON'T GO TO EXTREMES

The rank hatred of the Jews which lead them to slander Jesus and his mother is bad, and the over-infatuation of the Christians for Christ is also bad. Muhummed (pbuh) the Messenger of God condemned both these extremes, and elevated Jesus (pbuh) to his true status, as the Messiah, a great prophet and reformer.

Love him, respect him, revere him, follow him; but do not worship him! For worship is due to God alone, the Father in heaven: ALLAH![1]

This is true glorification — for,

> *"He shall glorify me!"*   **(HOLY BIBLE)** John 16: 14

Historically, morally and prophetically, Muhummed (pbuh) the last and final Messenger of God, **"The Spirit of Truth,"** is the only one to guide mankind into all truth. He is pre-eminently **the Natural Successor to Christ.**

Your further inquiries, comments and criticisms are welcome. Don't just sit there, for the sake of God, act now!

Ahmed Deedat

AHMED DEEDAT
(Servant of Islam)

EPILOGUE

Dear reader, it has been suggested that some Christian propagandists might lure you from your exposition of the preceding pages, by dangling before you the "Pentecostal" experience.

Pentecost was a Jewish festival day, celebrated on the fiftieth day after the beginning of corn harvesting. The Jews gathered in

---

1. **ALLAH:** The name for God Almighty in the semitic languages See Vol. III, Part 3 — **"What is His Name?"** from the IPCI.

Jerusalem from far and wide for the feast. Peter with **"the Eleven,"**[1] together with others were in one place, when suddenly they heard the roaring of a mighty windstorm in the skies above them where they were sitting. This electrified the people and they began to **"speak in tongues,"** in dialects and languages foreign to themselves. Some marvelled while others mocked, saying, **"They're drunk, that's all!"** It reminded them of the **"babbling"** at Babel (Genesis 11: 9).

The Christian missionaries contend that that was the fulfilment of what Jesus (pbuh) had prophesied in John chapters 14, 15 and 16. Astounding as the whole drama may sound, Peter, the one, the Master had appointed to *"feed my lambs . . . feed my sheep"* (John 21: 15-16), rose to defend the disciples, saying, "These men are not drunk! It's much too early for that! People don't get drunk so early in the morning!"

> *But this is that which was spoken*
> *by the prophet Joel . . .*[2]
>
> **(HOLY BIBLE)**   Acts 2: 16

Pentecost was the fulfilment of the prophecy of the prophet **Joel** and not of any predictions of Jesus (pbuh). Christendom believes that Peter was inspired to record the same. Both obviously tickled by the Holy Ghost! Not a **single word**[3] is recorded anywhere as to what these apostles of Christ had babbled or murmured on Pentecost day, yet as to the Comforter, he was to guide mankind *"into all Truth!"* Proving once again that the Comforter is **not** the Holy **Ghost!**

---

1. **"The Eleven"** (Acts 2: 14). No Bible commentator dare discuss as to who these eleven were, because Judas the traitor was long since dead. The Holy Ghost failed to inform Luke. That at best there could only be ten beside Peter and not **eleven!**

2. **"Prophet Joel:"** In **"The New English Bible,"** published by The Bible Societies in association with the Oxford University Press in their fourteenth impression of 1984, expunged the name **JOEL,** without an apology. He was too insignificant (?) a prophet, having written only two pages in a thousand of the Bible. If Christendom can edit out names of their own prophets, what will they not do to names like **Ishmael** and **Ahmed?**

3. On the contrary, hear what Muhummed (pbuh) the Comforter uttered in his trances in fulfilment of the prophecies. Get your **"Future World Constitution"** today! See inside back cover.

PART THREE

Muhummed

the Greatest

BY
AHMED DEEDAT

CHAPTER ONE

Everybody's Choice

**AND MOST CERTAINLY,
THOU (O MUHUMMED)
ART OF MOST SUBLIME
AND EXALTED CHARACTER.**

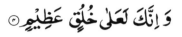

(SÚRA QALAM) Holy Qur'an 68:4 [1]

HOW THE TOPIC AROSE

About ten years ago, a distant cousin of mine — Mr. Mohamed Mehtar (Farooki) [2] gave me a typed quotation by the French historian, Lamartine. The quotation [3] purported to prove that Muhummed (pbuh), the prophet of Islam, was the greatest man that ever lived. Mr. Mehtar was in the habit of passing information on to me, believing that I might put the same to some good use at the proper time and place. Before this he had presented me with **"The Call of the Minaret"** an expensive book written by (Bishop Kenneth Cragg). By analysing this book I discovered the masterful deceit of the Christian orientalists.

Lamartine's tribute to our prophet inspired me and I had a great desire to share his thoughts about our **Nabee** with my Muslim brethren. The opportunity to do so was not long in coming.

I received a phone call from the Muslim community in Dann-hauser, a small town in Northern Natal, who were organising a birthday celebration of the Holy Prophet. They invited me to give a lecture on that auspicious occasion. So I deemed it an honour and a privilege, I readily agreed. When they inquired, in view of

---

1. I urge my Muslim brethren to memorize the verse in Arabic and its meaning.
2. Mr. Mehtar was for a long time editor of the Muslim newspaper **"The Indian Views,"** in South Africa.
3. A detailed exposition of the quotation will be found on page 137.

their advertising needs, as to the subject of my lecture, I suggested on the inspiration from Lamartine, **"Muhummed (pbuh) the Greatest."**

REPEATED LET-DOWNS

On my arrival in Dannhauser, I noticed a lot of posters advertising the meeting which in essence said that Deedat would be lecturing on the subject "MUHUMMED THE GREAT." I was somewhat disheartened and, on inquiring was told that the change in the title was due to a printer's error.

Some two months later, I got another, similar invitation. This time from the Muslim community of Pretoria the administrative capital of South Africa. The subject I had mooted was the same — **"Muhummed (pbuh) the Greatest."** To my dismay the topic was again changed to "MUHUMMED THE GREAT." Identical reasons and excuses were given. Both these incidents happened in South Africa, my own country. But, let me give you one more example of our inferiority complex — so much part of the sickness of the **Ummah.**

USA NO DIFFERENT

On my lecture tour of the mighty United States in 1977, I discovered that our soldiers in the New World also had feet of clay. Out of the many sad experiences I have had, I think that this one will suffice to prove the point.

The Muslims of Indianapolis were advised to organise a lecture for me on the subject **"What the Bible says about Muhummed (pbuh)".**[1] They agreed to advertise just that, but their timidity did not permit them to do so. They thought the topic was too provocative, so they, in their wisdom (?), toned it down to "A PROPHET IN THE BIBLE." A lifeless, insipid title you will

---

1. A book with the same title is available absolutely **FREE** from the IPCI.

no doubt agree. Which Hindu, Muslim, Christian or Jew would be intrigued to attend? What does **"A PROPHET"** mean? To most A PROPHET means **ANY** PROPHET, and who would be interested in attending a meeting where just **any** prophet in the Bible was debated? Job, Joel, Jonah, Ezra, Elisha, Ezekiel are just a few of the many mentioned in the Bible. As was to be expected the attendance left much to be desired.

INFERIORITY COMPLEX

What is the cause of this sickness? This inferiority complex? **"Yes!"** We are an emasculated people. Dynamism has been wrung out of us, not only by our enemies but by our own spiritless friends. We even dare not repeat Allah's Own testimony regarding his beloved —

> **And Most Certainly,**
> **Thou** (O MUHUMMED)
> **Art of most sublime**
> **And Exalted Character.**
>
> *Holy Qur'an 68:4*[1]

THE MOST INFLUENTIAL

Normally, it is quite, natural for anyone to love, praise, idolize or hero-worship one's leader, be it a guru, saint or prophet: and very often we do.

However, if I were to reproduce here[2] what great Muslims have said or written about our illustrious prophet, it could be played down as exaggeration, fancy or idolization by the sceptics and the opponents of Islam. Therefore, allow me to quote unbiased historians, friendly critics and even avowed enemies of that mighty Messenger of God — Muhummed (pbuh). If the tributes of

---

1. This verse, together with its Arabic text heads this chapter; memorize the verse with its meaning.

2. For an example, see Appendix "A" at the end of this book.

the non-Muslims do not touch your hearts, then you are in the wrong faith. Opt out of Islam! There is already too much dead-wood on the "ship" of Islam.

In recent times, a book has been published in America titled **"The 100,"** or the Top One Hundred, or the Greatest Hundred in History. A certain Michael H. Hart, described as a historian, mathematician and astronomer has written this novel book. He has searched history, seeking for men who had the greatest influence on mankind. In this book he gives us the hundred most influential men, including Asoka, Aristotle, Buddha, Confucius, Hitler, Plato, and Zoroaster. He does not give us a mere chart of the topmost **"one hundred"** from the point of view of their influence on people, but he evaluates the degree of their influence and rates them in order of their excellence from No. 1, through to No. 100. He gives us his reasons for the placing of his candidates. We are not asked to agree with him, but we cannot help admire the man's research and honesty.

The most amazing thing about his selection is that he has put our **Nabee-e-Kareem,** the Holy Prophet Muhummed (pbuh) as No. 1,[1] the first of his "100!" Thus confirming, unknowingly, God's Own testimony in His Final Revelation to the World:

MOST CERTAINLY, YOU HAVE
IN THE MESSENGER OF ALLAH[2]
AN EXCELLENT PATTERN (OF BEHAVIOUR)

لَقَدْ كَانَ لَكُمْ فِى
رَسُوْلِ اللهِ أُسْوَةٌ
حَسَنَةٌ

(SÚRA AHZÁB)   Holy Qur'an 33:21

JESUS (PBUH) No. 3!

Hart placing the Prophet of Islam as No. 1, has naturally pleased the Muslims. But his choice has shocked the Non-Muslims, more

---

1. With the kind permission of Mr. Hart, we have just reproduced the whole chapter on Muhummed (pbuh) from the **"Top 100"**. Get your **FREE** copy now from the I.P.C.I.

2. **Allah:** A proper noun for God Almighty in the Semitic languages; i.e. in the languages of Moses, Jesus and Muhummed (Peace be on them all). For more details obtain **"What is His Name?"** from the I.P.C.I.

specially the Jews and the Christians, who consider this as an affront. What? Jesus (pbuh) No. 3 and Moses (pbuh) No. 40! This is for them very difficult to stomach, but what says Hart? Let us hear his arguments —

SINCE THERE ARE ROUGHLY TWICE[1] AS MANY CHRISTIANS IN THE WORLD, IT MAY INITIALLY SEEM STRANGE THAT MUHAMMAD HAS BEEN RANKED HIGHER THAN JESUS.

THERE ARE TWO PRINCIPAL REASONS FOR THAT DECISION.

FIRST, MUHUMMAD PLAYED A FAR MORE IMPORTANT ROLE IN THE DEVELOPMENT OF ISLAM THAN JESUS DID IN THE DEVELOPMENT OF CHRISTIANITY.

ALTHOUGH JESUS WAS RESPONSIBLE FOR THE MAIN ETHICAL AND MORAL PRECEPTS OF CHRISTIANITY (INSOFAR AS THESE DIFFERED FROM JUDAISM), ST. PAUL WAS THE MAIN DEVELOPER OF CHRISTIAN THEOLOGY, ITS PRINCIPAL PROSELYTIZER, AND THE AUTHOR OF A LARGE PORTION OF THE NEW TESTAMENT.

MUHAMMAD, HOWEVER, WAS RESPONSIBLE FOR BOTH THE THEOLOGY OF ISLAM AND ITS MAIN ETHICAL AND MORAL PRINCIPLES.

IN ADDITION, HE PLAYED THE KEY ROLE IN PROSELYTIZING THE NEW FAITH, AND IN ESTABLISHING THE RELIGIOUS PRACTICES OF ISLAM.

Michael H. Hart in his book — *"THE 100"* pages 38/39

---

1. The latest estimate is that there are one thousand million Muslims in the world and one thousand two hundred million Christians.

PAUL THE FOUNDER OF CHRISTIANITY

According to Hart, the honour for founding Christianity is to be shared between Jesus (pbuh) and St. Paul. The latter he believes to be the real founder of Christianity.

I cannot help agreeing with Hart. Out of the total of 27 Books of the New Testament, more than half is authored by Paul. As opposed to Paul, the Master has not written a single word of the twenty-seven books. If you can lay your hands on what is called **"A Red Letter Bible,"** you will find every word alleged to have been uttered by Jesus (pbuh) — in red ink and the rest in normal black ink. Don't be shocked to find that in this so-called **"Injeel,"** the Gospel of Jesus, over ninety percent of the 27 Books of the New Testament is printed in black ink!

This is the candid Christian confession on what they call the **"Injeel."** In actual confrontation with Christian missionaries, you will find them quoting one hundred percent from Paul.

NO ONE FOLLOWS JESUS (PBUH)

Jesus (pbuh) said,
> **"If you love me, keep my commandments"**

John 14:15

He said further,
> **Whosoever therefore shall break one of these least commandments, and shall teach men so, he shall be called the least in the kingdom of heaven ..."**

(HOLY BIBLE) *Matthew 5:19*

Every Christian controversialist you question, "Do you keep the laws and the commandments?" will answer, **"No!"** if you ask further, "Why don't you?" he will if he is a Bible-thumper, invariably reply, **"The law is nailed to the cross!"** Meaning the law is done away with. **"We are now living under grace!"**

Every time you prod him with what his Lord and Master Jesus (pbuh) had said, he will confront you with something from Corinthians, Galatians, Ephesians, Philippians, etc. If you ask, "Who are they?" You will hear, "Paul, Paul, Paul!" "Who is your master? you question, and he will say, "Jesus!" But he will ever and anon contradict his own Jesus (pbuh) by his Paul!

No learned Christian will ever dispute the fact that the real founder of Christianity is St. Paul. Therefore, Michael H. Hart to be fair, had to place Jesus (pbuh), in slot number three.

WHY PROVOKE YOUR CUSTOMER?

This placing of Christ in the number three spot by Michael H. Hart poses a very serious question for us. Why would an American publish a book of 572 pages in America and selling in America for $15 each, go out of his way to provoke his potential readers?

Who will buy his books? Surely, not the Pakistanis and the Bangladeshis, neither the Arabs nor the Turks! Except for a few copies here and there, the overwhelming number of his customers will be from the 250 million Christians and the 6 million Jews of America. Then why did he provoke his customers? Did he not hear the dictum — **"the customer is always right!"** Of course he did. Then why his daring choice. But before I close this episode of Hart, I will allow him to make his one last apology for his "temerity.'

"MY CHOICE OF MUHAMMAD TO LEAD THE LIST OF THE WORLD'S MOST INFLUENTIAL PERSONS MAY SURPRISE SOME READERS AND MAY BE QUESTIONED BY OTHERS, BUT HE WAS THE ONLY MAN IN HISTORY WHO WAS SUPREMELY SUCCESSFUL ON BOTH THE RELIGIOUS AND SECULAR LEVEL."

Michael H. Hart

"The 100: A Ranking of the Most Influential Persons in History", New York: Hart Publishing Company, Inc., 1978, p.33.

WHO WERE HISTORY'S GREAT LEADERS
TIME, JULY 15, 1974

The world famous **"Time"**[1] carried the above rubric on its front cover. Inside the magazine were numerous essays as to **'What makes a great leader?' 'Throughout history, who qualifies?'** TIME asked a variety of historians, writers, military men, businessmen and others for their selections. Each gave his candidate according to his "light" as objectively as is humanly possible, depending on one's own awareness and prejudice.

WHO KNOWS DR. SALAZAR?

It is my habit and pleasurable duty to take non-Muslims on a guided tour[2] of the largest mosque in the Southern Hemisphere — **"The Jumma Musjid"**, Durban.

On one occasion I was hosting a Portuguese couple, a husband and wife team. At some stage during the discussion the Portuguese gentleman said that **"Dr. Salazar was the greatest man in the world!"** I did not debate the point with him as I personally knew little about Dr. Salazar except that he was a one-time dictator of Portugal albeit to many a great benefactor to his nation. My poor visitor was, however, speaking according to his own knowledge, point of view and prejudice.

MUHUMMED (PBUH) CANNOT BE IGNORED!

Among the contributors to the **"Time,"** it seems that none could ignore Muhummed (pbuh).

---

1. **"Time"** We are at loggerhead with this magazine. Believe it or not; they have spurned our paid advertisement as shown on the last page of this volume. The words **"FUTURE WORLD CONSTITUTION"** was referred back to us in their correspondence as "The Future World **CONFRONTATION."**

2. Obtain the Video Tape — **"NON-MUSLIMS IN YOUR MOSQUE,"** available on Pal and NTSC systems from the IPCI.

WILLIAM McNEILL, a United States historian, of the University of Chicago, records:

> "IF YOU MEASURE LEADERSHIP BY IMPACT, THEN YOU WOULD HAVE TO NAME JESUS, BUDDHA, MOHAMMED, CONFUCIUS, THE GREAT PROPHETS OF THE WORLD ..."

McNeill does not go into details, nor does he give us any explanation as to why he placed Jesus (pbuh) first and Muhummed (pbuh) number three. Perhaps it was by force of habit. It is very likely that McNeill is a Christian. However, we will not argue with him. Then comes —

JAMES GAVIN, described as a United States army man, a retired lieutenant general. He says —

> "AMONG LEADERS WHO HAVE MADE THE GREATEST IMPACT THROUGH AGES, I WOULD CONSIDER MOHAMMED, JESUS CHRIST, MAYBE LENIN, POSSIBLY MAO. AS FOR A LEADER WHOSE QUALITIES WE COULD MOST USE NOW, I WOULD CHOOSE JOHN F. KENNEDY."

The General does not say much more, yet we have to salute him. It calls for tremendous fortitude to pen the name Muhummed before that of Christ (peace be upon them both). It surely, was no slip of the pen.

JULES MASSERMAN, United States psychoanalyst and professor of the Chicago University, gives us, unlike the other contributors, the basis for making his selection. He gives us his reason for choosing his greatest LEADER of all times.

He wants us to find out, what we are really looking for in the man, the qualities that sets him apart. We may be looking for any sets of qualities. As in the case of Michael H. Hart, he was looking for a person wielding the **MOST influence.**[1]

However, Masserman does not want us to depend on our fancies or prejudices: he wants to establish objective standards for judging, before we confer greatness upon anybody.

He says that **"Leaders must fulfil three functions - -"**

No. 1   THE LEADER MUST PROVIDE FOR THE
WELL-BEING OF THE LEAD ...

The leader, whoever he is, must be interested in your welfare. He must not be looking for milking cows for his own greed like the Rev. Jim Jones of Jonestown, Guyana, of the **"Suicide Cult"** notoriety. You will remember him as the man who committed suicide together with 910 of his followers, all at the same time **EN MASSE!**

The United States Government was on his trail and he was on the verge of being caught for certain felonies. But before they could apprehend him, he thought it wise to eliminate himself, together with all his followers, so that no one would be left to testify against him. He laced lemonade with cynide and inspired his devotees to drink it, and so they did and they all died in disgrace! In the meantime, it was discovered that the Rev. Jim Jones had salted away fifteen million dollars and stacked it in his own account in banks throughout the world. All his victims were his milking cows and he was exploiting them to satisfy his own lust and greed. Masserman's hero must be found to benefit his sheep, his flock, and not himself.

No. 2   THE LEADER OR WOULD BE LEADER MUST
PROVIDE A SOCIAL ORGANIZATION IN WHICH
PEOPLE FEEL RELATIVELY SECURE ...

---

1.   Since Hart published his **"TOP 100"** many people have published books with the same theme. **"100 GREAT GOLFERS,"** or **"100 GREAT BATSMEN."** Many more will no doubt follow.

Unlike the Marxist, the Fascist, the Nazi, the Neo-Nazi, the Ashkenazi,[1] the Zionist, and their fellow-travellers, Professor Masserman, in his brief essay in the TIME magazine, did not spell this out. But his beliefs and feelings are abundantly clear. He is in search of a Leader who will provide a social order free of selfishness, and greed and racism: for all these "isms" carry within them the seeds of their own destruction.

> There's still with us much sorrow and sin,
> Injustice, oppression, wrong and hate.
> Still does Arrogance deaden Conscience,
> Rob struggling souls of e'en the crumbs
> Of Pity, and make, of loathsome flesh
> And crumbling dust, fair-seeming Idols
> For worship. Still does Ignorance blow
> A mighty Horn and try to shame
> True Wisdom. Still do men drive Slaves, - -
> Protesting smoothly the end of Slavery!
> Still does Greed devour the substance
> Of helpless ones within her power.
> Nay, more, - - the fine Individual Voice
> Is smothered in the raucous din
> Of groups and Crowds that madly shout
> What they call Slogans New, - -
> Old Falsehoods long discredited ...
>
> **Abdullah Yusuf Ali**

No. 3   THAT THIS LEADER MUST PROVIDE HIS
PEOPLE WITH ONE SET OF BELIEFS ...

It is easy to talk of the Fellowship of Faith and the Brotherhood of Man, but in South Africa today, there are a thousand different

---

1. **Askhenazi:** the Jews from Germany, Central Europe and Eastern Europe, mostly from Russia who are in unlawful occupation of Palestine. There is something prophetic in the name itself — the Jews are doing to the people of the occupied territories exactly what the Nazis did to them. What an irony!

sects and denominations among the Whites (people of European descent) and three thousand among the Blacks (of African descent).

The White Churches in my country are spawning "Black" Bishops, fast, but in the first three hundred years of European conquest, they did not produce a single Black Bishop. Even now, the Black, the White, the Coloured and the Indian cannot pray together in most of the Dutch Reformed Churches. The hatred between the Christian sects was aptly described by the Christian Emperor Julian, who said:

> "NO WILD BEASTS ARE SO HOSTILE TO MAN AS CHRISTIAN SECTS IN GENERAL ARE TO ONE ANOTHER."
>
> Sayed Amir Ali in his ***"Spirit of Islam,"*** page 1ii.

With the foregoing three standards, Masserman searches history and analyses Louis Pasteur, Salk, Gandhi, Confucius, Alexander the Great, Caesar, Hitler, Buddha, Jesus and the rest;[1] finally coming to the conclusion that —

> PERHAPS THE GREATEST LEADER OF ALL TIMES WAS MUHAMMED, WHO COMBINED ALL THREE FUNCTIONS. (and) TO A LESSER DEGREE, MOSES DID THE SAME

We cannot help marvelling at Masserman, that as a Jew he condescends to scrutinize even Adolf Hitler, the arch-enemy of his people. He considers Hitler to be a great leader. His race, the mighty German nation of 90 million people, was ready to march to destiny or destruction at his behest. Alas, he led them to ruin.

Hitler is not the question. The question is why would Masserman, as an American Jew, a paid servant of the Government

---

1. For Masserman's full essay see Appendix "C" on page 160.

proclaim to his countrymen of over two hundred million Jews and Christians that **not** Jesus, **not** Moses **but** Muhummed[1] was **"The greatest Leader of all times!"** ACCOUNT FOR THAT!

WHAT SAY THE SCEPTICS?

Michael H. Hart put Muhummed No. 1 on his list and his own Lord and Saviour Jesus Christ (pbuh) No. 3.

Why? **"Was he bribed!"** (?)

William McNeill considers Muhummed as worthy of honour in his list of the first three names of his.

Why? **"Was he bribed!"** (?)

James Gavin puts Muhummed (pbuh) before Christ (pbuh).

Why? **"Was he bribed!"** (?)

Jules Masserman adjudges Muhummed (pbuh) No. 1 and his own hero Moses (pbuh) a close second.

Why? **"Was he bribed"** (?)

> "ARE WE TO SUPPOSE THAT ALL THE GLOWING ADULATION OF MUHUMMED (PBUH) WAS A MISERABLE PIECE OF INTELLECTUAL LEGERDE-MAIN, HOCUS POCUS ... I, FOR MY PART, CANNOT FORM ANY SUCH SUPPOSITION ... ONE WOULD BE ENTIRELY AT A LOSS WHAT TO THINK OF MAN-KIND AT ALL. IF QUACKERY SO GREW AND FLOURISHED IN THE WORLD."[2]

Yet the scoffers bemoan anyone who has anything good to say about Muhummed (pbuh) or Islam AS HAVING BEEN BRIBED by the Arabs! They are giving too much credit to my brethren. I repeat: **"It is possible, but it is improbable!"**

During the Second World War, Norway produced only one "Quisling."[3] He was tried for treason and executed. It is unlikely

---

1. Blessings of God on all His Messengers.
2. With apologies to Thomas Carlyle and his ***"Hero and Hero-worship."***
3. **"Quisling"** has come to mean a person who is a traitor to his nation and his country.

that America and the Western world have just reached puberty to spawn a breed of Quislings nurtured by hot petro-dollars from the Middle East. Please do not demean your honest, courageous men, who without fear or favour are prepared to suffer obloquy for their convictions. We must all admire them!

We can now justifiably conclude that the God of Mercy, Who forever recognises the sincere efforts of His servants, is only fulfilling His Promise to Muhummed (pbuh) His Chosen Messenger —

***AND HAVE WE NOT RAISED HIGH THE ESTEEM** (IN WHICH) **THOU** (ART HELD)?*

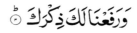

(*SÚRA INSHIRÁH*) *Holy Qur'an* 94:4

Alternative renderings:[1]

    (a) **Have We not exalted thy fame?**

    (b) **And have We not raised thy name for thee?**

    (c) **Have We not given you high renown?**

Friends and foe alike, as if by some secret compulsion are made to pay unsolicited tributes to this mighty Messenger of God. But the Almighty enlists even the devil into His service, as He had done in the time of Jesus (pbuh), (Matthew 4:1-11). Even the devil sometimes speaks Gospel truths.

Professor K.S. Ramakrishna Rao, a Hindu philosopher, in his book **"MUHUMMED — The Prophet of Islam,"**[2] quotes the arch-devil himself, yes, Adolf Hitler, to prove the unique greatness of Muhummed (pbuh).

---

1. These quotes are from different translations of the Holy Qur'an. There are no separate "Versions" of the Holy Qur'an. For **"What is a Version,"** obtain my book — **"Is the Bible God's Word?"**

2. Obtainable **FREE** from the IPCI.

The Professor, like Jules Masserman who had evaluated the Prophet of Islam on three grounds (see appendix "C" on page 160) also saw in Hitler's **"Mein Kampf"** a three-faceted jewel, a rare commodity which he found in our hero under discussion. Quoting Hitler, he says:

> "A GREAT THEORIST IS SELDOM A GREAT LEADER. AN AGITATOR IS FAR MORE LIKELY TO POSSESS THESE QUALITIES. HE WILL ALWAYS BE A BETTER LEADER. FOR, LEADERSHIP MEANS THE ABILITY TO MOVE MASSES OF MEN. THE TALENT TO PRODUCE IDEAS HAS NOTHING IN COMMON WITH THE CAPA-CITY FOR LEADERSHIP." Hitler continues, "THE UNION OF THE **THEORIST, ORGANISER,** AND **LEA-DER** IN ONE MAN IS THE RAREST PHENOMENON ON THIS EARTH; THEREIN CONSISTS GREATNESS." Professor Rao concludes, in his own words, **"IN THE PERSON OF THE PROPHET OF ISLAM THE WORLD HAS SEEN THIS RAREST PHENOMENON ON EARTH, WALKING IN FLESH AND BLOOD."**

SHARE THE ANGER

Before anyone assails the Professor of undue bias and **"bri-bery,"** let me give them a few more names of admirers of Muhummed (pbuh).

1. "MUHUMMAD WAS THE SOUL OF KINDNESS, AND HIS INFLUENCE WAS FELT AND NEVER FORGOTTEN BY THOSE AROUND HIM."

   A Hindu scholar — *Diwan Chand Sharma* in his **"The Prophets of the East,"** Calcutta 1935, p.122.

2. "FOUR YEARS AFTER THE DEATH OF JUSTINIAN, A.D. 569, WAS BORN AT MAKKAH, IN ARABIA THE MAN WHO, OF ALL MEN EXERCISED THE

GREATEST INFLUENCE[1] UPON THE HUMAN RACE . . . MOHAMMED . . ."

John William Draper, M.D., LLD., in his **"A History of the Intellectual Development of Europe,"** London 1875.

3. "I DOUBT WHETHER ANY MAN WHOSE EXTERNAL CONDITIONS CHANGED SO MUCH EVER CHANGED HIMSELF LESS TO MEET THEM."

R.V.C. Bodley in **"The Messenger,"** London 1946, p.9.

4. "I HAVE STUDIED HIM — THE WONDERFUL MAN — AND IN MY OPINION FAR FROM BEING AN ANTI-CHRIST, HE MUST BE CALLED THE SAVIOUR OF HUMANITY."

George Bernard Shaw, in **"The Genuine Islam,"** Vol. 1, No. 81936.

5. "BY A FORTUNE ABSOLUTELY UNIQUE IN HISTORY, MOHAMMED IS A THREEFOLD FOUNDER OF A NATION, OF AN EMPIRE, AND OF A RELIGION."

R. Bosworth-Smith in **"Mohammed and Mohammedanism,"** 1946.

6. "MOHAMMED WAS THE MOST SUCCESSFUL OF ALL RELIGIOUS PERSONALITIES."

Encyclopedia Britannica, 11th Edition

---

1. I wonder whether Michael H. Hart, as a historian, had stumbled across Draper's remark to inspire him to write his **"THE 100,"** a ranking of the Most Influential Persons in History? See page 105. Have you written for your **FREE** copy of the chapter on Muhummed (pbuh) from the **"TOP 100,"** yet?

CHAPTER TWO

From the Historical Past

It is not difficult to reproduce a further dozen or more eulogies by the admirers and critics of Muhummed (pbuh). Despite all their objectivity, jaundiced minds can always conjure up some aspersions. Let me take my readers deep down in past history.

It was Friday the 8th of May, 1840, that is about a hundred and fifty years ago, at a time when it was a sacrilege to say anything good about Muhummed (pbuh), and the Christian West was trained to hate the man Muhummed (pbuh) and his religion, the same way as dogs were at one stage trained in my country to hate all black people.[1] At that time in history, Thomas Carlyle, one of the greatest thinkers of the past century delivered a series of lectures under the theme — **"Heroes and Hero-worship."**

DEVELOPED SICKNESS

Carlyle exposed this blind prejudice of his people at the beginning of his talk. He made reference to one of the literary giants a Dutch scholar and statesman, by the name of Hugo Grotius,[2] who had written a bitter and abusive invective against the prophet of Islam. He had falsely charged that the Holy Prophet had trained pigeons to pick out peas from his ears, so that he could by this trick bluff his people that the Holy Ghost in the shape of a dove was revealing God's Revelation to him, which he then had them recorded in his Bible the Qur'an. Perhaps Grotius was inspired into this fairy-tale from his reading of his own Holy Scriptures:

---

1. By the way **"dogs are colour blind!"** Yet it can be done.
2. From page 57 of the book — "On Heroes Hero-worship and the Heroic in History" by *Thomas Carlyle,* London 1959.

Then Jesus, when he had been baptized (by John the Baptist in the Jordan River), **came up immediately from the water; and behold, the heavens were opened to him, and he saw the <u>Spirit of God Descending Like A Dove</u> and alighting upon him.**

(Emphasis added)   **(HOLY BIBLE)**   Matthew 3:16

WHERE'S THE AUTHORITY

Pococke, another respected intellectual of the time, like "doubting Thomas" (John 20:25), wanted proof about Muhummed (pbuh), the pigeons, and the peas? Grotius answered "THAT THERE WAS NO PROOF!"

He just felt like inventing this story for his audience. To him and his audience the "pigeons and peas" theory was more plausible than that of the Archangel dictating to Muhummed (pbuh). These falsities wrung the heart of Carlyle. He cried:

"THE LIES, WHICH WELL-MEANING ZEAL HAS HEAPED ROUND THIS MAN, ARE DISGRACEFUL TO OURSELVES ONLY."

Thomas Carlyle

THE HERO PROPHET

Carlyle was a man of genius and God gifted him with the art of articulation. In his own way, he wanted to put the records straight. He planned to deliver a lecture and he chose a very provocative topic **"The Hero as Prophet."** and he chose his hero-prophet to be the most maligned man of his time, "MUHUMMED (PBUH)!" Not Moses, David, Solomon, or Jesus but Muhummed![1] To placate his overwhelming Anglican (belong-

---

1.   May the Peace and Blessings of God be upon all his servants.

ing to the Church of England) fellow countrymen, he apologised —

> "AS THERE IS NO DANGER OF OUR BECOMING, ANY
> OF US, MAHOMETANS,[1] I MEAN TO SAY ALL THE
> GOOD OF HIM I JUSTLY CAN."

In other words he, as well as his elite audience, were free from the fear of converting to Islam, and could take a chance in paying some compliments to Muhummed (pbuh). If he had any fears regarding the strength of their faith, he would not have taken that chance.

In an era of hatred and spite towards everything Islamic and to an audience full of scepticism and cynicism, Carlyle unfolded many a glowing truth about his hero — Muhummed (pbuh). To the **"praiseworthy,"** indeed be praise. For that is what the very name Muhummed means — the Praised One — the Praiseworthy. There are times when Carlyle uses words and expressions which might not be too pleasing to the believing Muslim, but one has to forgive him as he was walking a cultural tightrope, and he succeeded eminently.

He paid our hero many ardent and enthusiastic tributes, and defended him from the false charges and calumnies of his enemies; exactly as the Prophet had done in the case of Jesus (pbuh) and his mother.[2]

HIS SINCERITY

1a. "THE GREAT MAN'S SINCERITY IS OF THE KIND
      HE CANNOT SPEAK OF : NAY, I SUPPOSE, HE
      IS CONSCIOUS RATHER OF INSINCERITY; FOR
      WHAT MAN CAN WALK ACCURATELY BY THE
      LAW OF TRUTH FOR ONE DAY? NO, THE

---

1. "Mahometans" means Muslims.
2. See **"Muhummed the Natural Successor to Christ"** by the author, Part 2 of this volume.

GREAT MAN DOES NOT BOAST HIMSELF SIN-
CERE, FAR FROM THAT; PERHAPS DOES NOT
ASK HIMSELF IF HE IS SO: I WOULD SAY
RATHER, HIS SINCERITY DOES NOT DEPEND
ON HIMSELF: HE CANNOT HELP BEING
SINCERE!"

Heroes and Hero-Worship, p.59

b. "A SILENT GREAT SOUL; HE WAS ONE OF
THOSE WHO CANNOT **BUT** BE IN EARNEST;
WHOM **N**ATURE HERSELF HAS APPOINTED TO
BE SINCERE. WHILE OTHERS WALK IN FOR-
MULAS AND HEARSAYS, CONTENTED ENOUGH
TO DWELL THERE, THIS MAN COULD NOT
SCREEN HIMSELF IN FORMULAS; HE WAS
ALONE WITH HIS OWN SOUL AND THE
REALITY OF THINGS . . . SUCH **SINCERITY,** AS
WE NAMED IT, HAS IN VERY TRUTH SOME-
THING OF DIVINE. THE WORD OF SUCH A
MAN IS A VOICE DIRECT FROM **N**ATURE'S
OWN **H**EART. MEN DO AND MUST LISTEN TO
THAT AS TO NOTHING ELSE; - - - ALL ELSE IS
WIND IN COMPARISON."

Heroes and Hero-Worship, p.71

In his lengthy speech Carlyle did not have the opportunity to
inform his audience about the sources of his inferences. I may
furnish just one incident from the life of the Prophet. An incident which reflects the highest degree of his sincerity in
recording a Revelation in the Holy Qur'an even if it seems to
reprove him for some natural and human zeal.

ADMONITION AS REVEALED

It was in the early days of his mission in Makkah. Muhummed
(pbuh) was deeply engrossed in trying to invite the leaders of
the Pagan Quraish to his teachings. Apparently one of them was

giving him an attentive hearing when a poor blind man by the name of **Abdullah ibn Umm-i-Maktum** tried to barge in into the discussion and wanted to draw attention to himself. The blessed Prophet said nothing, but a thought went through his mind (why don't you have a little patience, can't you see (sense) that because of your impatience I might lose these customers). I believe that lesser men, sinners and saints, will not be questioned for such lapses, but not so for Muhummed (pbuh). Did not God choose him and honour him with that lofty status as recorded?

> **And Most Certainly,**
> **Thou** (O MUHUMMED)
> **Art of most sublime**
> **And Exalted Character.**
>
> **(SÚRA QALAM)**   Holy Qur'an 68:4

HE FROWNED

Whilst in the midst of the conversation with his pagan fellow tribesmen, God Almighty sends Gabriel, the Angel of Revelation, with this admonition:

(THE PROPHET) FROWNED
AND TURNED AWAY,

عَبَسَ وَتَوَلَّیٰۤ ۙ

BECAUSE THERE CAME TO HIM
THE BLIND MAN (INTERRUPTING).

اَنْ جَآءَهُ الْاَعْمٰیٰ ؕ

BUT WHAT COULD TELL THEE
THAT PERCHANCE HE MIGHT GROW
(IN SPIRITUAL UNDERSTANDING)?

وَمَا يُدْرِیْكَ لَعَلَّهٗ يَزَّكّٰیٰۤ ۙ

OR THAT HE MIGHT RECEIVE
ADMONITION, AND THE TEACHING
MIGHT PROFIT HIM?

اَوْ يَذَّكَّرُ
فَتَنْفَعَهُ الذِّكْرٰیٰ ؕ

(SÚRA 'ABASA)   Holy Qur'an 80:1-4

The holy Prophet (pbuh) had naturally disliked the interruption. Perhaps the poor man's feelings were hurt. But he whose gentle heart ever sympathised with the poor and the afflicted, got new

Light (Revelation) from his Lord, and without the least hesitation, he immediately published it for all eternity!

Subsequently, everytime he met this blind man, he received him graciously and thanked him that on his account the Lord had remembered him. During Muhummed's (pbuh) absences from Madinah, the blind man was made the Governor of the City twice. Such was the sincerity and gratitude of Carlyle's Hero Prophet.

HIS FIDELITY[1]

2. "IT IS A BOUNDLESS FAVOUR. — — — HE NEVER FORGOT THIS GOOD KADIJAH. LONG AFTERWARDS, AYESHA HIS YOUNG FAVOURITE WIFE, A WOMAN WHO INDEED DISTINGUISHED HERSELF AMONG THE MOSLEMS, BY ALL MAN-NER OF QUALITIES, THROUGH HER WHOLE LONG LIFE; THIS YOUNG BRILLIANT AYESHA WAS, ONE DAY, QUESTIONING HIM: 'NOW AM NOT I BETTER THAN KADIJAH? SHE WAS A WIDOW; OLD, AND HAD LOST HER LOOKS: YOU LOVE ME BETTER THAN YOU DID HER?' — — — 'NO, BY ALLAH!' ANSWERED MAHOMET: 'NO, BY ALLAH! SHE BELIEVED IN ME WHEN NONE ELSE WOULD BELIEVE. IN THE WHOLE WORLD I HAD BUT ONE FRIEND, AND SHE WAS THAT!'"

Heroes and Hero-Worship, p. 76

It would have been easier to repel the temptation of the devil than to succumb to the ego of a young, loving, brilliant and beautiful wife like lady Ayesha Siddiqa. Why not let her hear the soft soothing balm of flattery; it will not harm anyone. Even the soul of Bibi Khadija, the mother of the Faithful, would look light-

---

1. A few poetic verses on fidelity will be found in Appendix "D" on page 160.

heartedly at the ruse. There is no shamming, no innocent "white lies" with Muhummed (pbuh). Traits of this kind show us the genuine man, brother of us all, brought visible through fourteen centuries, — — — the veritable son of our common mother.

'AL AMEEN, THE FAITHFUL'

3a. "A MAN OF TRUTH AND FIDELITY; TRUE IN WHAT HE DID, IN WHAT HE SPAKE AND THOUGHT. THEY NOTED THAT **HE** ALWAYS MEANT SOMETHING. A MAN RATHER TACITURN IN SPEECH; SILENT WHEN THERE WAS NOTHING TO BE SAID; BUT PERTINENT, WISE, SINCERE, WHEN HE DID SPEAK; ALWAYS THROWING LIGHT ON THE MATTER. THIS IS THE ONLY SORT OF SPEECH **WORTH** SPEAKING!"

Heroes and Hero-Worship, p. 69

b. "MAHOMET NATURALLY GAVE OFFENCE TO THE KOREISH, KEEPERS OF THE KAABAH, SUPERINTENDENTS OF THE IDOLS. ONE OR TWO MEN OF INFLUENCE HAD JOINED HIM: THE THING SPREAD SLOWLY, BUT IT WAS SPREADING, NATURALLY HE GAVE OFFENCE TO EVERYBODY."[1]

Heroes and Hero-Worship, p. 77

c. "NOT A MEALYMOUTHED MAN! A CANDID FEROCITY, IF THE CASE CALL FOR IT, IS IN HIM; HE DOES NOT MINCE MATTERS! THE WAR OF TABUC IS A THING HE OFTEN SPEAKS OF: HIS MEN REFUSED, MANY OF THEM, TO

---

1. The Jews hated the Prophet: the Christians hated the Prophet: the **Mushriks** (the Polytheists) hated the Prophet, and the **Munafiqeen** (the hypocrites) hated the Prophet. It is the nature of Falsehood to hate the Truth. Light eliminates Darkness, but darkness does not take kindly to Light.

MARCH ON THAT OCCASION; PLEADED THE HEAT OF THE WEATHER, THE HARVEST, AND SO FORTH; HE CAN NEVER FORGET THAT. YOUR HARVEST? IT LASTS FOR A DAY. WHAT WILL BECOME OF YOUR HARVEST THROUGH ALL **E**TERNITY? HOT WEATHER? YES, IT WAS HOT; 'BUT **H**ELL WILL BE HOTTER!' SOMETIMES A ROUGH SARCASM TURNS UP: HE SAYS TO THE UNBELIEVERS, YE SHALL NOT HAVE SHORT WEIGHT!"

Heroes and Hero-Worship, p. 95/6.

Remember, Thomas Carlyle uttered these words, and many more to a shocked and bewildered Christian audience in England, a hundred and fifty years ago. History did not record for us the lively arguments and debates which his lecture must naturally have caused. He kept to his promise: **"I mean to say all the good of him** (his Hero Prophet) **I justly can,"** and he went on in his talk to defend Muhummed (pbuh) against the false charges, slander and calumnies of his enemies:

CHARGE OF FALSITY

4a. "A FALSE MAN FOUND A RELIGION? WHY, A FALSE MAN CANNOT BUILD A BRICK HOUSE! IF HE DOES NOT KNOW AND FOLLOW **TRULY** THE PROPERTIES OF MORTAR, BURNT CLAY AND WHAT ELSE HE WORKS IN, IT IS NO HOUSE THAT HE MAKES, BUT A RUBBISH HEAP. IT WILL NOT STAND FOR TWELVE CENTURIES,[1] TO LODGE A HUNDRED-AND-EIGHTY MILLIONS;[2] IT WILL FALL STRAIGHT-AWAY . . . SPECIOSITIES ARE SPECIOUS[3] . . . IT

---

1. Now, fourteen centuries.
2. A thousand million today.
3. **Specious:** Having the ring of truth or plausibility but actually false.

IS LIKE A FORGED BANK NOTE; THEY GET IT
PASSED OUT OF **THEIR** WORTHLESS HANDS:
OTHERS, NOT THEY, HAVE TO SMART FOR IT.
NATURE BURSTS-UP IN FIRE-FLAMES, FRENCH
REVOLUTIONS AND SUCH-LIKE, PROCLAIMING
WITH THE TERRIBLE VERACITY THAT FORGED
NOTES ARE FORGED."

Heroes and Hero-Worship, p. 58

b. "IT GOES GREATLY AGAINST THE IMPOSTER
THEORY, THE FACT THAT HE LIVED IN THIS
ENTIRELY UNEXCEPTIONABLE, ENTIRELY QUIET
AND COMMON PLACE WAY, TILL THE HEAT OF
HIS YEARS WAS DONE. HE WAS FORTY BE-
FORE HE TALKED OF ANY MISSION FROM
HEAVEN . . ALL HIS 'AMBITION,' SEEMINGLY,
HAD BEEN, HITHERTO, TO LIVE AN HONEST
LIFE; HIS 'FAME,' THE MERE GOOD OPINION
OF NEIGHBOURS THAT KNEW HIM . . ."

Heroes and Hero-Worship, p. 70

c. "AMBITION? WHAT COULD ALL ARABIA DO
FOR THIS MAN; WITH THE CROWN OF GREEK
HERACLIUS, OF PERSIAN CHOSROES, AND ALL
THE CROWNS IN EARTH; — WHAT COULD
THEY ALL DO FOR HIM? IT WAS NOT OF THE
HEAVEN ABOVE AND OF THE HELL BENEATH.
ALL CROWNS AND SOVEREIGNTIES WHATSO-
EVER, WHERE WOULD **THEY** IN A FEW BRIEF
YEARS BE? TO BE SHEIK OF MAKKAH OR
ARABIA, AND HAVE A BIT OF GILT WOOD PUT
INTO YOUR HAND, — — — WILL THAT BE
ONE'S SALVATION? I DECIDEDLY THINK, NOT,
WE WILL LEAVE IT ALTOGETHER, THIS IM-
POSTER HYPOTHESIS, AS NOT CREDITABLE;
NOT VERY TOLERABLE EVEN, WORTHY CHIEF-
LY OF DISMISSAL BY US."

Heroes and Hero-Worship, p. 72/3

CHARGE OF SINNING

5. "FAULTS? THE GREATEST OF FAULTS, I SHOULD SAY, IS TO BE CONSCIOUS OF NONE. READERS OF THE BIBLE ABOVE ALL, ONE WOULD THINK, MIGHT KNOW BETTER. WHO IS CALLED THERE 'THE MAN ACCORDING TO GOD'S OWN HEART'? DAVID, THE **HEBREW KING** HAD FALLEN INTO SINS ENOUGH; BLACK-EST CRIMES; THERE WAS NO WANT OF SINS.[1] AND THEREUPON THE UNBELIEVERS SNEER AND ASK, IS THIS YOUR MAN ACCORDING TO GOD'S HEART? THE SNEER, I MUST SAY, SEEMS TO ME BUT A SHALLOW ONE. WHAT ARE FAULTS, WHAT ARE THE OUTWARD DE-TAILS OF A LIFE; IF THE INNER SECRET OF IT, THE REMORSE, TEMPTATIONS, TRUE, OFTEN-BAFFLED, NEVER-ENDED STRUGGLE OF IT BE FORGOTTEN? 'IT IS NOT IN MAN THAT WALK-ETH TO DIRECT HIS STEPS.' OF ALL ACTS, IS NOT, FOR A MAN, **REPENTANCE** THE MOST DIVINE? THE DEADLIEST SIN, I SAY, WERE THE SAME SUPERCILIOUS CONSCIOUSNESS OF NO SIN; THAT IS DEATH; THE HEART SO CON-SCIOUS IS DIVORCED FROM SINCERITY, HUMI-LITY, AND FACT; IS DEAD: IT IS 'PURE' AS DEAD DRY SAND IS PURE."

Heroes and Hero-Worship, p. 61

CHARGE OF "THE SWORD"

The greatest crime, the greatest "sin" of Muhummed (pbuh) in the eyes of the Christian West is that he did not allow himself to

---

1. This is the Jewish and Christian concept of God's prophets. They charge their prophets with incest, adultery and even murder. They impute horrendous crimes to them on the authority of the Holy Bible.

be slaughtered, to be "crucified" by his enemies. He ably defended himself, his family and his followers; and finally vanquished his enemies. Muhummed's (pbuh) success is the Christians' gall of disappointment: he did not believe in any vicarious sacrifice for the sins of others. He believed and behaved naturally. **"IN THE STATE OF NATURE, EVERYONE HAS A RIGHT TO DEFEND HIS PERSON AND POSSESSIONS, AND EXTEND HIS HOSTILITIES TO A REASONABLE AMOUNT OF SATISFACTION AND RETALIATION,"** says Gibbon, the master historian in his *"Decline and Fall of the Roman Empire."* His struggle and victory over the forces of unbelief and evil made the editors of the Encyclopedia Britannica to exclaim, Muhummed (pbuh) to be — — — **"THE MOST SUCCESSFUL OF ALL RELIGIOUS PERSONALITIES."**

How can the enemies of Islam account for Muhummed's phenomenal achievements except to decry that he spread his religion at the point of the sword? He forced Islam down peoples' throats!?

> 6a.   "HISTORY MAKES IT CLEAR HOWEVER, THAT THE LEGEND OF FANATICAL MUSLIMS SWEEPING THROUGH THE WORLD AND FORCING ISLAM AT THE POINT OF THE SWORD UPON CONQUERED RACES IS ONE OF THE MOST FANTASTICALLY ABSURD MYTHS THAT HISTORIANS HAVE EVER REPEATED."
>
> *De Lacy O'Leary* in
> **"Islam at the Crossroads"** London, 1923, p.8

You do not have to be a historian like O'Leary to know that the Muslims ruled Spain for 736 years. The longest the Christians ever ruled over Muslims was 500 years in Mozambique, a territory captured from an Arab governor by the name of **Musabin-baique,** a name they could not properly pronounce, hence the name Mozambique. Even today, after five centuries of Christian overlordship the country is still 60 percent Muslim.

However, after eight centuries in Spain the Muslims were totally eliminated from that country so that not even one man was left to give the **Azaan** (the Muslim call to prayer). If the Muslim had used force, military or economic there would not have been any Christian left in Spain to have kicked the Muslims out. One can blame the Muslim for exploitation if you like but one cannot charge them with using the sword to convert Spaniards to the Islamic religion.

Today, Islam is still spreading all over the world — and Muslims have NO sword!![1]

The Muslims were also the masters of India for a thousand years, but eventually when the sub-continent received independence in 1947, the Hindus obtained three-quarters of the country and the Muslims the balance of the one-quarter. Why? Because the Muslims did not force Islam down the Hindus' throat! In Spain and in India, the Muslims were no paragons of virtue, yet they obeyed the Qur'anic injunction to the letter —

*LET THERE BE NO COMPULSION
IN RELIGION:*

لَآ إِكْرَاهَ فِى الدِّيْنِ ۚ

*FOR TRUTH STANDS OUT
DISTINCT FROM ERROR:*

قَدْ تَّبَيَّنَ الرُّشْدُ مِنَ الْغَىِّ ۚ

(SÚRA BAQARA)   *Holy Qur'an 2:256*

The Muslim conquerors understood from this command that "compulsion" was incompatible with true religion: because

(a) Religion depends on faith and will, and these would be meaningless if induced by force. Force can conquer but cannot convert.

(b) Truth and Error have been so clearly shown up by the Mercy of God that there should be no doubt in the minds of any person of goodwill as to the fundamentals of faith.

---

1. See chart on page 133, **"the fastest growing faith on earth"**.

(c) God's protection is continuous and His Plan is always to lead us from the depths of darkness into the clearest light.[1]

Except for some eccentrics here and there, the Muslims as a whole adhered to the commandment of God in the lands over which they held sway.

But what can the enemy say about countries where no single Muslim soldier had set foot?

(i) INDONESIA: It is a fact that over a hundred million Indonesians are Muslim, yet no conquering Muslim army ever landed on any of its over two thousand islands.

(ii) MALAYSIA: The overwhelming number of its people in this country are Muslims yet no Muslim soldier had landed there either.

(iii) AFRICA: The majority of the people on the East coast of Africa as far down as Mozambique, as well as the bulk of the inhabitants on the West coast of the continent are Muslims, but history does not record any invading hoards of Muslims from anywhere. What sword? Where was the sword? The Muslim trader did the job. His good conduct and moral rectitude achieved the miracle of conversion.

"All what you say seems incontrovertible, Mr. Deedat," says the Christian controversialist, "but we are talking about Islam at its very beginning, the way in which your prophet converted the pagans to his faith! How did he do it if not with the sword?"

---

1. (a), (b) and (c) are Yusuf Ali's comments on verse 256. Obtain his translation with over 6000 explanatory footnotes from the IPCI.

ONE AGAINST ALL?

We can do no better than to allow Thomas Carlyle himself to defend his Hero Prophet against this false charge; — — —

7. "THE SWORD INDEED: BUT WHERE WILL YOU GET YOUR SWORD! EVERY NEW OPINION, AT ITS STARTING, IS PRECISELY IN A **MINORITY OF ONE.** IN ONE MAN'S HEAD ALONE, THERE IT DWELLS AS YET. ONE MAN ALONE OF THE WHOLE WORLD BELIEVES IT; THERE IS ONE MAN AGAINST ALL MEN. THAT HE TAKE A SWORD, AND TRY TO PROPAGATE WITH THAT, WILL DO LITTLE FOR HIM. YOU MUST FIRST GET YOUR SWORD! ON THE WHOLE, A THING WILL PROPAGATE ITSELF AS IT CAN. WE DO NOT FIND, OF THE CHRISTIAN RELIGION EITHER, THAT IT ALWAYS DISDAINED THE SWORD, WHEN ONCE IT HAD GOT ONE. CHARLEMAGNE'S CONVERSION OF THE SAXONS WAS NOT BY PREACHING."

Heroes and Hero-Worship, p. 80

At the age of forty when Muhummed (pbuh) declared his Divine mission from heaven, there was no political party, or royalty, and certainly no family or tribe to back him up. His people — the Arabs, immersed in idol-worship and fetishism were not by any means a docile people, they were no easy meat. They were a very volatile people. given to internecine and fratricidal wars: subject to **"all kinds of fierce sincerities"** (Carlyle). One man, single-handed, to wean such a people from barbarism required nothing short of a miracle. A miracle did happen. God alone could have made Islam and Muhummed (pbuh) to triumph through with flimsy, gossamer support. God fulfilling His promise:

> **And have We not raised high the esteem (in which) thou (O Muhummed art held)?**
>
> **(SÚRA INSHIRÁH)** *Holy Qur'an 94:4*

CHAPTER THREE

Fastest Growing Religion Today

THE SWORD OF THE INTELLECT

The enemy, the sceptic, the missionary and their passive camp followers will not stop bleating that "Islam was spread at the point of the sword!" but they will not venture to answer our question — — "WHO BRIBED CARLYLE!?" In 1840 when Carlyle defended Muhummed (pbuh) and refuted the allegation about the sword, there was nobody around to bribe. The whole Muslim world was in the gutters. The countries of Islam were all under subjugation by the Christians, except for a few like — Persia, Afghanistan and Turkey who were only nominally independent. There were no riches to flaunt and no petro-dollars to bribe with!

That was yesterday and many yesterdays ago, but what about today, in modern times? It is claimed **from the chart on the next page** that "Islam is the fastest growing religion in the world." The overall increase of all the sects and denominations of Christianity was a staggering 138 per cent with the incredible increase of Islam by 235 per cent in the same period of time of half-a-century. It is further affirmed that in Britain and the United States of America, Islam is the fastest growing faith. It is said that in Britain **"There are more Muslims than Methodists in the country."** You have a right to ask, "What sword?" The answer is, "THE SWORD INDEED!" (Thomas Carlyle)[1] **It is the sword of the intellect!** It is the fulfilment of yet another prophecy;—

IT IS HE (God Almighty) *WHO HAS SENT HIS MESSENGER* (Muhummed) *WITH GUIDANCE*

هُوَ الَّذِىٓ اَرْسَلَ
رَسُوْلَهٗ بِالْهُدٰى

---

1. See full quote on page 131, No. 7.

A CRUCIAL HALF CENTURY OF RELIGION

Islam

by Keith W. Stump

235%

We highlight the most significant developments.

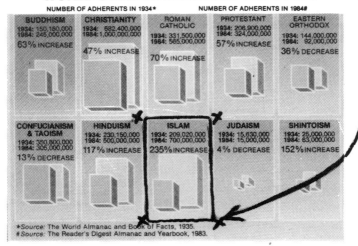

WORLD'S MAJOR RELIGIONS 1934/1984

NUMBER OF ADHERENTS IN 1934*   NUMBER OF ADHERENTS IN 1984#

BUDDHISM
1934: 150,180,000
1984: 245,000,000
63% INCREASE

CHRISTIANITY
1934: 682,400,000
1984: 1,000,000,000
47% INCREASE

ROMAN CATHOLIC
1934: 331,500,000
1984: 565,000,000
70% INCREASE

PROTESTANT
1934: 206,900,000
1984: 324,000,000
57% INCREASE

EASTERN ORTHODOX
1934: 144,000,000
1984: 92,000,000
36% DECREASE

CONFUCIANISM & TAOISM
1934: 350,800,000
1984: 305,000,000
13% DECREASE

HINDUISM
1934: 230,150,000
1984: 500,000,000
117% INCREASE

ISLAM
1934: 209,020,000
1984: 700,000,000
235% INCREASE

JUDAISM
1934: 15,630,000
1984: 15,000,000
4% DECREASE

SHINTOISM
1934: 25,000,000
1984: 63,000,000
152% INCREASE

*Source: The World Almanac and Book of Facts, 1935.
Source: The Reader's Digest Almanac and Yearbook, 1983.

The PLAIN TRUTH

AND THE RELIGION OF TRUTH (Islam)   وَدِينِ الْحَقِّ

THAT HE MAY MAKE IT PREVAIL   لِيُظْهِرَهُ عَلَى الدِّينِ كُلِّهِ
OVER ALL RELIGIONS,

AND ENOUGH IS GOD FOR A WITNESS.   وَكَفَى بِاللهِ شَهِيدًا ۝

(SÚRA FAT-Ḥ) *Holy Qur'an 48:28*

The destiny of Islam is spelt out here in the clearest terms. Islam is to master, overcome and supersede every other faith —

> **That He** (God Almighty) **make it** (Islam)
> **prevail over all religions . . .**

In Arabic the word is **Deen**[1] (literally meaning "Way of Life"), to supersede all, whether it be Hinduism, Buddhism, Christianism,[2] Judaism, Communism or any other **"ism."** This is the destiny of Allah's **Deen.**

The same Qur'anic Verse is repeated in chapter 61 verse 9 which ends with this slight variation —

> (Never mind) **Though the unbelievers**
> **might be averse to it** (Islam).

TRIUMPH OF ISLAM

Islam will prevail. It is the promise of God, and His Promise is true. But how? With the sword? Not even if we had the laser gun! Could we use it? The Holy Qur'an forbids us to use force as a means of converting! Yet the verse prophesies that Islam would be the most dominant of all religions. The triumphs of its doctrines have already started and is gaining hold over the religious ideology and doctrines of the various schools of thought in the world. Though not in the name of Islam, but in the name of reformation and amendments, the doctrines of Islam are being

---

1. Usually translated as Religion, which literally Islam is not.
2. In the time of Thomas Car'yle this was the term applied to Christianity.

fastly grafted into the various religious orders. Many things which are exclusively Islamic and which were formerly unknown, or which were being opposed before with tooth and nail by the other creeds, are now part of their beliefs.

**The Brotherhood of man
The abolition of the Caste system and
untouchability
The right of women to inherit
Opening the places of worship to all
Prohibition of all intoxicants
The true concept of the Unity of God
etc, etc.**

Just one word on the last subject above, before we proceed further. Ask any theist, polytheist,[1] pantheist,[2] or trinitarian: how many Gods he believes in? He will shudder to say anything other than ONE! This is the EFFECT of the strict monotheism of Islam.

THE CREED OF MOHAMED IS FREE FROM
THE SUSPICIONS OF AMBIGUITY AND THE
KORAN IS A GLORIOUS TESTIMONY TO
THE UNITY OF GOD.

Gibbon in his
"Decline and Fall of the Roman Empire."

VERDICT OF NON-MUSLIM ORIENTALS

Almost all the defenders of Muhummed (pbuh) who spoke out against the false theory that he spread his religion at the point of the sword, were Westerners. Let us now hear what some non-Muslim Easterners have to say on the subject:

---

1. **Polytheist:** One who believes in many gods.
2. **Pantheist:** The one who believes that everything is god. Of course the **"trinitarian,"** you already know.

8a.   THE MORE I STUDY THE MORE I DISCOVER THAT THE STRENGTH OF ISLAM DOES NOT LIE IN THE SWORD.

Mahatma Gandhi — the father of modern
India, in **"Young India."**

b.   THEY (Muhummed's critics) SEE FIRE INSTEAD OF LIGHT, UGLINESS INSTEAD OF GOOD. THEY DISTORT AND PRESENT EVERY GOOD QUALITY AS A GREAT VICE. IT REFLECTS THEIR OWN DEPRAVITY ...
THE CRITICS ARE BLIND. THEY CANNOT SEE THAT THE ONLY 'SWORD' MUHAMMAD WIELDED WAS THE SWORD OF MERCY, COMPASSION, FRIENDSHIP AND FORGIVE-NESS — THE SWORD THAT CONQUERS ENE-MIES AND PURIFIES THEIR HEARTS. HIS SWORD WAS SHARPER THAN THE SWORD OF STEEL.

Pandit Gyanandra Dev Sharma Shastri,
at a meeting in Gorakhpur (India). 1928

c.   HE PREFERRED MIGRATION TO FIGHTING HIS OWN PEOPLE, BUT WHEN OPPRESSION WENT BEYOND THE PALE OF TOLERANCE HE TOOK UP HIS SWORD IN SELF-DEFENCE. THOSE WHO BELIEVE RELIGION CAN BE SPREAD BY FORCE ARE FOOLS WHO NEITHER KNOW THE WAYS OF RELIGION NOR THE WAYS OF THE WORLD. THEY ARE PROUD OF THIS BELIEF BECAUSE THEY ARE A LONG, LONG WAY AWAY FROM THE TRUTH.

A Sikh journalist in **"Nawan Hindustan,"**
Delhi, 17 November 1947.

It was Rudyard Kipling who said, **"East is East and West is West, never the twain shall meet!"** He was wrong! In the defence of Muhummed (pbuh), **all,** who are not blinded by prejudice will converge.

THREE OTHER STANDARDS

Fourteen years after Thomas Carlyle had delivered his lecture on his **Hero Prophet,** a Frenchman by the name of Lamartine wrote the history of the Turks. Incidentally, the Turks being Muslims, Lamartine touched on some aspects of Islam and its founder. Like our Jules Masserman (see page 105) of current times, who had conceived three objective standards for discovering greatness of leadership; Lamartine had over a century ago thought of **three** other objective standards for conferring **GREATNESS.** We must give credit to the Westerner for this type of insight. Lamartine opines:

9. **IF GREATNESS OF PURPOSE, SMALLNESS OF MEANS AND ASTOUNDING RESULTS**[1] ARE THE THREE CRITERIA OF HUMAN GENIUS, WHO COULD DARE TO COMPARE ANY GREAT MAN IN MODERN HISTORY WITH MUHUMMED? (Lamartine ends his lengthy segment of literary masterpiece with the words): ... PHILOSOPHER, ORATOR, APOSTLE, LEGISLATOR, WARRIOR, CONQUEROR OF IDEAS, RESTORER OF RATIONAL BELIEFS, OF A CULT WITHOUT IMAGES: THE FOUNDER OF TWENTY TERRESTRIAL EMPIRES AND OF ONE SPIRITUAL EMPIRE, THAT IS MUHUMMED. **AS REGARDS ALL STANDARDS BY WHICH HUMAN GREATNESS MAY BE MEASURED, WE MAY WELL ASK, IS THERE ANY MAN GREATER THEN HE?**

   Lamartine, **"Historie de la Turquie,"** Paris 1854

The answer to his question, **"Is there any man greater than he?"** is reposed in the question itself. By implication he is

---

1. The full quotation from Lamartine's book will be found in appendix "B" page 159.

saying . . . "THERE IS NO MAN GREATER THAN MUHUMMED. MUHUMMED IS THE GREATEST MAN THAT EVER LIVED!"

And have We not raised high the esteem (in which) thou (O Muhummed art held)?

(SÚRA ISHIRÁH) *Holy Qur'an 94:4*

MOST CERTAINLY THOU HAST, O, MY LORD!

Before we absolve Lamartine of any favouritism, partiality, or of the charge of being bribed, we will scrutinize his three standards, and whether they can be justified in the case of Muhummed (pbuh).

1. GREATNESS OF PURPOSE

History of the time will tell you that it was the darkest period in the history of mankind when Muhummed (pbuh) was commanded to declare his mission. The need was for the raising of prophets in every corner of the world, or the sending of one Master Messenger for the whole of mankind, to deliver them from falsehood, superstition, selfishness, polytheism, wrong and oppression. It was to be the reclamation of the whole of humanity. And God Almighty in His wisdom chose His prophet from the backwaters of Arabia as His universal Messenger. Thus He records in His Noble Book —

AND WE SENT THEE NOT (O Muhummed), *BUT AS A MERCY UNTO* (all) *THE WORLDS.*

وَمَا أَرْسَلْنَاكَ اِلَّا
رَحْمَةً لِّلْعَالَمِينَ ۞

(SÚRA ANBIYÁA) *Holy Qur'an 21:107*

"There is no question now of race or nation, of a "chosen people" or the "seed of Abraham,"; or the "seed of David"; or of Hindu Arya varta; of Jew or Gentile. Arab or 'Ajam (Persian), Turk or Tajik, European or Asiatic, White or Coloured; Aryan,

Semitic, Mongolian, or African; or American, Australian, or Polynesian. To all men and creatures who have any spiritual responsibilty, the principles universally apply."

Abdullah Yusuf Ali[1]

JESUS (PBUH) DISCRIMINATES

Muhummed's (pbuh) immediate predecessor advised his disciples, **"Give not that which is holy unto the dogs"** (meaning non-Jews), **"Neither cast ye your pearls before swine"** (meaning non-Jews, Matthew 7:6). The Gospel writers are unanimous in recording that Christ lived by the precepts which he preached. In his lifetime he did not preach to a single non-Jew. In fact he spurned a gentile woman who sought his spiritual blessings (**"the woman was a Greek"** Mark 7:26). Then during the "passover" season in Jerusalem when the master with his disciples had congregated for the occasion, certain Greeks hearing of his reputation sought an audience with him for spiritual enlightenment, but Jesus (pbuh) gave them the "cold shoulder"[2] as narrated by St. John:

> *And there were certain Greeks among them that came up to worship at the feast:*
>
> *The same came therefore to Philip ... and desired him saying, Sir, we would see Jesus.*
>
> *Philip cometh and telleth Andrew: and again Andrew and Philip tell Jesus*
>
> *(HOLY BIBLE)* John 12:20-22

---

1. Get your copy now of Yusuf Ali's, English translation and commentary, with over 6000 annotations. Obtain a copy for your non-Muslim friend, also.

2. Means: a deliberately unkind or unfriendly treatment; a slight; a snub.

SELF-GLORIFICATION

The verses that follow do not even record the courtesy of **"Yea, yea;"** or **"Nay, nay;"** (Yes, yes or no, no of Matthew 5:37). They continue with his own praise —

> **And Jesus answered them** (Andrew and
> Philip), **saying, The hour is come, that
> the son of man** (referring to himself)
> **should be glorified.**
> **(HOLY BIBLE)** John 12:23

HIGHEST STANDARDS

Muhummed (pbuh) could never afford any such latitudes. Remember, how the Almighty reminded him of the highest etiquette required from him. Even the thought of being ruffled by the untimely intrusion of a blind man, was not accepted from him (see page 117 **"He frowned"**). As a universal Messenger, God set for him the most lofty standards:

> **And Most Certainly,
> Thou** ((O Muhummed)
> **Art of most sublime
> And Exalted Character.**
> **(SÚRA QALAM)** Holy Qur'an 68:4

And his diocese, his field of mission? The whole of mankind!

> **And We sent thee not
> (O Muhummed), but as
> a Mercy unto (all) the worlds.**
> **(SÚRA ANBIYÁA)** Holy Qur'an 21:107

UNIVERSAL MESSENGER

These are not mere platitudes; beautiful sentiments bereft of action. Muhummed (pbuh) practised what he preached. Among his first **Sahábás** (companions) and converts, beside the Arab can be counted **Bilal** the Abyssinian, **Salman** the Persian and **Abdullah Bin-Salaam** the Jew. The sceptics may say that his outreach was simply incidental but what can they say about the historical fact that before his demise, he sent out five epistles, one to each of the five surrounding countries, inviting them to accept the religion of Islam.

1. The Emperor of Persia
2. The King of Egypt
3. The Negus of Abyssinia
4. The Emperor Heraclius at Constantinople, and
5. The King of Yemen

Thus he set the example for the fulfilment of his impelling mission, his **"greatness of purpose,"** the reclamation of the whole of humanity into the Master's fold. Is there another example of such universality in another religion? Muhummed (pbuh) was not out to set or to break any records, he was simply carrying out the trust that was reposed in him by the Lord of Creation!

2. SMALLNESS OF MEANS

Muhummed (pbuh) was born with no silver spoon in his mouth. His life begins with infinitesimal support. His father had died before he was born. His mother dies by the time he was six years old. He was doubly-orphaned at this tender age, his grandfather Abdul-Muttalib takes charge of the child, but within three years he also died. As soon as he was able, he began to look after his uncle Abu Talib's sheep and goats for his keep. Contrast this poor, doubly-orphaned Arab child with some of the great religious personalities that preceded him, and you must marvel at what Destiny had in store for him!

Abraham (pbuh) the spiritual father of Moses, Jesus and Muhummed (May the peace of God be upon them all), was the son of a very successful businessman of his time. Moses (pbuh) was reared in the house of Pharaoh. Jesus (pbuh) though described as **"a carpenter and the son of a carpenter,"** was well endowed with learning as well as material means. Peter, Philip, Andrew, etc. all downed tools and followed him to be at his beck and call, not because he had any **halo**[1] on his head; there was no such thing, but because of his affluent attire and princely bearing. He could command mansions in Jerusalem for himself and his disciples even during the height of the festive season; and have sumptuous suppers arranged; and you could hear him reproach the materialistic Jews —

> *And when they found him (Jesus)*
> *on the other side of the sea, they*
> *said to him, "Rabbi, when did you*
> *come here?"*
>
> *Jesus answered them and said, "most*
> *assuredly, I say to you, you seek me,*
> *not because you saw the signs,*[2] *but*
> *because you ate of the loaves and*
> *were filled.*
>
> *(HOLY BIBLE)   John 6:25-26*

NOTHING TO OFFER

Muhummed (pbuh) had no bread nor meat to offer; no sugar-plums of any kind, in this world or the next! The only thing he could offer his bedraggled, poor shepherd people was trial and tribulations and the strait-jacketing of their lives here on earth and the good pleasures of God in the Hereafter. The life of the Prophet was an open book before them. He had shown them as to what he was; the nobility of his character, his integrity of purpose, his earnestness and fiery enthusiasm for the truth he

---

1. **Halo:** An imaginary luminous ring or disc surrounding the head of saintly men and women in religious paintings.

2. The veracity of the Messiah's message and his mission.

had come to preach revealed the hero; and they followed him. Mr. Stanley Lane Poole's estimate of our hero is so beautiful and yet so truthful that I cannot resist the temptation of quoting it here:

HE WAS AN ENTHUSIAST IN THAT NOBLEST SENSE WHEN ENTHUSIASM BECOMES THE SALT OF THE EARTH, THE ONE THING THAT KEEPS MEN FROM ROTTING WHILST THEY LIVE.

ENTHUSIASM IS OFTEN USED DESPITEFULLY, BECAUSE IT IS JOINED TO AN UNWORTHY CAUSE, OR FALLS UPON BARREN GROUND AND BEARS NO FRUIT. SO WAS IT NOT WITH MOHAMMED. HE WAS AN ENTHUSIAST WHEN ENTHUSIASM WAS THE ONE THING NEEDED TO SET THE WORLD AFLAME, AND HIS ENTHUSIASM WAS NOBLE FOR A NOBLE CAUSE.

HE WAS ONE OF THOSE HAPPY FEW WHO HAVE ATTAINED THE SUPREME JOY OF MAKING ONE GREAT TRUTH THEIR VERY LIFE-SPRING.

HE WAS THE MESSENGER OF THE ONE GOD; AND NEVER TO HIS LIFE'S END DID HE FORGET WHO HE WAS, OR THE MESSAGE WHICH WAS THE MARROW OF HIS BEING. HE BROUGHT HIS TIDINGS TO HIS PEOPLE WITH A GRAND DIGNITY SPRUNG FROM THE CONSCIOUSNESS OF HIS HIGH OFFICE, TOGETHER WITH A MOST SWEET HUMILITY, WHOSE ROOTS LAY IN THE KNOWLEDGE OF HIS OWN WEAKNESS."

It may easily be conceded that Muhummed (pbuh) was blessed with the flimsiest of human resources. In fact the odds were loaded against him. But what about his fortune towards the end of his earthly sojourn? He was the overlord of the whole of

Arabia! What about the endless means at his disposal then? We will allow a Christian missionary to answer that —

> HE WAS CAESAR AND POPE IN ONE; BUT HE WAS POPE WITHOUT THE POPE'S PRETENTIONS, AND CAESAR WITHOUT THE LEGIONS OF CAESAR: WITHOUT A STANDING ARMY, WITHOUT A BODYGUARD, WITHOUT A PALACE, WITHOUT A FIXED REVENUE; IF EVER ANY MAN HAD THE RIGHT TO SAY THAT HE RULED BY THE RIGHT DIVINE, IT WAS MOHAMMAD, FOR HE HAD ALL THE POWERS WITHOUT ITS INSTRUMENTS AND WITHOUT ITS SUPPORTS."

R. Bosworth Smith
"Mohammad and Mohammadanism", London 1874, p. 92

HIS HANDICAPS

His "weakness" was his strength. The very fact that he had no material means of support made him to put his entire trust in God, and God the Merciful did not forsake him. His success was all the more staggering. May not the Muslims justly say, the entire work was the work of God? **And Muhummed (pbuh) His instrument?**

3. OUTSTANDING RESULTS

In the words of Thomas Carlyle — **"One man against all men,"**[1] to a hundred and twenty four thousand at the Farewell Pilgrimage alone. How many were left behind of men, women and children, believers all?

On the 12th of RABI 1., in the 11th year after the *Hijra,*[2] approximating to the 8th of June 632 of the Christian Era, whilst

---

1. See full quotation by Thomas Carlyle on page 131.
2. *Hijra:* literally means Migration.

praying earnestly in whisper, the spirit of the great Prophet took flight to the **"blessed companionship on high"** *(Ibn Hisham).*

Hazrat Omar (May Allah be pleased with him), on receiving the sad news of the demise of the Holy Prophet, lost his bearings. He was so shocked that he blurted out "If anyone says that Muhummed is dead, I will chop off his head!" Hazrat Abu Bakr As-Siddiq presently verified that the Master had indeed departed from this world; and coming out from the Prophet's apartment announced to the gathering throng outside, that, **"Muhummed (pbuh) had indeed passed away. Those that worshipped Muhummed,"** he said, **"Let them know that Muhummed is dead, but those who worship Allah, let them know that Allah lives for ever!"**

This brought Omar al-Farooq (R.A.) back to his senses. Could this man who was to become the second great *Khaleefah* of Islam at this moment imagine that fourteen hundred years later there would be a **thousand million** followers of Muhummed (pbuh) at one time? Could he have visualized that the religion of the Prophet would be the fastest growing religion in the world?[1]

Christianity had a 600-year start on Islam. Numerically the Christians claim to outnumber the followers of any other faith; this is true but let us look at the picture in its true perspective —

> THERE ARE MORE **PROFESSING** CHRISTIANS IN THE WORLD THAN **PROFESSING** MUSLIMS, BUT THERE ARE MORE **PRACTISING** MUSLIMS IN THE WORLD THAN **PRACTISING** CHRISTIANS.
> (Emphasis added)
>
> R.V.C. Bodley (the American) in
> **"The Messenger: The Life of Mohammed."** U.S.A. 1969

---

1. See chart on page 133

I understand from the above that Mr. Bodley is trying to tell us that there are people in the world who, when filling their census forms, will tick off the term **Christian** under "Religion." It is not necessarily that they believe in the dogmas of Christianity. They could actually be atheists or **bush-Baptists,**[1] as opposed to being a Jew or Hindu or Muslim; coming from a Christian background they would for the purpose of convenience label themselves **"Christian."** From that point of view, and from the point of view that a person who practises what he believes, there would be more Muslims in the world than Christians.

Chronologically, Islam is six hundred years behind Christianity, but amazingly it is a very close second, and is catching up fast — the fastest growing religion in the world today (see chart on page 133). **"One Billion"** The figure is outstanding and the sincerity and practice of the Believers astonishing!

Taking into account his own three objective standards: (a) **"greatness of purpose;"** (b) **"smallness of means;"** and (c) **"outstanding results;"** does Lamartine dare to produce another candidate greater than Muhummed (pbuh)? He further awes his readers with the multifarious roles of Muhummed (pbuh) in which he excelled, ie. **"Philosopher, Orator, Apostle, Legislator, Warrior, Conqueror of Ideas, the Restorer of Rational Beliefs, of a Cult without Images, the Founder of twenty Terrestrial Empires and of one Spiritual Empire, that is Muhummed. As regards ALL standards** (I repeat "ALL") **by which Human Greatness may be measured, we may well ask, "IS THERE ANY MAN GREATER THAN HE?"** (Emphasis added).

No! Muhummed (pbuh) was the greatest man that ever lived! According to Lamartine the French historian. And God Almighty questions —

---

1. **"bush-Baptist":** There are forty different Baptist Churches in the United States of America. But bush-Baptists are people with strong religious feelings yet will not go to any Church; and will not affiliate with any sect or denomination.

And have We not raised high
the esteem (in which) thou
(O Muhummed art held)?

(SÚRA ISHIRÁH)   Holy Qur'an 94:4

MOST ASSUREDLY THOU HAST, O MY LORD!

THE QUALITY OF MERCY

The Christian propagandists make the wild boast that there is nothing in the history of mankind to compare with the merciful and forgiving cry of Jesus (pbuh) on the cross ...

"Father, forgive them, for they know
not what they do."

(HOLY BIBLE)   Luke 23:34

Amazing as it may sound, of the four writers of the Canonical Gospels, only St. Luke was inspired by the Holy Ghost (?) to pen these words. The other three — Matthew, Mark and John never heard these words or they felt them to be too insipid or not important enough for recording. St. Luke was not even one of the twelve disciples selected by Jesus (pbuh). According to the revisers of the Revised Standard Version (RSV) of the Bible, these words are not in the most ancient manuscripts which by implication means that they are an interpolation.

In "The New King James Version," (Copyrighted by the Thomas Nelson Publishers in 1984), we are told that these words are "not in the original text" of the Greek manuscripts of St. Luke. In other words they have been fabricated by some pious gentleman. Although the quotation is unauthentic, we will still entertain it because it demonstrates great piety of loving one's enemies and of unsurpassed forgiveness as preached by the Master himself.

For forgiveness to be of any worth, the forgiver must be in a position to forgive. If the victim of injustice is still in the clutches of his enemies; in that helpless position and he would cry out, "I FORGIVE YOU!" it would be meaningless. But if the aggrieved party had turned the tables on his enemies and was in a position of taking revenge or exact retribution, and yet say "I forgive you!", only then would it mean something!

MUHUMMED'S (PBUH) CLEMENCY

Contrast the alleged forgiveness from the "cross" with the historical bloodless conquest of Makkah by Muhummed (pbuh) at the head of ten thousand "saints"[1] (his companions).

> "THE CITY WHICH HAD TREATED HIM SO CRUELLY, DRIVEN HIM AND HIS FAITHFUL BAND FOR REFUGE AMONGST STRANGERS, WHICH HAD SWORN HIS LIFE AND THE LIVES OF HIS DE-VOTED DISCIPLES, LAY AT HIS FEET. HIS OLD PERSECUTERS RELENTLESS AND RUTHLESS, WHO HAD DISGRACED HUMANITY BY INFLICTING CRUEL OUTRAGES UPON INOFFENSIVE MEN AND WOMEN, AND EVEN UPON THE LIFELESS DEAD, WERE NOW COMPLETELY AT HIS MERCY. BUT IN THE HOUR OF HIS TRIUMPH EVERY EVIL SUFFERED WAS FORGOTTEN, EVERY INJURY INFLICTED WAS FORGIVEN, AND A GENERAL AMNESTY WAS EXTENDED TO THE POPULATION OF MAKKAH ..."

Sayed Amir Ali in "The Spirit of Islam."

Calling before him the populace of the vanquished city, he addressed them with **"What do you expect at my hands today?"** His people had known him too well, even from his childhood so they replied, "Mercy, O generous brother and nephew!" Tears came into the eyes of the Prophet, and he said,

---

1. A fulfilment of another prophecy in Muhummed (pbuh). "...**He came from mount Paran** (that is in Arabia). **and he came with ten thousand saints** ..." Deuteronomy 33:2.

"I will speak to you as Joseph spoke unto his brethren, I will not reproach you today; go you are free!"

And now a scene was enacted of which there is really no parallel in the history of the world. Hosts upon hosts came forward and adopted the religion of Islam. God almighty testifies as to the lofty and exalted behaviour of His Messenger —

> **Ye have indeed in the Messenger**
> **of Allah a beautiful pattern (of**
> **conduct)**
>
> *(SÚRA AHZÁB)* *Holy Qur'an 33:21*

How well has Lamartine[1] unknowingly echoed these sentiments —

> "AS REGARDS **ALL STANDARDS** BY WHICH
> HUMAN GREATNESS MAY BE MEASURED, WE
> MAY WELL ASK, IS THERE ANY MAN GREATER
> THAN HE?"

In reply, we too can say once more, **"No! there is no man greater than Muhummed (pbuh). Muhummed (pbuh) was the greatest man that ever lived!"**

So far, our hero has earned the unsolicited and ungrudging tributes from many non-Muslims of different religious persuasions and from varying intellectual fields of endeavour. But all this still remains incomplete without the Master's verdict; Muhummed's (pbuh) predecessor — Jesus Christ (pbuh). We will now apply his own standard for evaluating greatness.

JOHN THE BAPTIST

John the Baptist,[2] known throughout the Muslim world as Hazrat **Yahya** Alaihis-salaam (Peace be upon him) was, a contemporary

---

1. Full quotation of Lamartine will be found in Appendix "B" on page 158.
2. **"JOHN"** not to be confused with John the disciple of Jesus (pbuh). A very common name among the Jews and Arabs, even today, like Tarik Aziz the current Iraqi Minister of Foreign Affairs. Real name Tarik **Hanna** Aziz; **"Hanna"** short for Yuhanna meaning John. No one in the non-Arab Muslim world knowing that our friend is a Christian Marxist.

prophet of the Messiah. They were also cousins. Here is what the Master has to say of him:

> *Verily I say unto you, Among them*
> *that are born of women there hath*
> *not risen a greater than John the*
> *Baptist:*
>
> (HOLY BIBLE)   Matthew 11:11

Every son of man is **"born of women."** By this very fact John the Baptist is greater than Moses, David, Solomon, Abraham or Isaiah; none of the Israelite prophets excluded. What gives John this ascendency over every other prophet? It could not be any miracle, because the Bible records none to his credit. It could not be his teachings, because he brought no new laws or regulations. Then what makes him the greatest? Simply because he was the heralder, a precursor, a harbinger of the happy news of the coming of the Messiah. This is what made John the greatest, but Jesus (pbuh) claims that he himself was even greater than the greatest (ie. John). Why?

> *But I have greater witness than*
> *that of John* (the Baptist): *For The*
> *Works which the Father hath given*
> *me to finish:* (Emphasis added)
>
> (HOLY BIBLE)   John 5:36

It is the **"witness,"** the commission which God Almighty had entrusted him with, which makes Jesus (pbuh) greater than even John. Applying these very standards as enunciated by the Master, we find that —

1. John the Baptist was the greatest of all the Israelite prophets, because he heralded the mighty Messiah (Jesus pbuh).

    Similarly Jesus (pbuh) would be greater than even John because he heralded **"The Spirit**

of Truth, the Comforter," who was to guide mankind into **all Truth** (of the Gospel of St. John, chapter 16).[1]

2. The diocese, the mission of Jesus (pbuh), or **"the works which God had given him to accomplish,"** was limited to the Lost sheep of the House of Israel (Matthew 15:24), whereas the mission of Muhummed (pbuh) was universal. He had been told —

> **And we have sent thee not**
> **(O Muhummed), but as a**
> **Mercy unto (all) the worlds.**
>
> ***(SÚRA ANBIYÁA)*** *Holy Qur'an 21:107*

In keeping with his grand commission, Muhummed (pbuh) consistently delivered his Message to one and all who would hear, irrespective of race, class or creed, He welcomed them all in the religion of God, without any discrimination. He had no thought of dividing the creatures of God into **"dogs and pigs"** (Matthew 7:6) or into **"sheep and goats"** (Matthew 25:32). He was the Messenger of the One True God, who was sent as a Mercy unto all mankind, nay, unto the whole universe (H.Q. 21:107 above). And, he never forgot this mission even right up to his dying day.

Towards the end of his earthly sojourn, when he could look back to a hectic and dangerous past, now crowned with success; he now feels that he could sit back and enjoy the fruits of his toil; he dreams of a life free from turmoil and full of satisfaction and relaxation. Not for him! There is no time to rest or relax. There is work still to be done. God Almighty reminds him --

WE HAVE NOT SENT THEE
(O MUHUMMED) *BUT TO THE*
WHOLE OF MANKIND,

وَمَآ أَرْسَلْنَٰكَ إِلَّا كَآفَّةً لِّلنَّاسِ

---

1. For a detailed explanation about this prophecy, obtain today your FREE copy of the book **"MUHUMMED (pbuh) the Natural Successor to CHRIST (pbuh)"** from the IPCI.

AS A GIVER OF GLAD TIDINGS
AND AS A WARNER,

بَشِيرًا وَنَذِيرًا

BUT MOST OF MANKIND
STILL DO NOT KNOW.

وَلَكِنَّ أَكْثَرَ النَّاسِ لَا يَعْلَمُونَ ۞

(SÚRA SABÁ) Holy Qur'an 34:28[1]

How was he to respond to this new challenge in his ripening old age? There were no electronic gadgets of modern communication methods at his disposal; there were no telex and fax machines which he could exploit. What could he do? Being an **ummi** (unlettered), he called the scribes and dictated five letters, one each to the Emperor at Constantinople, the King of Egypt, the Negus of Abyssinia, the King of Yemen and to the Emperor in Persia. He called forth five *Sahaaba* (his holy companions) with five Arab steeds and set them out in five different directions inviting the nations of the world to the universal religion of God.

I had the good fortune of seeing one of those holy epistles in the Topkapi Museum in Istanbul (old Constantinople) Turkey. That letter is collecting dust! Materially the Turks have preserved the parchment. But the Message is collecting dust, as I have said.

The letter begins, **"From Muhummed the Messenger of God, to Heraclius the Emperor at Constantinople: Accept Islam and be benefited."**

Followed by this exhortation from the Book of God — —

SAY: "O PEOPLE OF THE BOOK![2]

COME TO COMMON TERMS
AS BETWEEN US AND YOU:

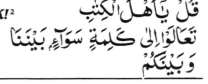

قُلْ يَا أَهْلَ الْكِتَابِ
تَعَالَوْا إِلَى كَلِمَةٍ سَوَاءٍ بَيْنَنَا
وَبَيْنَكُمْ

---

1. This is your last chance to memorize the text and the translation of this verse. If you are lackadaisical, we can only mourn your loss.

2. **"People of the Book,"** stands for the Jews and the Christians. You will never have it so good for learning Allah's **Kalaam.** Don't ignore this opportunity. Memorize the verses as they occur.

THAT WE WORSHIP *NONE BUT GOD;*	اَلَّا نَعْبُدَ اِلَّا اللّٰهَ
THAT WE ASSOCIATE *NO PARTNERS WITH HIM;*	وَلَا نُشْرِكَ بِهٖ شَيْئًا
THAT WE ERECT NOT, *FROM AMONG OURSELVES,* *LORDS AND PATRONS* *OTHER THAN GOD."*	وَّلَا يَتَّخِذَ بَعْضُنَا بَعْضًا اَرْبَابًا مِّنْ دُوْنِ اللّٰهِ ؕ
IF THEN THEY TURN BACK, *SAY YE: "BEAR WITNESS* *THAT WE (AT LEAST) ARE* *MUSLIMS (BOWING TO GOD'S WILL)"*	فَاِنْ تَوَلَّوْا فَقُوْلُوا اشْهَدُوْا بِاَنَّا مُسْلِمُوْنَ ۝

(*SÚRA ÁL-i-'IMRÁN*) *Holy Qur'an 3:64*

After the above Qur'anic insertion in the letter, it is concluded with felicitation in the Prophet's own words, ending with a seal on which is inscribed — **"There is no other object of worship but Allah, and Muhummed is His Messenger."**

The letter in Turkey arouses our curiosity; and interest with regards to its preservation, but the preservation itself is lost upon the sightseer. The same Qur'anic Message is in almost every Muslim home; being read and re-read a thousand times over without the reader being moved to deliver its Message to the adressees!

Glance once more at the above verse. It is addressed to the **"ahle-Kitaab,"** — the People of the Book, the Jews and the Christians. But, for over a thousand years we have utterly ignored that great directive at our own peril. We are sitting on that Message like a cobra on a pile of wealth, keeping the rightful heirs at bay. This utter neglect will continue to inflict untold suffering to the **Ummah** for generations to come.

After over fourteen hundred years of our reading, and chanting the Qur'an in every rhythmic style, we still hear this poignant cry:

> **But Most of mankind still
> do not know.** [1]
>
> *(SÚRA SABÁ)*   *Holy Qur'an 34:28*

This is the concluding phrase of the verse revealed fourteen hundred years ago. It was the factual situation of the then religious world. The question which must be asked is: "Is it any different today?" **Not at all!** There are today more **Mushriks** in the world than there are believers in the One True God.

Is there any hope of changing this situation? Allah commanded His Prophet then as He is commanding us now through the first seven verses of Sura **Muddaththir** (chapter 74).

1. *O THOU WRAPPED UP*
    (IN A MANTLE)!

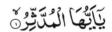

> "As usual, there is these wonderful early mystical verses (including the ones that follow), a triple thread of thought:
>
> (a) A particular occasion or person is referred to;
>
> (b) a general spiritual lesson is taught, and
>
> (c) a more profound mystical reverie is suggested.
>
> **As to (a),** the Prophet was now past the stage of personal contemplation. Wearing his mantle; he was now to go forth and boldly deliver his Message and publicly proclaim Allah The One True God. His heart had always purified, but now all his outward doings must be dedicated to God, and conventional respect for ancestral customs or worship must be thrown aside. The work of his Messengership was the most generous that could flow from his personality, but no reward or

---

1. For the full context of this verse, see page 152.

appreciation was to be expected from his people, but quite the contrary; there would be much call on his patience, but his contentment would arise from the good pleasure of God.

As to (b), similar stages arise in a minor degree in the life of every good man, for which the Prophet's life is to be a universal pattern.

As to (c), the **Sufis** understand, by the mantle and outward wrappings, the circumstances of our phenomenal existence, which are necessary to our physical comfort up to a certain stage; but we soon outgrow them, and our inner nature should then boldly proclaim itself; not that it brings any credit or reward with men; the very hope of expectation of such would be inconsistent with our higher nature, which should bear all checks and rejoice in the favour of God."

2. *ARISE AND DELIVER THY WARNING!*   قُمْ فَأَنذِرْ ۝

3. *AND THY LORD DO THOU MAGNIFY!*   وَرَبَّكَ فَكَبِّرْ ۝

4. *AND THY GARMENTS KEEP FREE FROM STAIN!*   وَثِيَابَكَ فَطَهِّرْ ۝

5. *AND ALL ABOMINATION SHUN!* (a)   وَالرُّجْزَ فَاهْجُرْ ۝

"(a) **Rujz** or **Rijz** means abomination and is usually understood to mean idolatry. It is even possible that there was an idol called **Rujz**. But these days it has a wider significance as including a mental state opposed to true worship, a state of doubt or indecision."

6. **NOR EXPECT, IN GIVING,
ANY INCREASE (FOR THYSELF)!** (b)

وَلَا تَمْنُنْ تَسْتَكْثِرُ

> "**(b)** The legal and commercial formula is that
> you give in order to receive what is worth **to you**
> a little more than you give, but expect nothing
> from the receiver. You serve God and God's
> creatures."

7. **BUT, FOR THY LORD'S (CAUSE)
BE PATIENT AND CONSTANT!** (c)[1]

وَلِرَبِّكَ فَاصْبِرْ

(SÚRA MUDDATHTHIR) Holy Qur'an 74:1—7

> "**(c)** Our zeal for God's Cause itself requires that
> we should not be impatient, and that we should
> show constancy in our efforts for His Cause. For
> we have faith, and we know that He is All-Good,
> All-Wise, and All-Powerful, and everything will
> ultimately be right."

Abdullah Yusuf Ali[2]

To the Arabs in general and to our Holy Prophet in particular **"a
mantle"** was the protective covering used for protection against
the sun, wind and sand. He was so to say girding himself,
rolling up his sleeves, to accomplish his task. Although most of
the Muslims in the world do not cover themselves with shawls
(mantles), in their day to day living, they carry a host of mantles
in the way of inferiority complexes.

> WHAT CAN WE DO TO MAKE GOD'S LIGHT
> SHINE FORTH THROUGH THE DARKNESS
> AROUND US?
> WE MUST FIRST LET IT SHINE IN OUR OWN
> TRUE SELVES

---

1. Remember to memorize Allah's **Kalaam** with its meaning!

2. The English translation and the commentaries was by Abdullah Yusuf Ali. Obtain your
volume from the IPCI at a specially subsidised price. **Also order a volume for your
non-Muslim friend.**

WITH THAT LIGHT IN THE NICHE OF OUR
INMOST HEARTS
WE CAN WALK WITH STEPS BOTH FIRM AND SURE:
WE CAN HUMBLY VISIT THE COMFORTLESS
AND GUIDE THEIR STEPS. NOT WE, BUT THE
LIGHT WILL GUIDE! BUT OH! THE JOY OF
BEING FOUND WORTHY TO BEAR THE TORCH,
AND TO SAY TO OUR BRETHREN: "I TOO WAS
IN DARKNESS, COMFORTLESS, AND BEHOLD, I
HAVE FOUND COMFORT AND JOY IN THE
GRACE DIVINE!"
THUS SHOULD WE PAY THE DUES OF
BROTHERHOOD, — —
BY WALKING HUMBLY SIDE BY SIDE,
IN THE WAYS OF THE LORD,
WITH MUTUAL AID AND COMFORT,
AND HEARTFELT PRAYER,
BACKED BY ACTION,.
THAT GOD'S GOOD PURPOSE
MAY BE ACCOMPLISHED
IN US ALL TOGETHER!

Abdullah Yusuf Ali

وَ لَكِنَّ اَكْثَرَ النَّاسِ لَا يَعْلَمُوْنَ ۝

BUT MOST OF MANKIND
STILL DO NOT KNOW

Thus spake, inspired our Holy Prophet,
Muhummed (pbuh) on whom we invoke
God's blessings for ever and ever —

AAMEEN!

APPENDIX "A"

He attained the height of eminence by his perfection;

كَشَفَ الدُّجٰى بِجَمَالِهٖ

He dispelled the darkness (of the world) by his grace;

حَسُنَتْ جَمِيْعُ خِصَالِهٖ

Excellent were all his qualities;

صَلُّوْ عَلَيْهِ وَاٰلِهٖ

Pray for blessings on him and his descendants.

Shaikh Sa'di Sheeraazi (RA)

APPENDIX "B"

Muhummed (PBUH) The Greatest

"If greatness of purpose,
smallness of means
and astounding results

are the three criteria of human genius, who could dare to compare any great man in modern history with Muhummed?

The most famous men created arms, laws and empires only. They founded, if anything at all, no more than material powers which often crumbled away before their eyes. This man Muhammed moved not only armies, legislations, empires, peoples and dynasties, but millions of men; and more than that the altars, the gods, the religions, the ideas, the beliefs and the souls.

On the basis of a Book, every letter of which has become law, he created a spiritual nationality which blended together peoples of every tongue and of every race ...

The idea of the unity of God, proclaimed amidst the exhaustion of fabulous theologies, was in itself such a miracle that upon its utterance from his lips it destroyed all the ancient superstitions ...

His endless prayers, his mystic conversations with God, his death and his triumph after death: all these attest not to an imposture but to a firm conviction which gave him the power to restore a dogma. This dogma was twofold, **the unity of God and the immateriality of God;** the former telling what God is, the latter telling what God is not ...

. . . PHILOSOPHER, ORATOR, APOSTLE, LEGISLATOR, WARRIOR, CONQUEROR OF IDEAS, RESTORER OF RATIONAL BELIEFS, of a cult without images; the founder of twenty terrestrial empires and of one spiritual empire, that is Muhammed. **AS REGARDS ALL STANDARDS BY WHICH HUMAN GREATNESS MAY BE MEASURED, WE MAY WELL ASK, IS THERE ANY MAN GREATER THAN HE?"**

(Lamartine, *Historie de la Turquie, Paris 1854, Vol II pp. 276-277*).

APPENDIX "C"

<u>JULES MASSERMAN, U.S. psychoanalyst:</u>

TIME, JULY 15, 1974

Leaders must fulfil three functions — — — provide for the well-being of the led, provide a social organization in which people feel relatively secure, and provide them with one set of beliefs. People like Pasteur and Salk are leaders in the first sense.

People like Gandhi and Confucius, on one hand, and Alexander, Caesar and Hitler on the other, are leaders in the second and perhaps the third sense. Jesus and Buddha belong in the third category alone. **PERHAPS THE GREATEST LEADER OF ALL TIMES WAS MOHAMMED, WHO COMBINED ALL THREE FUNCTIONS.** To a lesser degree Moses did the same. (Emphasis added)

APPENDIX "D"

Fidelity is said to be a human attribute,

Which makes the modern gentleman distinguished from the brute,

But that supreme fidelity, inborn in every hound,

Which is the mark of man's best friend,

In man, it's rarely found!

A South African Poet.

PART FOUR

AL-QUR'AN

The Miracle of Miracles

THE HOLY
QUR'AN
Translation and commentary
by
A. YUSUF ALI

Published by
Islamic Propagation Centre
International

BY
AHMED
DEEDAT

CHAPTER ONE

A Standing Challenge

SAY: IF THE WHOLE, *OF MANKIND AND JINNS* [1] *WERE TO GATHER TOGETHER*	قُلْ لَّبِنِ اجْتَمَعَتِ الْإِنْسُ وَالْجِنُّ
TO PRODUCE *THE LIKE OF THIS QUR'AN,*	عَلَى أَن يَأْتُوا بِمِثْلِ هَذَا الْقُرْآنِ
THEY COULD NOT PRODUCE *THE LIKE THEREOF,*	لَا يَأْتُونَ بِمِثْلِهِ
EVEN IF THEY BACKED UP *EACH OTHER WITH* *HELP AND SUPPORT.* [2]	وَلَوْ كَانَ بَعْضُهُمْ لِبَعْضٍ ظَهِيرًا ۞

(BANI ISRÁ-ÍL)   Holy Qur'an 17:88

WHAT IS A MIRACLE

I think it is necessary that we have a clear picture of what we mean by a miracle. Here are some definitions:—

> **"An event that appears so inexplicable by the laws of nature, that it is held to be supernatural in origin or an act of God."**

> **"A person, thing or event that excites admiring awe."**

---

1. **Jinns** — "I think, from a collation and study of the Qur'anic passages, that the meaning is simply **a spirit, or an invisible or hidden force.**" A. Yusuf Ali. Obtain his text, translation and commentary from the IPCI. In his INDEX under **"Jinns"** he gives five Qur'anic references and as many annotations on the subject.

2. The proof of the Qur'an is in its own beauty and nature, and the circumstances in which it was promulgated. **The doubters of the world are challenged to produce a Book like it and has produced none.** It is the only revealed Book whose text stands pure and uncorrupted today, after 1400 years!

"An act beyond human power, an impossibility."

It is logical that greater the impossibility, greater the miracle. For example, should a person expire before our very eyes and is certified dead by a qualified medical man, yet later on a mystic or a saint commands the corpse to 'arise!', and to everybody's astonishment the person gets up and walks away, we would label that as a miracle. But if the resurrection of the dead took place after the corpse had been in the mortuary for three days, then we would acclaim this as a greater miracle. And if the dead was made to arise from the grave, decades or centuries after the body had been decomposed and rotted away, then in that case we would label it the greatest miracle of them all!

A COMMON TRAIT

It has been a common trait of mankind since time immemorial that whenever a Guide from God appeared to redirect their steps into the Will and Plan of God; they demanded supernatural proofs from these men of God, instead of accepting the Message on its merit.

For example, when Jesus Christ (pbuh) began to preach to his people — "The Children of Israel" — to mend their ways and to refrain from mere legalistic formalism and imbibe the true spirit of the Laws and Commandments of God, his "people" demanded Miracles from him to prove his **bona fides,**[1] as recorded in the Christian Scriptures:

> *Then certain of the Scribes and the Pharisees answered, saying Master, we would have a SIGN* (Miracle) *from thee.*
>
> *But he answered and said unto them, "An evil and adulterous generation seeketh after*

---

1. **Bona fides** — his authenticity, his genuineness.

> *a SIGN* (Miracle) *and there shall no SIGN* (Miracle) *be given to it, but the SIGN* (Miracle) *of the Prophet Jonas:*[1] (Emphasis added)
> **(Holy Bible)** *Matthew 12:38-39*

Though on the face of it, Jesus (pbuh) refuses to pamper the Jews here, in fact, he did perform many miracles as we learn from the Gospel narratives.

The Holy Bible is full of supernatural events accredited to the Prophets from their Lord. In reality all those **"signs"** and **"wonders"** and **"miracles"** were acts of God, but since those miracles were worked through His human agents, we describe them as the Miracles of Prophets, i.e. Moses or Jesus (peace be upon them) by whose hands they were performed.

QUIRK CONTINUES

Some six hundred years after the birth of Jesus Christ (pbuh), Muhummed (pbuh) the Messenger of God was born in Makkah in Arabia. When he proclaimed his Mission at the age of forty, his fellow countrymen, the *MUSHRIKS*[2] of Makkah made an identical request for Miracles, as had the Jews, from their promised Messiah. Textbook style, it was as if the Arabs had taken a leaf from the Christian records. History has a habit of repeating itself!

AND THEY SAY: وَقَالُوْا

WHY ARE NOT SIGNS[3] SENT DOWN TO HIM FROM HIS LORD? لَوْلَاۤ اُنْزِلَ عَلَيْهِ اٰيٰتٌ مِّنْ رَّبِّهٖ ۭ

(SÚRA 'ANKABÚT)   *Holy Qur'an 29:50*

---

1. What was the outcome of the **"only sign"** that Jesus (pbuh) was prepared to give? Obtain your **FREE** copy of the Book — **"What was the Sign of Jonah?"** from the IPCI which furnishes a detailed exposition.

2. **MUSHRIK** — pagans, idol worshippers, polytheists.

3. **"Signs"** The Arabic word used is **'AAYAAH'** which literally means 'signs', and which is really more to the point. The Holy Qur'an does not mention the word **'MU'JAZAH'** (miracle).

SIGNS! WHAT SIGNS?

"MIRACLES? CRIES HE, WHAT MIRACLES WOULD YOU HAVE? ARE NOT YOU YOURSELVES THERE? GOD MADE *YOU*, 'SHAPED YOU OUT OF A LITTLE CLAY.' YE WERE SMALL ONCE, A FEW YEARS AGO YE WERE NOT AT ALL. YE HAVE BEAUTY, STRENGTH, THOUGHTS, 'YE HAVE COMPASSION ON ONE ANOTHER.' OLD AGE COMES ON YOU, AND GREY HAIRS; YOUR STRENGTH FADES INTO FEEBLENESS: YE SINK DOWN, AND AGAIN ARE NOT. *YE HAVE COMPASSION ON ONE ANOTHER* : THIS STRUCK ME MUCH: ALLAH MIGHT HAVE MADE YOU HAVING NO COMPASSION ON ONE ANOTHER, — HOW HAD IT BEEN THEN! THIS IS A GREAT DIRECT THOUGHT, A GLANCE AT FIRST-HAND INTO THE VERY FACT OF THINGS ..."

"On Heroes and Hero-Worship and the Heroic in History" by Thomas Carlyle

"THIS STRUCK ME MUCH"

This, that — **"Ye have Compassion on one another,"** impressed Thomas Carlyle most from his perusal of an English translation. I presume, the verse that motivated this sentiment is:

1. **And among His signs is this, that He created for you mates from among yourselves,**

   That ye may dwell in TRANQUILLITY WITH THEM. and He has put love and mercy between your (hearts):

   Verily in that are signs for those who reflect.
   (Emphasis added)

   (SÚRA RÚM)   *Holy Qur'an 30:21*
   Translation by A. Yusuf Ali.

2. **And one of his signs it is, that he hath created wives for you or your own species**

   That YE MAY DWELL WITH THEM, and hath put love and tenderness between you.

   Herein truly are signs for those who reflect. (Emphasis added)

   Translation by Rev. J.M. Rodwell (M.A.)

3. **By another sign he gave you wives from among yourselves,**

   That ye might LIVE IN JOY WITH THEM, and planted love and kindness into your hearts.

   Surely there are signs in this for thinking men. (Emphasis added)

   Translation by N.J. Dawood

The first example is from the translation by A. Yusuf Ali, a Muslim. The second is by a Christian priest the Rev. Rodwell and the last example is by an Iraqi Jew, N.J. Dawood.

Unfortunately Thomas Carlyle had no access to any one of these because none of them had seen the light of day in his time. The only one available to him in 1840 was as he said on page 85 of his book under reference —

> 'WE ALSO CAN READ THE KORAN[1]; OUR TRANSLATION OF IT, BY SALE, IS KNOWN TO BE **A VERY FAIR ONE.**'' (Emphasis added)

TAINT IS IN THE MOTIVE

Carlyle is very charitable to his fellow countryman. The motives of George Sale who pioneered an English Translation of the Holy

---

1. The Arabic word is **Qur'an,** it starts with a "Q" and not a "K"

Qur'an, were suspect. He makes no secret of his antagonism to the Holy Book of Islam. In his preface to his translation in 1734 he made it known that it was his **avowed intention to expose the man Mohammed and his forgery:** He records:

> "WHO CAN APPREHEND ANY DANGER FROM SO MANIFEST A FORGERY? ... THE PROTESTANTS ALONE ARE ABLE TO ATTACK THE KORAN WITH SUCCESS; AND FOR THEM, I TRUST, PROVIDENCE HAS RESERVED THE GLORY OF ITS OVERTHROW."

George Sale

And he set to work with his prejudiced translation. You will be able to judge how **"fair"** and scholarly George Sale was from the very verse which **"Struck"** (Carlyle) **"much!"** Compare it with the three examples already given by a Muslim, a Christian and a Jew:

> *And of his signs another is,*
> *that he had created for you, out of*
> *yourselves, wives that YE MAY*
> *COHABIT WITH THEM, and hath put*
> *love and compassion between you.*

(Emphasis added)

I do not think that George Sale was "a male chauvinist pig" of his day to describe our mates, wives or spouses as sexual objects. He was only keeping to his promise, which Carlyle overlooked. The Arabic word which he (Sale) perverted is *"li-tas-kunoo"* which means to find peace, consolation, composure or tranquility; and not **"cohabit"** meaning **"To live together in a sexual relationship when not legally married."** (The Reader's Digest Universal Dictionary).

Every word of the Qur'anic text is meticulously chosen, chiselled and placed by the All-Wise Himself. They carry God's "finger-print", and are the Signs of God. And yet, the spiritually jaundiced ...

ASK FOR A SIGN

What Signs? They mean some special kinds of signs or miracles such as their own foolish minds dictate. Everything is possible for God, but God is not going to humour the follies of men or listen to their false demands. He has sent His Messenger to explain His Signs clearly, and to warn them of the consequences of rejection. Is that not enough? The trend of their demand is generally as follows:

In specific terms they asked that he — Muhummed (pbuh) — 'Put a ladder up to heaven and bring down a book from God in their very sight' — **"THEN WE WOULD BELIEVE,"** they said. Or "Ye see the mountain yonder, turn it into gold' — **"THEN WE WOULD BELIEVE."** or 'Make streams to gush out in the desert' — **"THEN WE WOULD BELIEVE."**

Now listen to the soft, sweet reasoning of Muhammed (pbuh) against the unreasonable and sceptical demands of the **MUSH-RIKS** — **"Do I say to you, verily I am an angel? Do I say to you, verily in my hands are the treasures of God? Only, what is revealed to me do I follow."**

Listen further to the most dignified reply he is commanded by his Lord to give the Unbelievers.

SAY (O MUHUMMED):
'THE SIGNS (MIRACLES)
ARE INDEED WITH ALLAH:

قُلْ إِنَّمَا الْآيَاتُ عِنْدَ اللّهِ

AND MOST CERTAINLY
I AM ONLY A CLEAR WARNER!'

وَإِنَّمَا أَنَا نَذِيرٌ مُّبِينٌ ۞

(SÚRA 'ANKABÚT)   *Holy Qur'an 29:50*

In the following *AAYAAH*[1] (verse) the Holy Prophet is made to point to the Holy Qur'an itself as an answer to their hypocritical

---

1. **AAYAAH** In the Holy Qur'an stands for "a sign" as well for "a verse." There are over six thousand **AAYAAHS** or verses in the Book of God, and every verse is a sign of God.

demand for some special kind of **"Sign"** or **"Miracle"** for which their foolish, pagan mentality craved. For indeed all miracles are "signs"; and it is their disbelief, their scepticism, their lack of faith which motivates their request for a sign. They are asked to — 'Look at the Qur'an" And again, **"Look at the Qur'an!"**

IS IT NOT ENOUGH FOR THEM	اَوَلَمۡ يَكۡفِهِمۡ
THAT WE[1] HAVE SENT DOWN TO THEE (O MUHUMMED!) THE BOOK (AL-QUR'AN)	اَنَّا اَنۡزَلۡنَا عَلَيۡكَ الۡكِتٰبَ
WHICH IS REHEARSED TO THEM?	يُتۡلٰى عَلَيۡهِمۡ ط
VERILY, IN IT (THIS PERSPICUOUS BOOK)	اِنَّ فِىۡ ذٰلِكَ
IS A MERCY AND REMINDER	لَرَحۡمَةً وَّذِكۡرٰى
TO THOSE WHO BELIEVE.[2]	لِقَوۡمٍ يُّؤۡمِنُوۡنَ ۝

SÚRA 'ANKABÚT) *Holy Qur'an 29:51*

TWO PROOFS

As proof of the Divine Authorship and the miraculous nature of the Holy Qur'an, two arguments are advanced by the Almighty Himself:

1. **"THAT WE"** (God Almighty) have revealed to **YOU** (O! Muhummed!) **"THE BOOK** to **YOU"** who art absolutely an

---

1. **WE** is a plural of respect and honour and not of numbers. In every Eastern language, including Hebrew, this is their method of grammar. In the English Language it is called the "Royal Plural."

2. Memorize the verse with its meaning while the Book is still in your hands.

unlearned person. An **"UMMI"** Prophet. One who cannot read or write. One who cannot sign his own name. Let Thomas Carlyle[1] testify regarding the educational qualifications of Muhummed —

"ONE OTHER CIRCUMSTANCE WE MUST NOT FORGET: THAT HE HAD NO SCHOOL-LEARNING; OF THE THING WE CALL SCHOOL-LEARNING NONE AT ALL."

Moreover the Divine Author (God Almighty) Himself testifies to the veracity of Muhummed's (pbuh) claim that he could never have composed the contents of the Holy Qur'an; he could not have been its author:

AND THOU (O MUHUMMED)
WAS NOT (ABLE)
TO RECITE A BOOK

وَمَا كُنْتَ تَتْلُوا

BEFORE THIS (BOOK
CAME),

مِنْ قَبْلِهِ مِنْ كِتَبٍ

NOR ART THOU (ABLE)
TO TRANSCRIBE IT
WITH THY RIGHT HAND:

وَلَا تَخُطُّهُ بِيَمِينِكَ

IN THAT CASE, INDEED,
WOULD THE TALKERS OF
VANITIES HAVE DOUBTED[2]

إِذًا لَّارْتَابَ الْمُبْطِلُونَ ۝

(SÚRA 'ANKABÚT)   *Holy Qur'an 29:48*

The Author of the Qur'an is reasoning with us, that had Muhummed (pbuh) been a learned man, and had he been able to read and write, then in that case the babblers in the market-places might have had some justification to doubt his

---

1. Already referred to on page 166.

2. Get into the habit of learning off by heart the verses with their meanings as they occur in this Book.

claim that the Holy Qur'an is God's Word. In the event of Muhummed (pbuh) being a literate person, the accusation of his enemies that he had probably copied his Book (Al-Qur'an) from the writings of the Jews and the Christians, or that perhaps he had been studying Aristotle and Plato, or that he must have browsed through the **"Torat,"** the **"Zabur"** and the **"Injeel"**[1] and had rehashed it all in a beautiful language, might have carried some weight. Then, "THE TALKERS OF VANITIES" **might have had a point.** But even this flimsy pretence has been denied to the unbeliever and the cynic: a point hardly big enough to hang a fly upon![2]

2.   'The Book'? Yes, the **"BOOK"** itself, carries its own evidence proving its Divine Authorship. Study the Book from any angle. Scrutinize it. Why not take up the Author's challenge if your doubts are genuine?

DO THEY NOT CONSIDER
THE QUR'AN (WITH CARE)?

أَفَلَا يَتَدَبَّرُونَ الْقُرْآنَ

HAD IT BEEN FROM
OTHER THAN ALLAH,

وَلَوْ كَانَ مِنْ عِنْدِ غَيْرِ اللَّهِ

THEY WOULD SURELY
HAVE FOUND THEREIN
MUCH DISCREPANCY[3]

لَوَجَدُوا فِيهِ اخْتِلَافًا كَثِيرًا ۝

(SÚRA NISÁA)   Holy Qur'an 4:82

---

1.   **TORAT/ZABUR/INJEEL:** These are the Arabic terms of the original revelations God granted Moses, David and Jesus (peace be upon them all) respectively.

2.   The Bible was not translated into Arabic until the tenth century of the Christian Era, so no Arab living before the year 1000 would have had the opportunity to examine the written text of the Bible in his own language.

3.   If you cannot muster enough enthusiasm to learn the verses with their meanings, why not hand over the Book to someone who will make better use of it?

CONSISTENCY

It is inconceivable that any human author would remain consistent in his teachings and his preachings for a period of over two decades. From the age of forty, when Muhummed (pbuh) received his first call from Heaven to the age of sixty-three when he breathed his last, for twenty-three years the Holy Prophet practised and preached Islam. In those twenty-three years, he passed through the most conflicting vicissitudes of life. Any man, during the course of such a mission, would be forced by circumstances to make "honourable" compromises, and cannot help contradicting himself. No man can ever write the same always, as the Message of the Holy Qur'an is: CONSISTENT WITH ITSELF, **throughout!** Or is it that the unbelievers' objections are merely argumentative, refractory, against their own better light and judgement?

Furthermore, the Holy Qur'an contains or mentions many matters relating to the nature of the universe which were unknown to man before but which subsequently through evolution and discoveries of Science have fully confirmed — a field where an untutored mind would have most certainly lost in wild and contradictory speculations!

SELF-EVIDENT PROOF

Again and again when miracles were demanded from the Prophet of God by the cynical and frivolous few, he is made to point to the Qur'an — Message from High — as **"The Miracle."** THE MIRACLE OF MIRACLES! And men of wisdom, people with literary and spiritual insight, who were honest enough to themselves, recognised and accepted Al-Qur'an as a genuine miracle.

Says the Holy Qur'an:

NAY, HERE ARE
SIGNS SELF-EVIDENT

بَلْ هُوَ اٰيَتٌ بَيِّنٰتٌ

IN THE HEARTS
OF THOSE ENDOWED
WITH KNOWLEDGE:[1]

فِىْ صُدُوْرِ الَّذِيْنَ اُوْتُوا الْعِلْمَ

AND NONE BUT
THE UNJUST REJECT
OUR SIGNS.[2]

وَمَا يَجْحَدُ بِاٰيٰتِنَا اِلَّا الظّٰلِمُوْنَ ۞

(SÚRA 'ANKABÚT)   *Holy Qur'an 29:49*

---

1. **"Knowledge"** ('ilm) means both power of judgement in discerning the value of truth and acquaintance with previous revelations. It implies both literary and spiritual insight. To men so endowed, God's revelations and Signs are self-evident. They commend themselves to their hearts, minds, and understandings, which are typified in Arabic by the word *sadr*, "breast".

2. Now the argument is carried a stage farther. Such rejection is also a mark of injustice, a deliberate perversity in going against obvious Signs, which should convince all honest men.

CHAPTER TWO

Science and the Qur'anic Revelations

UNGRUDGING TRIBUTES

Today, there are in the world some one thousand million Muslims who unhesitatingly accept that the Holy Qur'an is the **"WORD OF GOD"** and that it is a **"Miracle."**

Why should they not, when even avowed enemies are paying unsolicited tributes regarding the miraculous nature of this Book of God. The Rev. R. Bosworth-Smith in his book **"Mohammed and Mohammedanism"**[1] opines about the Qur'an:

(a) "A MIRACLE OF PURITY OF STYLE, OF WISDOM AND OF TRUTH.

Another Englishman — A.J. Arberry, in the preface of his English translation of the Holy Qur'an — says:

(b) "WHENEVER I HEAR THE QUR'AN CHANTED, IT IS AS THOUGH I AM LISTENING TO MUSIC, UNDERNEATH THE FLOWING MELODY, THERE IS SOUNDING ALL THE TIME THE INSISTENT BEAT OF A DRUM, IT IS LIKE THE BEATING OF MY HEART."

From these words and the rest of his preface he sounds like a Muslim, but regretfully he died outside the pale of Islam. And yet another Briton, Marmaduke Picktall in the foreword to his translation of the Holy Qur'an, describes it as:

(c) "THAT INIMITABLE SYMPHONY, THE VERY SOUND OF WHICH MOVE MEN TO TEARS AND ECSTASY."

---

1. There is no such thing as **"Mohammedanism"**, and no such thing as a **"Mohammedan."** The name of the Religion is **Islam** and its followers are **Muslims.**

This Author embraced Islam before translating the Qur'an, and we are not in a position to verify whether he wrote the previous effect before or after his conversion.

(d) "NEXT TO THE BIBLE[1] IT (The Qur'an) IS THE MOST ESTEEMED AND MOST POWERFUL RELIGIOUS BOOK IN THE WORLD."

> J. Christy Wilson in *"Introducing Islam"* New York 1950

(e) "THE KORAN IS THE MOHAMMEDAN BIBLE, AND IS MORE REVERENCED THAN ANY OTHER SACRED BOOK, MORE THAN THE JEWISH OLD TESTAMENT OR THE CHRISTIAN NEW TESTAMENT."

> J. Shillidy, D.D., in *"The Lord Jesus in the Koran,"* Surat 1913, p.111

We can quite easily adduce a dozen more eulogies to the above list. Friends and foes alike pay ungrudging commendations to the Last and Final Revelation of God — the Holy Qur'an. The contemporaries of Muhummed (pbuh) saw in its beauty and majesty, the nobility of its Call and the magnanimity of its Message, the Sign and Miracle of God's Handiwork, and accepted Islam. To all the tributes and testimonies the unbeliever and the sceptic may say that these are all subjective feelings. He might further seek refuge in the pretext that he does not know Arabic. He is heard to say, "I do not see what you see, nor do I feel as you feel. How am I to know that God exists and that it is He Who inspired His Messenger Muhummed (pbuh) with that beautiful Message; the Qur'an?" He continues "I am not averse to the beauty of its philosophy, its practical ethics and high morality, I am prepared to concede that Muhummed (pbuh) was a sincere man and that he gave many beautiful precepts for human welfare. What I cannot subscribe to is what you Muslims claim, **'a supernatural authority for his dicta'.''**

---

1. Coming from a Christian critic of Islam, we will not take exception to his placing the Qur'an in the second place.

REASONED LOGIC

To this kind of sympathetic, yet sceptical mentality, the Author of the Book (Al-Qur'an) uses various types of arguments to resolve his doubts. To the atheists and agnostics, the cynics and the sceptics, who have a super-abundance of scientific knowledge and who consider themselves to be "intellectual giants," the point is driven home that they are in reality like stunted "dwarfs." They are like the dwarf who may have acquired abnormal development in any one particular direction at the expense of other parts of his faculty, like an oversized head on a puny body, the Supreme Creator questions him.

But before we pose God's question to him, let me satisfy my own curiosity. "You men of science who have studied astronomy and who study our Universe through your mighty telescopes as if scrutinising an object in the palm of your hand; tell me how did this Universe come into being?" This man of science though lacking in spiritual insight, is nevertheless most generous in sharing his knowledge. He readily responds. "Well," he begins, "Billions of years ago our Universe was a single piece of matter, and there happened a **"Big Bang"** in the centre of that huge lump of matter and mighty chunks of matter began flying in all directions. Out of that "big bang" our solar system came into being as well as the galaxies, and since there is no resistance in space to that primordial momentum generated by the initial explosion, the stars and the planets swim along in their orbits ..."

At this juncture, my memory tickles me — Our materialist friends appear to have been secretly imbibing their knowledge from the *Súra Yaa-Seen:*[1]

AND THE SUN RUNS HIS COURSE وَالشَّمْسُ تَجْرِى

---

1. **Yaa-Seen:** is the 36th chapter of the Holy Qur'an. The verses here are laid out for you to memorize in a very easy form, together with their meanings. Take advantage of it!

**FOR A PERIOD DETER-
MINED FOR HIM:**

لِمُسْتَقَرٍّ لَّهَا

**THAT IS THE DECREE
OF (HIM) THE EXALTED IN
MIGHT THE ALL-KNOWING.**

ذٰلِكَ تَقْدِيرُ الْعَزِيزِ الْعَلِيْمِ ۝

**AND THE MOON, WE HAVE
MEASURED FOR HER MANSIONS
(TO TRAVERSE)**

وَ الْقَمَرَ قَدَّرْنٰهُ مَنَازِلَ

**TILL SHE RETURNS LIKE THE
OLD (AND WITHERED) LOWER
PART OF A DATE — STALK.**

حَتّٰى عَادَ
كَالْعُرْجُوْنِ الْقَدِيْمِ ۝

**IT IS NOT PERMITTED
TO THE SUN TO OVER
TAKE THE MOON,**

لَا الشَّمْسُ يَنْبَغِيْ لَهَآ اَنْ تُدْرِكَ الْقَمَرَ

**NOR CAN THE NIGHT
OUTSTRIP THE DAY:**

وَلَا الَّيْلُ سَابِقُ النَّهَارِ

**EACH (JUST) SWIMS ALONG
IN (ITS OWN) ORBIT
(ACCORDING TO LAW).**

وَ كُلٌّ فِيْ فَلَكٍ يَّسْبَحُوْنَ ۝

(SÚRA YÁ-SÍN)   HOLY QUR'AN 36:38-40

The atheistic scientist continues. "Ours is an **'expanding'** universe. The galaxies are receding away from us at a faster and faster rate, and once they reach the speed of light,[1] we will not be able to see them anymore. We must construct bigger and better telescopes as quickly as possible to study the sights, if not we will miss the bus!"

"When did you discover these fairy Tales?" we ask. "No, these are not fairy tales but scientific facts!" our friend assures us. "All right, we accept your facts for what you say they are, but when

---

1. Light is said to travel at a speed of a hundred and eighty six thousand miles per second (7.5 times around the world in one second!).

did you really stumble upon these facts?" "Only yesterday!" he replies. Fifty years, after all, is only 'yesterday' in the history of the human race. "An unlettered Arab in the desert over 1400 years ago could never have had your knowledge of the **'big bang'** and of your 'expanding universe,' could he?" we ask. "No never!" he retorts boastingly. "Well, then listen to what this **ummi**[1] Prophet uttered under inspiration:"

DO NOT THE UNBELIEVERS (THE ATHEISTS AND THE AGNOSTICS) SEE	اَوَلَمْ يَرَ الَّذِيْنَ كَفَرُوٓا
THAT THE HEAVENS AND THE EARTH	اَنَّ السَّمٰوٰتِ وَالْاَرْضَ
WERE JOINED TOGETHER (AS ONE UNIT OF CREATION) BEFORE WE CLOVE THEM ASUNDER? ...	كَانَتَا رَتْقًا فَفَتَقْنٰهُمَا

(*SÚRA ANBIYÁA*)   HOLY QUR'AN 21:30

AND IT IS HE (GOD AL-MIGHTY) WHO CREATED THE NIGHT AND THE DAY,	وَهُوَالَّذِىْ خَلَقَ الَّيْلَ وَ النَّهَارَ
AND THE SUN AND THE MOON:	وَالشَّمْسَ وَالْقَمَرَ
ALL (THE CELESTIAL BODIES) SWIM ALONG, EACH IN ITS ROUNDED COURSE.	كُلٌّ فِىْ فَلَكٍ يَّسْبَحُوْنَ

(*SÚRA ANBIYÁA*)   HOLY QUR'AN 21:33

'BIG BANG' THEORY

Can't you see that the words **"The Unbelievers"** in the first quote above are specifically addressed to **You** — the men of

---

1. **Ummi:** means unlettered, unlearned. '**"And the Book is given to him that is NOT LEARNED, saying, Read this, I pray thee: and he sayeth, I am not learned"** Isaiah 29:12. See how this prophecy finds fulfilment in Muhummed (pbuh). Obtain your FREE COPY OF *"What the Bible says about Muhummed (pbuh)"* from the IPCI.

science — the geographers, the astronomers, who, after having made amazing discoveries and conveyed these discoveries to mankind, still remain so 'BLIND' as not to 'SEE' its Author? **"With our Sciences and Encyclopaedias, we are apt to forget the Divineness, in those laboratories of ours"**[1] says Thomas Carlyle.

Where on earth could a camel driver in the desert have gleaned **'Your facts' fourteen hundred years ago,** except from the Maker of the **'Big Bang'** Himself?

ORIGIN OF LIFE

"And **You** biologists who seem to have your fingers on all organic life, and yet have the temerity to deny the existence of the Source of that Life, i.e. God: tell me, according to your vaunted research; **where and how did life originate?"**

Like his 'unbelieving' astronomer companion in science, he too begins — "Well, billions of years ago primaeval matter in the sea began to generate protoplasm out of which came the amoeba; and out of that mire in the sea came all **living** things. In one word ALL LIFE came from the sea, i.e. **Water!"**

"And when did you discover this fact that all living things came from water?" The answer is no different from that of his fellow scientist the astronomer — **"Yesterday!"** "No man of learning, no philosopher or poet could ever have guessed your biological discovery fourteen centuries back, could he?" we ask, and our biologist is as emphatic as the astronomer. **"No, never!"** says he. "Well, then, you just listen to this untutored son of the desert!"

AND WE MADE FROM WATER[2]
EVERY LIVING THING   وَجَعَلْنَا مِنَ الْمَاءِ كُلَّ شَيْءٍ حَيٍّ

---

1. From **"Heroes and Hero Worship"** by Thomas Carlyle.

2. Protoplasm is the basis of all living matter, and "the vital power of protoplasm seems to depend on the constant presence of water" (Lawson's Text Book of Botany, London 1922). Textbooks on Zoology are also clear on this point. For further explanation see Yusuf Ali's translation and commentary, available from the IPCI.

WILL THEY (THE UNBELIEVERS,
THE ATHEISTS AND THE AGNOSTICS)　　اَفَلَا يُؤْمِنُوْنَ ۞
THEN NOT BELIEVE?

(SÚRA ANBIYÁA)　*Holy Qur'an 21:30*

The above statement is further elaborated in the Book of God:

AND ALLAH HAS CREATED
EVERY ANIMAL FROM　　وَ اللهُ خَلَقَ كُلَّ دَآبَّةٍ مِّنْ مَّآءٍ ۚ
WATER: [1]

OF THEM THERE ARE
SOME THAT CREEP ON　　فَمِنْهُمْ مَّنْ يَّمْشِىْ عَلٰى بَطْنِهٖ ۚ
THEIR BELLIES;

SOME THAT WALK ON　　وَمِنْهُمْ مَّنْ يَّمْشِىْ عَلٰى رِجْلَيْنِ ۚ
TWO LEGS;

AND SOME THAT WALK　　وَمِنْهُمْ مَّنْ يَّمْشِىْ عَلٰى اَرْبَعٍ
ON FOUR.

ALLAH CREATES WHAT　　يَخْلُقُ اللهُ مَا يَشَآءُ
HE WILLS;

FOR VERILY ALLAH HAS
POWER OVER ALL THINGS.　　اِنَّ اللهَ عَلٰى كُلِّ شَىْءٍ قَدِيْرٌ ۞

(SÚRA NÚR)　*Holy Qur'an 24:45*

It will not be difficult for you to note that these words of the
Omnipotent, Omniscient Creator of the Universe were addressed
to YOU men of knowledge in answer to your scepticism TODAY.
Their real import was beyond the dwellers of the desert fourteen
centuries ago. The Author (God Almighty) is reasoning with
YOU, you men of science, how can **YOU** not believe in God?
YOU should be the LAST to deny His existence and yet you are
the FIRST! What sickness has overtaken **YOU** that you allow
your egos to overshadow your sense of logic?

---

1. See Note No. 2 at bottom of page 180

AND to the botanists and the zoologists and the physicists who, despite their amazing insight into the nature of things, refuse to acknowledge a Master Creator. Let them then account for these utterances of Muhummed (pbuh) the mouthpiece of God.

GLORY BE TO HIM *(GOD ALMIGHTY)*	سُبْحٰنَ الَّذِیْ
WHO CREATED IN *PAIRS* ALL THINGS*	خَلَقَ الْاَزْوَاجَ كُلَّهَا
THAT WHICH THE EARTH PRODUCES *(THE VEGETABLE KINGDOM),*	مِمَّا تُنْبِتُ الْاَرْضُ
AS WELL AS THEIR OWN (HUMAN) *KIND (THE ANIMAL KINGDOM)*	وَمِنْ اَنْفُسِهِمْ
AND (OTHER) THINGS OF WHICH *THEY HAVE NO KNOWLEDGE* *(LIKE OF PHYSICS)* [1]	وَمِمَّا لَا یَعْلَمُوْنَ ۝

(*SÚRA YÁ-SÍN*)   Holy Qur'an 36:36

* "CREATED IN PAIRS" *"The mystery of sex runs through all creation, — in man, in animal life, in vegetable life, and in other things of which we have no knowledge. Then there are pairs of opposite forces in nature, e.g. positive and negative electricity, etc. The atom itself consists of a positively charged nucleus or proton, surrounded by negatively charged electrons. The constitution of matter itself is thus referred to as pairs of opposite energies."* (Comment by A. Yusuf Ali) [2]

---

1. Here is another verse from YÁ-SÍN. Further to footnote No. 1 on page 171, a special plea is made to Muslim readers who already know the Sura in Arabic, to now master its English meaning as well. Equip yourself for all the good work!

2. Obtain your volume of Yusuf Ali's translation with over 6000 such explanatory notes at a subsidised price from the IPCI.

SIGNS OF GOD

The verses of this **"Perspicuous Book,"** the Holy Qur'an are evidently self-explanatory. Students of the Qur'an saw the unmistakable Finger of God in every discovery that man made. These were the **"Signs,"** the **"Miracles"** from his Beneficent Lord and Cherisher so as to remove his doubts and strengthen his faith.

... IN THESE ARE SIGNS FOR
A PEOPLE OF LEARNING.

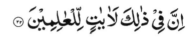

(SÚRA RÚM) *Holy Qur'an 30:22*

What an irony! It is the **'people of learning'** who are actually rebellious! Their vast material knowledge has inflated them with pride. They lack the genuine humility which goes together with all true knowledge.

In the words of a modern Frenchman:

"THE ABOVE OBSERVATION (HIS OWN THESIS) MAKES THE HYPOTHESIS ADVANCED BY THOSE WHO SEE MUHAMMAD AS THE AUTHOR OF THE QUR'AN UNTENABLE. HOW COULD A MAN, FROM BEING ILLITERATE, BECOME THE MOST IMPORTANT AUTHOR, IN TERMS OF LITERARY MERITS, IN THE WHOLE OF ARABIC LITE-RATURE?

"HOW COULD HE THEN PRONOUNCE TRUTHS OF A SCIENTIFIC NATURE THAT NO OTHER HUMAN BEING COULD POSSIBLY HAVE DEVE-LOPED AT THAT TIME, AND ALL THIS WITH-OUT ONCE MAKING THE SLIGHTEST ERROR IN HIS PRONOUNCEMENT ON THE SUBJECT?"

See **"The Bible, the Qur'an and Science"** p. 125 by Maurice Bucaille

EARLY INSPIRATION

The seeds of this booklet, **"AL-QUR'AN — The Miracle of Miracles,"** was probably sown by the Roving Ambassador of Islam, the silver-tongued orator — Maulana Abdul Aleem Siddiqui. I was only a schoolboy when he visited South Africa on a lecture tour in 1934. Among his many erudite speeches, I heard him talk on **'Cultivation of Science by the Muslims."** Subsequently, a booklet under the same title was published by the World Federation of Islamic Missions, Karachi, Pakistan, which brings back the earlier joy and thrill of the discourse I heard in my teens. In memory of that great servant of Islam, I reproduce here, for posterity, a few words of what the Maulana had to say on the relationship between the Holy Qur'an and the branches of scientific knowledge:

EXHORTATIONS TO THE SCIENCES

"The stress which the Holy Qur'an has laid on the scientific study of the universe is a phenomenon unique in the religious literature of the world. Repeatedly it calls our attention to the multifarious phenomena of nature occuring around us. Repeatedly it exhorts the Muslims that the pursuit of scientific knowledge is one of their religious duties. Repeatedly it emphasises the great truth unknown to the pre-Qur'anic world that everything in nature is for the service of man and should be harnessed by him for his use. It exhorts us to study the structure and function of the human organism, the structure, functions and distribution of animals, the form, structure, functions, classification and distribution of plants, and these are problems of BIOLOGY.

"It exhorts us to study the order of nature and the general properties of matter as affected by energy, which is the problem of modern PHYSICS.

"It exhorts us to study the properties of substances both elementary and compound and the laws of their combination and action one upon another which is the problem of modern CHEMISTRY.

"It exhorts us to study the structure and mineral constitution of the globe, the different strata of which it is composed, the changes that take place in its organic and inorganic matter, etc, etc., which are the problem of modern GEOLOGY.

"It exhorts us to study the general description of the earth, its physical divisions into seas, rivers, mountains, plains, etc., and the minerals, plants and animals in each, and its political divisions which are the problems of modern GEOGRAPHY.

"It exhorts us to study the causes which bring about the alternation of day and night, the variation of the seasons, the movement of the planets and other celestial phenomena, which are the problems of modern ASTRONOMY."

"It exhorts us to study the movements of winds, the formation and evolution of clouds and the production of rain, and other similar phenomena, which are the problems of modern METEOROLOGY."

For centuries, Muslims were world leaders in the field of scientific learning. Then slowly, the leadership began to slip away from their hands. Muslims had failed in their leadership role and materialistic Europe moved forward to fill the vacuum in leadership created by the Muslims.

Further, the Maulana records the contribution made by the Muslims as follows:

"The intellectual upheaval created by Islam was a gigantic one. There is not a single department of learning which the Muslim scholars have left untouched and which they have not carved out a high position for themselves.

"In truth, Islam intends the Muslim community to be a community of intellectuals, and the cultivation of science and all other forms of learning is one of the primary aims of Islam. Had it not been for the Muslims, Europe would never have seen its way to the Renaissance and the modern scientific era would never have dawned. Those nations who have received their knowledge of science from Europe are in fact indirectly the disciples of the Islamic community of the past. Humanity owes to Islam a debt which it can never repay and gratitude which it can never forget."

The silver-tongued orator (the Maulana) ended his masterful exposition of the topic — "CULTIVATION OF SCIENCE BY THE MUSLIMS," with the words:

"Before I conclude, let me affirm once more that the Muslim community is out and out a creation of Islam which in its turn is rooted in Divine revelation. Nothing but belief in and the practice of Islam can make an individual a Muslim. Islam has laid it down as a religious duty that a Muslim should enquire into the reality of objects around him, so that his scientific enquiry may lead him to the knowledge of his Creator. Scientific enquiry in Islam is not an end but a means to the attainment of a higher end. And this is really the true end of humanity. 'TO ALLAH WE BELONG AND TO ALLAH IS OUR RETURN'

Holy Qur'an 2:156

MY ABORTED LECTURE

I had the privilege of hearing the above speech in 1934 from the lips of the master himself. In the late thirties I had the speech in my hands as a booklet. I memorized it with some changes and modifications, whilst still working in a Muslim shop at Adams Mission Station. I was so enthused that I made arrangements

with Adam's College to speak to the students and their lecturers on
the same subject. At that time I might not have fully grasped the
enormity of my task but I will never know for sure as my Muslim
Boss came to my rescue? He threatened me with dismissal if I did
not cancel my first public lecture. I backed out. My employer was no
doubt ignorant of Allah's warning. I too, knew no better. I cannot
say what stand I would have taken then if I was programmed with
this admonition:

قُلْ اِنْ كَانَ اٰبَآؤُكُمْ

SAY: IF IT BE YOUR FATHERS;

وَ اَبْنَآؤُكُمْ

OR YOUR SONS,

وَاِخْوَانُكُمْ

OR YOUR BROTHERS,

وَاَزْوَاجُكُمْ وَعَشِيْرَتُكُمْ

OR YOUR MATES,
OR YOUR RELATIONS;

وَ اَمْوَالُ اقْتَرَفْتُمُوْهَا

OR THE WEALTH THAT
YE HAVE AMASSED;

وَتِجَارَةٌ تَخْشَوْنَ كَسَادَهَا

OR THE LOSSES YE FEAR
IN YOUR BUSINESSES:

وَ مَسَاكِنُ تَرْضَوْنَهَآ

OR THE DWELLINGS IN
WHICH YOU TAKE DELIGHT —

اَحَبَّ اِلَيْكُمْ مِّنَ اللّٰهِ

IF YOU LOVE (ANY OF THESE)
MORE THAN YOU LOVE ALLAH,

وَ رَسُوْلِهٖ

OR HIS MESSENGER,

وَجِهَادٍ فِيْ سَبِيْلِهٖ

OR THE STRIVING IN
HIS CAUSE;

فَتَرَبَّصُوْا حَتّٰى يَأْتِيَ اللّٰهُ بِاَمْرِهٖ

THEN WAIT UNTIL ALLAH
BRINGS ABOUT HIS DECISION:

وَاللّٰهُ لَا يَهْدِے الْقَوْمَ الْفٰسِقِيْنَ ۝

AND ALLAH GUIDES
NOT A REBELLIOUS
PEOPLE[1]

(SÚRA TAUBA)   Holy Qur'an 9:24

---

1. (a) A video tape on the topic — **"Da'wah or Destruction?"** is available from the IPCI
   (b) Write for your FREE video catalogue.
   (c) Memorize the verse together with its meaning. If you are rightly programmed, you
        will have the right responses in every challenging situation. **Insha-Allah!**

Thanks (?) to our timid brother, my first ever lecture to Christian missionaries and trainee priests which I had so assiduously planned, memorized and rehearsed came to nothing. Perhaps I was set back ten years in my career in public speaking. There are millions like my Muslim boss who are just as terrified by material considerations enumerated in the above verse who not only will not deliver the Message of Islam themselves but obstruct those prepared to do the job. Yet they display in their bearing the utmost piety: to no avail — Allah describes such as **"Perverted transgressors!"**

TAKE UP THE CHALLENGE

In the foregoing speech the Maulana had drawn our attention to the Qur'anic exhortations for us to ponder on, Biology, Physics, Chemistry, Geology, Meteorology etc. Scholars like Maurice Bucaille, Keith Moore and Sheikh Zindani have written on different scientific aspects of the Holy Qur'an in recent times. But the scope is limitless. The noble Qur'an is an ocean of Knowledge. In this world of specialization Muslim scientists must take up the challenges hinted at by the Maulana in the mid-thirties. They do not have to dabble in every field. To each his own particular speciality. The youth of Islam is hungry for information and articles and small tracts on different scientific subjects in order to whet their appetites. Encyclopaedias may follow. **Insha-Allah!**

I do not have to apologise for leaving the exposition of Qur'anic sciences to Muslim scientists. Even non-Muslims should be encouraged to explore the depths of Wisdom as enshrined in the book of God. For my part, as a layman, I will share with you the miraculous nature of the Holy Qur'an in what appears to me to be in simple, ordinary facts.

CHAPTER THREE

Al-Qur'an Absolutely Unique In Its Recording

Among all the extant religious literature of the world, the Holy Qur'an is absolutely unique. Its recording and preservation are miraculous! Because it stands out distinctly from the ordinary human pattern of narration; the short-sighted and the inimical say that it is incoherent or incongruous. The pattern definitely is different. It is unique. It is miraculous. Let me substantiate what I assert.

HUMAN STYLE

Every other religious book is set on the pattern of, **"Once upon a time ..."** or **"The fox and the grapes ... the wolf and lamb,"** etc, etc. i.e.

1a. *IN THE BEGINNING* (Once Upon a Time) *God created the heaven[1] and the earth ...* (Emphasis added) *(HOLY BIBLE)* Genesis 1:1[2]

b. *IN THE BEGINNING* (Once Upon a Time) *was the word, and the word was with God, and the word was God[3] ...* (Emphasis added) *(HOLY BIBLE)* John 1:1

---

1. The first verse of the Bible speaks about "the heaven and the earth" in the singular. In the Holy Qur'an the word earth is always singular whereas the word heavens is in the plural. Some thing to ponder upon!

2. The word **"Genesis"** itself means the beginning, this is, after all how every human tale ought to start. It should begin with the "beginning!"

3. In the original Greek manuscripts of the new Testament there is no such thing as a capital letter and a small letter. The Christian theologians have contrived capitals according to their religious prejudices into their translations of the Bible i.e. God and god.

c. ***THIS IS THE GENEALOGY*** (The Origin, The Beginning) ***of Jesus Christ, the son of David, the son of Abraham ...*** (Emphasis added)

(HOLY BIBLE)   *Matthew 1:1*

2. ***NOW AFTER THE DEATH OF MOSES THE SERVANT OF THE LORD IT CAME TO PASS*** (So It Happened, Once Upon a Time), ***that the Lord spake unto Joshua*** ... (Emphasis added)

(HOLY BIBLE)   *Joshua 1:1*

3. ***NOW AFTER THE DEATH OF JOSHUA IT CAME TO PASS*** (So It Happened, Once Upon a Time), ***the children of Israel asked the Lord ...*** (Emphasis added)

(HOLY BIBLE)   *Judges 1:1*[1]

4. ***NOW IT CAME TO PASS*** (So It Happened, Once Upon a Time) ***in the days when the judges ruled, that there was famine in the land ...*** (Emphasis added)

(HOLY BIBLE)   *Ruth 1:1*[2]

5. ***NOW THERE WAS A CERTAIN MAN*** (Once Upon a Time) ***of Ramathaimzophim, of the mount Ephraim ...*** (Emphasis added)

(HOLY BIBLE)   *1 Samuel 1:1*[3]

6. ***NOW IT CAME TO PASS*** (So It Happened, Once Upon a Time) ***after the death of Saul ... (Emphasis added)***

(HOLY BIBLE)   *2 Samuel 1:1*

---

1. The editors of the RSV (the Revised Standard Version) of the Bible; supported by 32 scholars of the highest emminence; backed by 50 co-operating denominations, concluded their verdict regarding its authorship — NOT God but **"Possibly** Samuel!"

2. Their verdict again — "Not **definitely** known, **perhaps** Samuel!" Most definitely NOT God!

3. Amazingly, the inspired editors of the RSV say about the authorship of the Book of Judges — **"Possibly** Samuel," and for the Book of Ruth — **"Perhaps** Samuel", but when they come to the Book of Samuel (?) himself they declare — Author — **"Unknown!"**

7. *NOW* (Once Upon a Time) ***King David was old*** (Gone Cold) ***and stricken in years, and they covered him with clothes, but he gat no heat.***   **(HOLY BIBLE)**   *1 King 1:1* [1]

8. *NOW* (Once Upon a Time) ***in the first year of Cyrus King of Persia ...***
           (HOLY BIBLE)   *Book of Ezra 1:1* [2]

9. *NOW IT CAME TO PASS* (So It Happened Once Upon a Time) ***in the days of Aha-suerus ...*** **(Emphasis added)**
           (HOLY BIBLE)   *Book of Esther 1:1*

10. *NOW IT CAME TO PASS* (So It Happened, Once Upon a Time) ***in the thirtieth year, in the fourth month, in the fifth day of the month ...*** (Emphasis added)
           (HOLY BIBLE)   *Ezekiel 1:1*

If these examples do not confuse and bewilder you, then nothing else will! You are inevitably struck with the **"once upon a time"** syndrome. You have cultivated a predilection for man made stories, even if they be true. The style, the pattern, the narration is what I am speaking about. This is how humans think, talk and write. No blame on them for humans will be humans!

All the above references are from the authorised King James Version (KJV) which is the most popular version among the Christians of the world. You must have noted that every verse in the above quotations is 1:1, 1:1, meaning the **first** chapter and the **first** verse of **every book** of the Bible. Which start with **NOW,** NOW, now!". Try it out, see for yourself how many more

---

1. The same (editors' verdict) — Author — **"Unknown!"**
2. Again they unashamedly confess — Author — **"Probably** written or edited by Ezra!" Note their guarded semantics — "Possibly, perhaps, probably, etc." Get my book **"Is the Bible God's Word?"** from the IPCI for a fuller insight.

such beginnings you can find in the **"Book of Books,"**[1] I must, however warn you that your Bible Concordances will not help you. You will have to page through the Bible the same way as I did.

CONCORDANCES WON'T HELP

I consulted two Bible Concordances. The one was published by the Jehovah's Witnesses — The fastest growing Christian sect in Christendom. The second is **"Young's Analytical Concordance to the Bible."** Both these concordances boast over 300 000 entries each. The latter has no less than 277 **now's** listed, but there is not a single "NOW" (once upon a time) of the examples given above. You can guess the reason![2]

I do not want to tax your patience any further. I realise that you will want proof. **"Alright now,** please tell us **your** story about **your** Qur'anic revelation!":

"It was the night of the 27th of the month of Ramadaan that Muhummed (pbuh) the prophet of Islam, was in cave of Hira, in the outskirts of the City of Makkah. He used to retire to Mount Hira for peace, quiet and contemplation. He used to worry about the problems of his people — their drunkenness, adulteries, idolatries, wars, their rank injustices and cruelties. So much so that Gibbon, the master historian, was constrained to record in his **"Decline and Fall of the Roman Empire"**:

> "THE HUMAN BRUTE (THE ARAB), ALMOST
> WITHOUT SENSE, IS POORLY DISTINGUISHED
> FROM THE REST OF THE ANIMAL CREATION."

The recluse of Hira was yearning for a solution. He was wont to retire to his retreat often alone, but sometimes with his dear wife **Umm-ul-Mo'mineen** (Mother of the Faithful) **Khadija-tul-Kubra.**

---

1. **Book of Books:** A title of the Holy Bible.
2. Because they represent childish redundancies (**"ONCE UPON A TIME"**), which ill-befits the word of God even according to their own standards.

THE FIRST CALL

One night — the night of **Lailatul-Qadr** — (the Night of Power and Excellence) when Divine peace rests on creation, and all nature is lifted up towards its Lord — in the middle of that night the book of God was opened to the thirsting soul. Gabriel, the angel of God, appears to him, and commands him in his mother tongue. اِقْرَأ **Iqra'**, which mean "read!" or "recite" or "rehearse!" or "proclaim" aloud! Muhummed (pbuh) was too terrified and was totally unprepared for this shock. This was no graduating or gowning ceremony. In fear and trepidation he cries out مَا أَنَا بِقَارِءٍ **Maa-ana-beqaa-Ri'in** "I am not learned!" The angel repeats the command **Iqra'** for the second time, with the identical response from Muhummed (pbuh). Gabriel embraces him hard and commands him the third time:

READ! IN THE NAME OF
THY LORD AND CHERISHER
WHO CREATED ...

اِقْرَأ بِاسْمِ رَبِّكَ
الَّذِى خَلَقَ ۚ

Muhummed (pbuh) now grasps that what he was required to do, was repeat what was being said, since this Arabic word **Iqra'** means all these things — read, recite or repeat! Following the above first verse of **Súra Al-'Alaq** (Chapter 96 of the Holy Qur'an), four more verses were repeated and recited on Muhummed's (pbuh) first call and subsequently recorded in written form in the Holy Qur'an ... (see page 194).

"Hold it, Mr Deedat!" I can almost hear you shriek. All this that you are telling us about your **'Qur'anic revelation'** is no different from the other numerous examples you have to prove to have had a human hand in it. Were they all fallible and not divine?"

Exactly! I am happy that you see clearly how the subjective mind of man thinks, talks, and records. From the time you asked me (above page 192) **"please tell us your STORY about your**

Qur'anic revelation," and I began to respond — "**It was the night of the 27th of the month of Ramadaan ...**" up to — "**and subsequently recorded in written form in the Holy Qur'an**" were my own words, borrowed from the Holy Qur'an, from the Books of Tradition, from history and from the lips of learned men, I heard over the decades. The Qur'anic Scripture has no such taint from the hands of men. This is how it is preserved. I list below the **first** five verses of the first revelation to Muhummed (pbuh), for your critical observation and study —

Iqraa, or Read! or Proclaim!
Or *'Alaq*, or The Clot of Congealed Blood.

In the name of God, Most Gracious, Most Merciful.

١ - اِقْرَأْ بِاسْمِ رَبِّكَ الَّذِىْ خَلَقَ ۝

1. Proclaim! (or Read!)[6203]
    In the name[6204]
    Of thy Lord and Cherisher,
    Who created—

٢ - خَلَقَ الْاِنْسَانَ مِنْ عَلَقٍ ۝

2. Created man, out of
    A (mere) clot
    Of congealed blood:[6205]

٣ - اِقْرَأْ وَرَبُّكَ الْاَكْرَمُ ۝

3. Proclaim! And thy Lord
    Is Most Bountiful,—

٤ - الَّذِىْ عَلَّمَ بِالْقَلَمِ ۝

4. He Who taught
    (The use of) the Pen,—[6206]

٥ - عَلَّمَ الْاِنْسَانَ مَالَمْ يَعْلَمْ ۝

5. Taught man that
    Which he knew not.[6207]

(SÚRA 'ALAQ) Holy Qur'an 96:1-5

A UNIQUE RECORD

Every Qur'anic **text**, in Arabic or in a **translated** form in any language will follow this pattern. There are no ifs and buts. You will **NOT** find in the text or translation that Muhummed (pbuh) "WAS FORTY YEARS OLD WHEN HE RECEIVED HIS FIRST CALL." You will **NOT** find that "HE WAS IN THE CAVE OF

MOUNT HIRA." You will **NOT** find that "HE SAW THE ANGEL GABRIEL." Or that "HE WAS TERRIFIED," or how he reacted and responded to the command **"Iqra'!"** That when the angel departed after having completed the first five verses, "MUHUM-MED RAN HOME SOME THREE MILES SOUTH TO MAKKAH TO HIS DEAR WIFE KHADIJA AND RELATED WHAT HAD HAPPENED AND REQUESTED HER TO COVER HIM UP, COVER HIM UP!" All this is what I call a **"Once upon a time!"** style. The Holy Qur'an narrates nothing of this, it is absolutely unique in its narration and its preservation. In short it is **Miraculous!**

Further, unlike any human endeavour of literary art, where every thing begins with the beginning: the first word and the first verse of the Qur'anic inspiration is **not** the **first chapter** and the **first verse** of the Holy Qur'an — IT OCCUPIES THE NINETY-SIXTH CHAPTER OF THE HOLY QUR'AN, as the divine Author (GOD ALMIGHTY) had instructed His Chosen Messenger Muhummed (pbuh). No religious Book on earth is like it or follows this pattern, because no alleged Revelation was preserved in its pristine purity when it was **revealed!**

A CANADIAN PSYCHOLOGIST

I had the privilege of sharing my thoughts on the first call of Muhummed (pbuh), as contained in the first five verses of **Súra Al-'Alaq** (chapter 96) as seen on page 194, with a young man from Canada. I was taking him on a guided tour of the largest Mosque in the southern hemisphere. Whilst chatting, I enquired as to his occupation. He said that he was doing a post-graduate course, majoring in psychology. "Psychology?" I said, and immediately drew his attention to the first five verses of the chapter under discussion. I asked him as to how he would account for the Message and experience of Muhummed (pbuh), speaking about **"Reading, Writing and learning things un-known before,"** things which were not his immediate problem nor the problem of his people. How could the subjective mind of man, as if out of the blue[1] rehearse these words. I said, "Account for it!" He said that he could not. He confessed that he had already grappled with that problem. I said, "In that case we would have to accept the man at his word." And I quoted the first verses from **Súra Najm:**

BY THE STAR[2] *WHEN IT GOES DOWN, —*	وَالنَّجْمِ إِذَا هَوٰىۙ
YOUR COMPANION[3] *IS* *NEITHER ASTRAY NOR* *BEING MISLED.*	مَا ضَلَّ صَاحِبُكُمْ وَمَا غَوٰىۙ
NOR DOES HE SAY (AUGHT) *OF (HIS OWN) DESIRE.*	وَمَا يَنْطِقُ عَنِ الْهَوٰىؕ
IT IS NO LESS THAN INSPIRATION[4] *SENT DOWN TO HIM:*	اِنْ هُوَ اِلَّا وَحْيٌ يُّوْحٰىۙ
HE WAS TAUGHT BY ONE *MIGHTY IN POWER.*[5]	عَلَّمَهٗ شَدِيْدُ الْقُوٰىۙ

(SÚRA NAJM)   Holy Qur'an 53:1-5

And Muhummed (pbuh) is repeatedly made to tell the people:

SAY: I AM BUT A MAN *LIKE YOURSELVES,*	قُلْ اِنَّمَاۤ اَنَا بَشَرٌ مِّثْلُكُمْ
(BUT) THE INSPIRATION *HAS COME TO ME,*	يُوْحٰۤى اِلَيَّ

---

1. **Blue:** as from nowhere!

2. **"By the Star":** an oath, an adjuration.

3. Meaning Muhummed (pbuh) the Messenger of God.

4. **Inspiration:** Our concept of the revelation to Muhummed (pbuh) is a verbal inspiration. The words of the Holy Qur'an were so to say **"put into his mouth"** (Deut. 18:18). Get your FREE copy of **"What the BIBLE says about MUHUMMED (pbuh)"** from the IPCI

5. This is referred to by the Commentators to the archangel Gabriel through whom the revelation came.

THAT YOUR
GOD IS ONE GOD ...

أَنَّمَا إِلَٰهُكُمْ إِلَٰهٌ وَاحِدٌ

(SURA KAHF) *Holy Qur'an 18:110*

The young Canadian politely responded, "I will have to give this matter serious thought."

If only we would familiarize ourselves with the facts from the Holy Qur'an, we would be able to open a conversation with the specialists in any science.

MIRACLE OF JOURNALISM

Being a beehive of activity, the IPCI Centre attracts a lot of people for dialogue and discussions, including the journalist and the newspaperman. As soon as I discover that my interviewer's field of activity is journalism, I tell him that I would like to show him the Holy Qur'an as a **"Miracle of Journalism!"** No one refuses to hear. I begin with the story of the Holy prophet Moses (pbuh), in the style and pattern of **"Once upon a time."** It can't be helped. Yet we cannot afford the luxury of the details of **"Moses and the Bulrushes,"** or even the details of "his childhood, mother, and his sister," (Holy Qur'an 20:38-40 and 28:7-13). We have to skip the details. I begin with —

HIS MISHAP IN THE CITY

Moses (pbuh) came upon two men fighting, a man belonging to his own tribe and the other an enemy of his people. He went to help the Jew against the Egyptian and in the altercation slapped the tyrant too hard so that he died.

Moses (pbuh) then fled the country into the Sinai Desert and found himself among the Midianites. Here he helped two damsels in distress and was offered a job by their father Jethro. After having completed his indenture for a period of over eight years, Moses (pbuh) was beginning to get bored with his rustic existence. For a man who had grown up with royalty in the midst of the hustle and bustle of the city, he was getting restless. He wanted a change and asked for permission to become independent from his in-laws. Jethro was a very reasonable, and a practical man. He grants Moses (pbuh) leave.

MOSES PIONEERS A TREK

Moses (pbuh) left with his wife and children, together with his share of the sheep and the goats which he used to herd for his father-in-law.

After some time he found himself with his family in the Sinai. He had lost direction from the last habitation with whom he had rested. He had run out of stocks of the braised meat that he was carrying. There was still enough Matzos the dried unleavened bread of the Jews. The problem was the meat. He had to slaughter a sheep or a goat. That would be easy. The difficulty was to start a fire which was a laborious task. It could take as long as half a day of rubbing two dissimilar materials. Obviously there were no matches or ligthers in those days. He was procrastinating. Putting things off for today, or tomorrow and his meat problem would be solved, he thought ... **"Where is the promised miracle!"** Mr. Deedat?

So far I have given only the background to the story. The miracle is to condense all the above and more in just four terse verses — four short sentences in the most beautiful prose. But to appreciate the feat, I must draw your attention to what I would like you to notice in what is to me, the acme of journalism.

NEWSPAPER PLACARDS

I live some thirty kilometres north of the City of Durban, where I have my offices. Prior to the construction of the N2 (Freeway) linking the City of Durban, I usually took the beach (seaside) road to Durban. This route took me past the amphitheatre on the Durban beachfront. At the intersection of the amphitheatre I regularly observed a news vendor offering the morning paper — **"The Natal Mercury,"** for sale. He had a placard daily with headline to attract buyers. Again and again on reading the placard, I made up my mind not to buy the newspaper that day, but on parking my car in central Durban on passing other news vendors, I nevertheless bought the paper.

After numerous such changes of decision, I began to question myself as to the reasons for my change of mind. I discovered that though the same newspaper was being offered for sale the placards were different. On the beachfront the placards were made appealing to European clientele whereas the placards in the area I passed were directed to the Asian community. By extension the placard for the African and the Coloured areas would be slanted to induce them to buy the same paper.

So the master journalist would be the one who could invent a single placard that would appeal to the four major race groups[1] each day.

That would be the masterpiece of journalism! Journalists no doubt all agree with this reasoning. Let us then analyse the Holy Qur'an on this basis.

UNIVERSAL APPEAL

Muhummed (pbuh), the prophet of Islam is in Madeenah, and is surrounded by Jews, Christians, Muslims, **Mushriks**[2] and **Munaafiqs**[3] in the City. The Holy Prophet is to broadcast his news (Divine Revelation) to all these various people. What must he write on his placard to attract the attention of each of these varied groups? He is made to proclaim:

---

1. Under the **"Apartheid"** system, the four groups live in separate areas.
2. **"Mushriks"**: the pagans, the idolators of Makkah.
3. **"Munaafiqs"**: the hypocrites, running with the hare and hunting with the hounds.

HAS THE STORY OF MOSES REACHED YOU? [1]

وَهَلْ اَتٰىكَ حَدِيثُ مُوْسٰى

(SÚRA TÁ-HÁ) Holy Qur'an 20:9

Can you imagine the excitement? The Christians and the Jews would be waiting to hear further, wanting Muhummed (pbuh) to make a fool of himself, for they reason within themselves what could this Arab know about Moses (pbuh) since he is an **ummi** (unlettered). The Muslims are thirsty for knowledge, they would be yearning — please tell us everything you can about Moses (pbuh).

The **Mushriks** (The polytheists) and the **Munaafiqs** (the hypocrites) were lolling their tongues to enjoy the three-sided debate on Moses (pbuh): between the Muslims, the Christians and the Jews. Everybody is **"all-ears"** (acutely attentive)! Muhummed (pbuh) [2] continues

BEHOLD, HE SAW A FIRE!

اِذْ رَاٰ نَارًا

Dramatisation! You can almost visualize the scene. Muhummed (pbuh) is talking telegraphically. It took about two thousand years after the birth of Jesus Christ (pbuh) for the largest Christian and Jewish nations on earth (the mighty United States) [3] to reach the height of perfection in the advertising field to formulate the slogan, in the words of the Western Union Telegraph Company, **"Don't Write — Telegraph!"** Which school of journalism did Muhummed (pbuh) attend to master this super American sizzlemanship? [4] He is made to carry on:

---

1. I urge my Muslim brethren to memorise the Qur'anic text with its meaning.

2. Actually, these are not the words of Muhummed (pbuh) but the veritable Words of God as dictated to the Prophet. We say, **"Muhummed continues,"** because this is what the unbeliever is thinking. Then let him give **full credit** to God's human mouthpiece.

3. The mightiest Christian nation on earth is the USA because it boasts a Christian population of over 200 million. The USA is also the largest Jewish nation because there are more Jews in America than in Israel or in any other country.

4. **Sizzlemanship:** The art of American high-pressure salesmanship.

SO HE SAID TO HIS FAMILY,	فَقَالَ لِاَهْلِهِ امْكُثُوَا
"TARRY YE; I PERCEIVE A FIRE;	اِنِّيَ اٰنَسْتُ نَارًا
PERHAPS I CAN BRING YOU SOME BURNING BRAND THEREFROM,	لَعَلِّيَ اٰتِيْكُمْ مِّنْهَا بِقَبَسٍ
OR FIND SOME GUIDANCE AT THE FIRE."	اَوْ اَجِدُ عَلَى النَّارِ هُدًى ⊙

(SÚRA TÁ-HÁ)   *Holy Qur'an 20:10*

DICTATING SHORTHAND

Please compare the above with any other English translation of the Holy Qur'an by friend or foe, and you will find the same brevity and economy of words. Muhummed (pbuh) was not doing any exercise in precis writing. He was only articulating God's Words as they were whispered into his heart and mind through the medium of the Archangel Gabriel. We must remember that there was no Arabic Bible, in the sixth century of the Christian era, when the Holy Prophet dictated the Qur'an.

Now do yourself a favour. Please contrast this Qur'anic Revelation with the Biblical story as contained in the second Book of the Holy Bible, the **Book of Exodus,** chapters 1, 2 and 3 which discusses this very aspect of the life of the Holy Prophet Moses (pbuh) we are dealing with here. I quote the beginning of the story from the Bible —

> *NOW*[1] *these are the names of the children of Israel, which came into Egypt; every man and his household came with Jacob.*

---

1. **"NOW!"** Here we start again — the **"Once upon a time"** story! Give another glance to all the other examples on the preceding pages 189 to 191.

Reuben, Simeon, Levi, and Judah, Is-sa-char, Ze-bu-lun, and Benjamin, Dan, and Naph-ta-li, Gad, and Asher,

And all the souls that came out of the loins of Jacob were seventy souls: for Joseph was in Egypt already,

(HOLY BIBLE) Exodus 1:1-5

MOSES SET-UP

Simply warming up! Is this how God speaks? Please compare these five verses from the Bible with the four verses from the Holy Qur'an reproduced below.

To continue with the Qur'anic narrative, Moses (pbuh) was hungry for two things whilst wondering in the Sinai with his flock and family. He wanted 'fire' to cook his meat, and 'direction' to some hospitable community in the desert. Allah was unfolding his plan. Moses (pbuh) was being 'SET-UP' for his mission from the illusion of burning coal to the reality of the spiritual fire burning in the souls of mankind for thousands of years and a true direction for the guidance of humanity.

The 'fire' that Moses (pbuh) saw, was no ordinary fire. To him it meant an easy kindling of his own fire, the fire also indicated the presence of other human beings from whom he could get information: and guidance.

BUT WHEN HE CAME
TO THE FIRE, A VOICE
WAS HEARD: "O MOSES!

فَلَمَّآ أَتٰهَا نُودِیَ یٰمُوسٰی ۞

"VERILY I AM THY LORD!

اِنِّیۤ اَنَا رَبُّكَ

THEREFORE (IN MY PRESENCE)
PUT OFF THY SHOES:

فَاخْلَعْ نَعْلَیْكَ

THOU ART IN THE SACRED VALLEY OF TUWA."

اِنَّكَ بِالْوَادِ الْمُقَدَّسِ طُوًے ۞

(*SÚRA TÁ-HÁ*)   *Holy Qur'an 20:11-12*

The spiritual history of Moses (pbuh) begins here and this was his spiritual birth. In Biblical terminology — **'This day have I begotten thee!'** This is how God spoke to David (pbuh) about his appointment, in the Book of Psalms 2:7

The whole Qur'anic passage above is full of the highest mystic meaning, which is reflected in the short rhymed verses in the original. Both the rhythm and the meaning in the text suggest the highest mystery. For easier comparison I reproduce the four verses together —

*Has the story of Moses
reached you?*

*Behold, he saw a fire:
so he said to his family,
"tarry ye; I perceive a fire,
perhaps I can bring you some
burning brand therefrom,
or find some guidance at the fire."*

*But when he came to the fire,
a voice was heard: "O Moses!*

*Verily I am thy Lord!
therefore (in my presence)
put off thy shoes: for thou art
in the sacred valley of Tuwa.**

(*SÚRA TÁ-HÁ*)   *Holy Qur'an 20:9-12*

* **Tuwa** was the valley just below Mount Sinai, where subsequently Moses (pbuh) was to receive the Law. In the parallel mystic meaning, we are selected by trials in this humble life, whose valley is just as sacred and receive God's glory just as much as the heights of the Mount *(Tur)* Sinai, if we but have the insight to perceive it. And the **'shoes'** were to be put off as a mark of respect. In the parallel mystic meaning again, Moses (pbuh) was now to put away his mere worldly interests, and anything of mere worldly utility, he having been chosen by the Most High God.

WHAT IS YOUR VERDICT?

How is one, inured to folklore and fairy tales to evaluate this pure elixir from Heaven? Even a sympathetic critic like Thomas Carlyle, one of the greatest thinkers of the past century could not fathom its incisive brevity and perspicuousness. He called the Qur'anic reading —

"A WEARISOME CONFUSED JUMBLE CRUDE, INCONDITE; — INSUPPORTABLE STUPIDITY ..."

Incondite, meaning a badly constructed literary or artistic composition: and **'unsupportable stupidity?'** After contrasting the Qur'anic and the Biblical narrations, how would your verdict go? I have yet to come across a journalist who failed to recognise the brilliance of Muhummed (?) (peace be upon him), in dictating direct facts, without any attempt on his part at analysing or interpreting it: exactly as a master journalist would do for today's newspaper or magazine. **It is nothing short of the miraculous! Do you agree?**

CHAPTER FOUR

Miraculous Book of Telegrams

The Holy Qur'an can be appropriately described as '**A Book of Telegrams.**' For this is how the Book was revealed in the form of telegraphically addressed Messages in answer to the questions on:

1. ALCOHOL AND GAMES OF CHANCE

THEY ASK THEE CONCERNING WINE AND GAMBLING.	يَسْئَلُوْنَكَ عَنِ الْخَمْرِ وَالْمَيْسِرِ
SAY: [1] *"IN THEM IS GREAT SIN,*	قُلْ فِيْهِمَا اِثْمٌ كَبِيْرٌ
AND SOME PROFIT, FOR MEN;	وَّمَنَافِعُ لِلنَّاسِ ۖ
BUT THE SIN IS GREATER THAN THE PROFIT."	وَاِثْمُهُمَا اَكْبَرُ مِنْ نَّفْعِهِمَا ۗ
AND THEY ASK THEE HOW MUCH THEY ARE TO SPEND (IN CHARITY);	وَيَسْئَلُوْنَكَ مَا ذَا يُنْفِقُوْنَ ۗ
SAY: [2] *"WHAT IS BEYOND YOUR NEEDS,"*	قُلِ الْعَفْوَ ۗ
THUS DOTH ALLAH MAKE CLEAR TO YOU HIS SIGNS:	كَذٰلِكَ يُبَيِّنُ اللهُ لَكُمُ الْاٰيٰتِ
IN ORDER THAT YE MAY REFLECT —	لَعَلَّكُمْ تَتَفَكَّرُوْنَ ۙ

(SÚRA BAQARA) *Holy Qur'an 2:219* [3]

---

1. **"SAY!"** That is Muhummed (pbuh) is commanded to **answer:** "Tell them!" O Muhummed! "Proclaim, express it in words, utter aloud, pronounce, speak out!"

2. The same command with the same import.

3. I cannot urge too strongly upon my Muslim brethren to memorize the verses with their meaning and share it with all who will give you a hearing.

QUR'AN AND HADITH

The above is just one example of how God speaks! Other examples are to follow. Can any sincere seeker of truth be convinced in any easier way? The answer is **'No!'** Yet He (God) Reasons with the recalcitrant in the following words: —

Say: "Are the blind equal
With those who see?"

           (SÚRA RA'D) *Holy Qur'an 13:16*

Of course not!

Now compare the above Words of God Almighty on the subject of 'WINE' (intoxicants) with the words of His Chosen Messenger Muhummed Mustafa (pbuh), NOT FORGETTING that the above verse 2:219 and what follows from the **Hadith** below were heard from the lips of the Prophet (pbuh) and recorded by his Companions:

Ibn Anas (RA) reported that the Messenger of Allah cursed every one who was associated in any way with the production and consumption of any kind of intoxicating beverages. He said:

1. **Cursed is he who grows grapes for brewing.**[1]

2. **Cursed is he who sells its.**

3. **Cursed is he who crushes it.**

4. **Cursed is he who bottles its,** and

5. **Cursed is he who drinks it,** or words to this effect.

The Holy Prophet (pbuh) is also reported to have said:

"Whatever intoxicates if taken in greater quantity is also forbidden in smaller quantity."

---

1. It is the brewing or fermenting that invites the curse. Otherwise, the planting of fruit trees for the purpose of eating or selling their fruits is an act of virtue for which Allah will reward us.

There is no excuse in the House of Islam for a nip or a tot, unlike Paul's advice to Timothy —

> *"Drink no longer water, but use a little wine for thy stomach's sake and thine often infirmities.*
>
> *(HOLY BIBLE)*   1 Timothy 5:23

Or Solomon's sanguine yet humorous recommendation for enslaving and subjugating a conquered people:

> *"Give strong drink[1] unto him that is ready to perish, and wine unto those that be of heavy hearts."*
>
> *"Let them drink, and forget his poverty, and remember his misery no more."*
>
> *(HOLY BIBLE)*   Proverbs 31:6-7

Lest we forget, please look again at the Qur'anic diction and the words of the Prophet (pbuh) above, and you cannot help agreeing that the two are worlds apart in style, structure, and sublimity though articulated by the same lips.

Another example of replying telegraphically to a question regarding the —

2.   NEW MOONS

They ask thee concerning the new moons.

Say: they are but signs to mark fixed periods of time in (the affairs) of men, and for pilgrimage.

(SÚRA BAQARA)   Holy Qur'an 2:189

---

1. **"Hard liquor is for sick men at the brink of death and wine for those in deep depression."** Is the alternative rendering of the verse in the **"Living Bible,"** not a sure death to the dying?

"There were many superstitions connected with the New Moon, as there are to the present day. We are told to disregard such superstitions. As a measure of time, where the lunar calendar is used, the New Moon is one great sign, for which people watch with eagerness. Muslim festivals, including the Pilgrimage are fixed by the appearance of the New Moon."

A. Yusuf Ali [1]

A telegram, in an identical vein to the question of —

3. C-H-A-R-I-T-Y

They ask thee (O Muhummed!) what they should spend (in charity).

Say: whatever ye spend that is good, Is for parents and kindred and orphans and those in want and for wayfarers.

And whatever ye do that is good, — Allah knoweth it well

(SÚRA BAQARA) Holy Qur'an 2:215

"Three question arise in charity:

(a) What shall we give?

(b) To whom shall we give?

(c) How shall we give?

The answer is here, giving anything that is good, useful, helpful, valuable. It may be property or money; it may be a helpful hand; it may be advice, it may be a kind word: **"WHATEVER YE DO THAT IS GOOD" is charity.** On the other hand, if you throw away what is useless, there is no charity in it. Or if you give something with harmful intent, e.g. a sword to a madman, or a

---

1. The comment on the verse is by Abdullah Yusuf Ali. Obtain his monumental translation and commentary from the IPCI at a highly subsidised price. A veritable encyclopaedia of over 1800 pages with over 6000 footnotes.

drug or sweets or even money to some one whom you want to entrap or corrupt, IT IS NO CHARITY BUT A GIFT OF DAMNATION."

TO WHOM SHOULD YOU GIVE?

It may be tempting to earn the world's praise by a gift that will be talked about, but are you meeting the needs of those who have the first claim on you? If you are not, YOU ARE A PERSON WHO DEFRAUDS CREDITORS: it is not charity!

"Every gift is judged by its unselfish character: the degree of need or claim is a factor which you must consider; if you disregard it, there is something selfish behind it.

HOW SHOULD IT BE GIVEN?

As in the sight of Allah; it shuts out all pretence, show, and insincerity."

A. Yusuf Ali

Muhummed (pbuh) received yet another telegram in answer to the query in the nature of :—

4. THE SOUL

**They ask thee (O Muhummed!)
concerning (the nature of) the soul.**

**Say: "The soul is by the command
of my Lord:
and of the knowledge of it very
little is communicated to you, (O Men!)"**

(SÚRA BANI ISRÁ-ÍL) Holy Qur'an 17:85

I cannot help over-emphasising the fact that THE RECITATION OF THE HOLY QUR'AN IS UNLIKE ANY OTHER BOOK ON EARTH. IT SPEAKS STRAIGHT AND TO THE POINT. THERE ARE NO IFS AND BUTS, NO PREVARICATIONS, NO BEATING

ABOUT THE BUSH. In the whole vast volume you will not get the type of script out of which a "box-office hit," or a record breaking film like the **"Ten Commandments," "Samson and Delilah,"** or a **"David and Bath-sheba"** can be produced for the silver screen — the cinema. In this regard the Holy Bible is the script writer's delight. It is all there for easy transmuting into pots of gold!

While we are at it, let me remind my readers that search as you may you will not find within the covers of the Holy Qur'an even the name of Muhummed's (pbuh) father or mother. You will not discover the names of his wives or the names of his daughters, nor the names of his beloved companions. Amazingly! though you will find a whole chapter dedicated to Mary, the mother of Jesus Christ (pbuh) ... **Súra Maryam,** or Mary, chapter 19 of the Holy Qur'an. **Jesus (pbuh) is mentioned in this Book of God no less than twenty-five times, whereas the name of the Prophet (pbuh) only five times.** Reason? Are Jesus and his mother more important than Muhummed and his mother (peace be upon them all)? "No! not at all" Then why this inordinate coverage? Simply because the integrity of Jesus and his mother (peace be upon them) was at stake. There were various false charges, insinuations and innuendos against mother and son which had to be cleared. Hence the story of the annunciation, the immaculate conception and the birth of Jesus (pbuh) had to be recorded. Nobody ever questioned the genealogy of the Prophet of Islam at any time, therefore not a word was wasted in the whole book about the Prophet's birth or parentage. **The Qur'an is not a biography of Muhummed (pbuh)!** This is difficult for the unbeliever to understand.

Let us give one more example of the telegraphic communication from the Holy Qur'an on the subject of the Last Day, the End of Time, that is —

5. THE FINAL HOUR

**They ask thee (O Muhummed!) about
the (final) hour — when will
be its appointed time?**

**Say: "the knowledge thereof is
with my Lord (alone): none but He
can reveal as to when it will occur.**

**Heavy were its burden through the
heavens and the earth.
Only, all of a sudden will it come
to you."**

(SÚRA A'RÁF) *Holy Qur'an 7:187*

It will be worth while to compare this one verse above
with the whole of chapter thirteen of the Gospel of St.
Mark, which uses all of the thirty-seven verses there to
reach the conclusion of the single ***aayah*** (verse) above. A
simple test to distinguish man-made books from the Word
of God. You will find the Qur'an free from frills and
verboseness!

Many other examples can be given from the Book of God
to prove that its narration is not in the style of men; that
it is an absolutely unique Book. In fact a volume can be
written on this theme itself. However we will end this
chapter with one last example from the Holy Qur'an. It is a
classical short chapter of only four verses. All the four
verses put together are less in wording than the five
examples of a single verse each given above. I give you
on the next page a replica of that short ***súra*** (chapter).

Ikhlas, or Purity (of Faith).

In the name of God, Most Gracious, Most Merciful.

1.   Say : He is God,[6296]
     The One and Only ;[6297]

2.   God, the Eternal, Absolute ;[6298]

3.   He begetteth not,
     Nor is He begotten ;[6299]

4.   And there is none
     Like unto Him.[6300]

(*SÚRA IKHLÁS*)   Holy Qur'an 112:1-4

In the English translation on previous page, you will note five numbers to the four verses, Nos. 6296 to 6300. In the complete translation of A. Yusuf Ali,[1] you will find his learned commentary. You may or may not agree with his elucidations. They are not infallible. The word of God **IS THE ARABIC TEXT** you see above, and the **English** is accepted as the best human effort at translation.

I will now give you my own observation from the angle of Revelation that we are discussing, eg., Divine inspiration — Word of God, under the title:

6.   ACID TEST OF THEOLOGY

On the authority of the Messenger of Allah, it is universally accepted that a Muslim reciting the above four verses in its original form, three times, will derive the spiritual blessings of reading the whole Qur'an. What makes this short *Súra* (chapter) so invaluable? It is not the sound, nor the music of that

---

1.   You will do yourself and your Muslim and non-Muslim friends a great favour by making this translation available to them.

inimitable symphony which move men to ecstasy and tears. It is the Message, that acid test of religion which gives it that high and sublime status.

There is not a theology, or a concept of God which is out of the purview of these four short verses. They are the touchstones about the knowledge of God. Through these you can accept or reject any idea of God, or know right from wrong. This is exactly like the **"touchstone"** the jewellers use for testing gold. Ask a jeweller friend how a touchstone works. How did our Qur'anic touchstone come about?

FROM THE "HEAD COMPUTER"

Arrangements were under way for me to visit Zambia on a lecture tour in mid-1975. I received a phone call from Lusaka that an air ticket was sent to Durban which I could pick up from the headquarters of the South African Airways in the city centre. I walked up to the airways office and approached the information counter and told the man in charge that I had come to pick up my air ticket which had been sent from Lusaka. He told me to see one of the ladies, out of a dozen that were seated in a semi-circle, each with a computer terminal with a visual screen in front. As most of them were attending to other customers, I asked "Which one?" The officer was obviously irritated and flayed his hands and said roughly, "Any one!" pointing in the direction of the seated ladies.

At that moment, I could not understand the reason for this otherwise polite gentleman getting ruffled with my humble and innocent question. I was looking forward to receiving a long booklet of ticket vouchers. I had handled and used them a few times before in my life so there was no mistaking in what I was anticipating. How can any one of those women have my ticket? I wondered. But the irritated tone of the man's voice left me no choice but to seek further information as indicated.

Sheepishly, I approached the first lady that I saw free to serve and told her of my mission. I was informed about a ticket waiting to be picked up. She asked me my name which I spelled out for her. As I spelt it, she began typing it on the keyboard before her. She was watching the screen as she typed. I could not see the wording from where I stood. She nodded her head and said, "Yes", suggesting that she had got it. I said that I wanted to leave Durban for Johannesburg on the Tuesday evening. She offered me a 6 p.m. flight which I accepted, and she punched a few more words on the keyboard. I told her, further, that I wanted to leave Johannesburg to arrive in Lusaka at about 3 p.m. the next day. That was the instruction from my hosts there as they wanted the news media and the TV news to cover my arrival. She typed some more words and enquired whether I wanted to go to Lusaka via Gaborone or Maputo.

I said, it didn't matter as long as I arrived at my destination on Wednesday at 3 p.m. She hit the keyboard again and scanning the screen said, "I am sorry but you are booked on Zambian Airlines and we cannot transfer your ticket to another airline because we cannot contact Zambian Airlines today as they are closed on account of a national holiday in that country." So I was asked to return the next day. Very interesting! I thought, but I was sorely disappointed as the ticket was almost within my reach but not within my grasp. I still imagined that she had the tickets in her desk drawer.

IGNORANCE REMOVED

In my puzzlement, I asked her, "Where did you get all that information from?" She said, "It was from the Head Computer in Johannesburg." She was kind enough to explain further that every other computer in the country with similar end terminals had access to that computer at the press of a button. I enquired that whilst she was trying to book me on that 6 p.m. flight to

Johannesburg, and if there was only one seat left, and if there were other terminals trying for that seat, what would happen? She said the first one within the second would get the seat and the rest would draw a blank. I thanked her profusely and left the airways building.

On my way back to my office, my mind began to buzz with ideas. This is how it happened, I thought. I mean the **wahy** (the Revelation of God to Muhummed (pbuh) His Chosen Messenger, came from the "Head Computer" — THE PRESERVED TABLET!

NAY, THIS IS
A GLORIOUS QUR'AN,

بَل هُوَ قُرْاٰنٌ مَّجِيدٌ ۞

(INSCRIBED) IN
A TABLET PRESERVED!

فِى لَوْحٍ مَّحْفُوظٍ ۞

(SÚRA BURÚJ) *Holy Qur'an 85:21-22*

This "**Tablet**" is not like the one Moses (pbuh) used for inscribing the Ten Commandments, a tablet of stone. It is unlike the ones teachers use in schools, called "blackboards" or "green boards". Neither it is the Tablet of a computer screen or the silicone chip. It is God's Own tablet guarded and protected; it is not to be understood in any material sense for it is not made of stone or metal, IT IS SPIRITUAL! How does it operate? We can only guess —

CHRISTIANS FROM NAJRAN

Whilst Islam was getting a firm foothold in Madeenah, the reputation of the Messenger of God spread throughout the length and breadth of Arabia. A community of Arab Christians living in Najran, around Yemen, heard that an Arab in Arabia was now claiming Divine inspiration and had proclaimed himself to be the mouthpiece of God — a Prophet. A deputation set out for Madeenah to cross-examine the Prophet, to match their wits against his to test his knowledge about God and religion in general.

On their arrival they were housed in the **Musjid-e-Nabawi** (the mosque of the Prophet): a simple structure of mud walls with a thatched roof of palm leaves. The Christians, ate and slept in the Mosque and had discussions with the Messenger of Allah for three days and three nights in the mosque. The details of the dialogue can be found in the Books of Traditions.

During the course of the dialogue, the spokesman for the Christians, amongst many other things, posed the question, **"Now tell us O Muhummed, what is your concept of God?"** The Prophet did not prevaricate, he did not beat around the bush, fumbling for words and ideas, to gather his thoughts, as anyone of us would have done if we did not have a ready answer. Muhummed (pbuh), so to speak, presses his spiritual buttons (there were no buttons to press) but as I said; **"So to speak."** as if, like the lady above, in the airways office contacting the "Head Computer" He is seeking an answer from Allah through the "PRESERVED TABLET", the head computer of all revelational knowledge. He is asking, again I said, so to speak "O my Lord! What shall I say?" Came the answer —

> **Say: (O Muhummed) He is Allah
> the one and only;**
>
> **Allah, the eternal absolute;**
>
> **He begetteth not,
> nor is He begotten,**
>
> **And there is none
> like unto him.**
>
> (**Súra Ikhlás**) *Holy Qur'an 112:1-4*

After uttering the above formula on the Purity of Faith, the conversation returned to the usual discourse of words. No Arab worth his name could have missed the difference in tone and intensity between the two discourses. The words above were not the Prophet's but were God's words. They were literally being put into his mouth. While he recited them, he was only being used as a mouthpiece of God, like the "speaker" in the radio. This data material was programmed into his own, God-given, computer, into his heart and mind a decade earlier in Makkah, under identical circumstances. At that time he was being prodded by the Jews who were trying to trip him on the subject of the **"identity and genealogy of God."** Not unlike the Pharisees of old who were dogging the footsteps of Jesus, their awaited Messiah (pbuh).

The foregoing is a perfect example of how God Almighty sent His revelation to his chosen Messenger — by verbal inspiration — and how His Messenger had it protected and preserved, and how His human mouthpiece used and re-used that Message, and how we, the followers of the Prophet (pbuh), are to have that Message imbibed to use it at every opportunity.

In the religious literature of the world there is nothing to compare with even this short chapter of **Súra Ikhlaas** quoted above! If this chapter 112 is the acid test of theology — God's concentrated word, then the rest of the Qur'anic text is its explanation, with which we are to discover the Qualities of God, and avoid the pitfalls into which men and nations have fallen repeatedly in trying to understand God.

CHAPTER FIVE

God — Unique In His Attributes

God Almighty is absolutely unique in His Person and in His attributes. In no way is he to be compared, or comparable, with any other person or thing that we know or can imagine. In the last verse of the **Súra** quoted in the preceding chapter, we are reminded that not only **"Is nothing like Him, but nothing is in the likeness of Him that can be imagined."** Then how can we know Him? We will realise him through His attributes.

The last and Final Revelation of God — the Holy Qur'an gives us ninety-nine attributes of God with the crowning name —ALLAH! These ninety-nine attributes or names called the **Asma-ul-husna** (the Most Beautiful names) are interspersed throughout the whole Qur'anic text, like a beautiful necklace of pearls with a magnificent pendant — Allah.

Here is a sample segment of that necklace:

HE IS ALLAH, **BESIDES WHOM THERE IS** **NO OTHER GOD;**	هُوَ اللهُ الَّذِىْ لَاۤ اِلٰهَ اِلَّا هُوَ
THE SOVEREIGN, THE HOLY ONE, **THE SOURCE OF PEACE** **(AND PERFECTION),**	اَلْمَلِكُ الْقُدُّوسُ السَّلٰمُ
THE GUARDIAN OF FAITH, **THE PRESERVER OF SAFETY,**	الْمُؤْمِنُ الْمُهَيْمِنُ
THE EXALTED IN MIGHT, **THE IRRESISTIBLE, THE SUPREME:**	الْعَزِيْزُ الْجَبَّارُ الْمُتَكَبِّرُ ط
GLORY TO ALLAH: (HIGH IS HE) **ABOVE THE PARTNERS THEY** **ASCRIBE TO HIM,**	سُبْحٰنَ اللهِ عَمَّا يُشْرِكُوْنَ ۝

HE IS ALLAH, THE CREATOR,
THE EVOLVER, THE BESTOWER
OF FORMS (OR COLOURS).

هُوَ اللّٰهُ الْخَالِقُ الْبَارِئُ الْمُصَوِّرُ

TO HIM BELONG THE
MOST BEAUTIFUL NAMES:

لَهُ الْاَسْمَآءُ الْحُسْنٰى ط

ALL THAT IS IN THE
HEAVENS AND THE
EARTH, DOTH DECLARE
HIS PRAISE AND GLORY:

يُسَبِّحُ لَهُ مَا فِي السَّمٰوٰتِ وَالْاَرْضِ ۚ

AND HE IS THE EXALTED
IN MIGHT, THE WISE.

وَهُوَ الْعَزِيزُ الْحَكِيمُ ۞

(SÚRA HASHR)　*Holy Qur'an 59:23-24*

"THE MOST BEAUTIFUL NAMES"

In the two verses quoted above, we count thirteen of the ninety-nine attributes interspersed throughout the Holy Qur'an. Even the most jaundiced and inimical opponent of Islam will be forced to admit that even in its translated form the attributes and the phraseology are beautiful and unique. In its original Arabic the wordings and their construction are absolutely inimitable and sublime.

How could an **ummi,** an unlettered person, among an **ummi** — unlearned nation contrive such a rhapsody of God fourteen hundred years ago? We must remember that there were no encyclopaedias or treatises that Muhummed (pbuh) could consult even if they were lying around in the deserts of Arabia. From where, then, did Muhummed (pbuh) get this treasure trove of theology? He said, **"It is all given to me by God through inspiration!"** How else can we account for it?

It would be a good experiment to ask the most learned of our learned friends to conjure up some attributes of God for us. I assure you that with all their acquired knowledge the professors of theology and the doctors of divinity will not be able to recount even a dozen. The worldly-wise will say that **"You see, Muhummed was a genius, and after all a genius can excel ten times better than us!"** To which we respond: "It is true that a genius can do ten times better than us. The Prophet (pbuh) gave us ninety-nine attributes, but what makes his list **MIRACULOUS** and **DIVINE** is the one he left out of his list" The word **"Father"**, that is Miracle!

THE FATHER IN HEAVEN

In our human list, no contributor will fail to utter the word FATHER in the first half-a-dozen attributes. The miracle of Muhummed's (pbuh) list[1] is not the "ninety-nine " but this particular one which he (?) kept out of his (?) Qur'an. The word **"father"** as an attribute of God was dangled before him for the twenty-three years of his prophetic life. He eschewed it. He kept it out of his vocabulary (consciously or unconsciously) for over two decades and hence out of the theology of Islam.

You have a right to ask me, "What about the Christians' Lord's Prayer?" Yes, what about it? Read it Mr Deedat! So I read:

> *"O our father which art in heaven, hallowed be thy name; thy kingdom come, thy will be done on earth as it is in heaven."*

"What is wrong with that?" you ask. "Nothing!" Then why are the Muslims so allergic to it? I am not so jaundiced as our opponents. We have to acknowledge that the Christian prayer is a beautiful prayer but there are certain deficiencies in it. You see my child will never ever learn God's name through this prayer. What is His Name?[2] In all the twenty-seven books of the New

---

1. This is **not** Muhummed's list. The Qur'an is **not** his handiwork. I am using these terms in a manner of speaking to the unbeliever.

2. A book under the same title: **"What is His Name?"** is available from the IPCI FREE of charge.

Testament God's name does not occur even once! **"Father"** is given here as a substitute. This is not His Name! As an attribute, meaning — Lord, God, Creator, Provider, I can take no exception to it. **"The loving Father in Heaven. O our Heavenly Father!"** etc. We Muslims take exception to the new meaning, the acquired connotation of the word **Father.**

ONLY BEGOTTEN SON ETC.

In Christian theology, this simple, innocent word "Father" has acquired a novel meaning. He is, according to Christianity, the One Who **BEGOT** the son Jesus. They say in their catechism[1] "Jesus is the very God of very God, **begotten** of the Father, **begotten** NOT made." If words have any meaning, what does this mean? Of course it means what is says! God has many sons according to the Holy Bible. Adam, Israel, Ephraim, David, Solomon, etc ... But all these are metaphorical sons. God Almighty as the Creator and Cherisher is metaphorically the father of His every creature; every animal or human being: but Jesus (pbuh), the Christians say, is not like these. He was **BEGOTTEN,** not **MADE!** This according to Islam is the most abominable utterance, attributing to God an animal nature — the lower animal function of sex!

MEANINGS CHANGE

In the beginning the word "Father" for God did not carry any blasphemous associations, but words do change in their meanings at times. I will give you just two as examples: **"Comrade"** and **"gay."**

> **"Comrade":** originally a beautiful and innocent word, meaning — a friend, an associate or a companion derived from the Old French **comrade,** roommate or soldier sharing the same room. But today the same word stinks in the nostrils of the Americans as a "commy", a communist, a member

---

1. Catechism: A short book giving, in question-and-answer form, a brief summary of the basic principles of a religion, especially Christianity.

of the Marxist-Leninist party, any radical viewed as a subversive or revolutionary who should be eliminated as a pest or parasite. If any foolish friend addresses you today as COMRADE in the United States, he could jeopardise your career, as well as your life!

"Gay:" What is wrong with this word? Nothing at all! I learnt this word in my early schooling as showing or characterised by **cheerfulness** and **light-hearted excitement;** a merry person. I was taught to sing —

"GENTLE LORDS AND LADIES GAY
ON THE MOUNTAIN DAWNS THE DAY."

I have forgotten the balance of the poem. Here, I understood the meaning of the word "gay" to mean **happy** and **joyous.** I did not have the slightest inkling that one day such an innocuous word which children learn at school would in time acquire a filthy, dirty meaning of being homosexual: sodomites and catamites in its very primary sense. So "LADIES GAY" would mean today — LADIES LESBIAN! In like manner the respectable word "Father" has become contaminated by the belief of — **"the only BEGOTTEN of the Father!"** etc.

RABB OR ABB?

God Almighty through Muhummed (pbuh) has protected Islam and the Muslims by keeping the word "Father" *(ABB)* for God, out of its religious vocabulary. It is a miraculous fact that though the Holy Qur'an lists ninety-nine attributes to God, including the word **RABB** which means — Lord, Cherisher, Sustainer, Evolver, etc, (this attribute **Rabb** occurs dozens of times in the Book of God) — But the easier word **Abb,** meaning "Father" in Arabic and in Hebrew, is not used even once, thus preserving the Muslims from the blasphemy of the only BEGOTTEN son! To whom must we give credit for this feat: Allah or Muhummed (pbuh)? The Holy Prophet (pbuh) disclaims any credit, always saying that all this is given to him by inspiration, the words ye hear are not his, they are **God's Word** as dictated to him!

CHAPTER SIX

Solving Controversy

The Holy Qur'an is one huge Miracle. It is a Book of Miracles which may be expounded from innumerable points of views. I have tried from some simple aspects to share with you that which I, as a layman was enthralled with. There is no end to this research. I leave this task to my more learned brethren, and the erudite scholars of Islam. May I live to see their efforts. Let me end with this, my final example, for this short publication.

CALL TO SWAZILAND

A few years ago, a controversy arose in Swaziland. King Sobuza lost his Queen elect. The Christian Churches in the country began quibbling on the subject of the period of waiting before a man can remarry. It was not such a serious problem for discussion because the King still had eight more wives. So the topic changed to **"How long must a woman wait if her husband dies."** As the debate was raging furiously in the tiny Kingdom, the benevolent King ordered a synod of all the Churches in the country to thrash out the problem.

Mr. Moosa Borman, a Swazi brother who had embraced Islam, sought permission from the King to have his "Church" (Islam) also represented in the debate. With the King's blessings, I too was honoured to attend the discussion.

One Sunday morning, in the King's kraal, representatives of the various denominations of Christianity gathered to arrive at some consensus on the period of widowhood.

Speaker after speaker delivered his discourse. God Almighty had gifted the African, each and everyone is a potential Billy Graham or Jimmy Swaggart!

At the end of each sermon the audience applauded enthusiastically. The next speaker came and he brushed off his predecessor with the expression **"paalish"** (meaning porridge), implying rubbish, garbage! and performed to resounding applause. From morning to evening the performance went on. Around 5 p.m. my turn came. With the volume of the Holy Qur'an you see on the cover of this booklet, in my hands, I began, "From morning till night, we have been fumbling for an answer, as to how long is a woman to wait before remarrying after the demise of her husband: and we have heard what the Old Testament says and what the New Testament says, **a-n-d** what the New Testament says and what the Old Testament says, but we have not yet got the answer! because the solution to our problem is in the —

"LAST TESTAMENT"

"The Last Testament' was a bombshell for the Christian priests and preachers. They had never heard the expression THE LAST TESTAMENT in their lives. "Quoting OLD and NEW, NEW, and OLD will not help because the answer is in the LAST TESTAMENT of God to mankind!" I brandished the Book above my head, and read only the English of the Holy Qur'an, chapter 2 verse 234. A reference which is very easy to remember — 2:234, just 2234!

> **If any of you die**
> **and leave widows behind,**
>
> **They shall wait**
> **concerning themselves**
> **four months and ten days:**
>
> **When they have**
> **fulfilled their term,**
> **there is no blame on you**

**if they dispose of themselves
in a just and reasonable manner.**

**And God is well acquainted
with what ye do.**

(SÚRA BAQARA)   Holy Qur'an 2:234

I asked the audience, "FOUR MONTHS AND TEN DAYS, do you need any interpretation!?" They all answered in chorus, "NO!", I explained to the learned clergy the wisdom behind the period of "four months and ten days." In the preceding verses, in this Last and Final Testament of God, we are told about the period of waiting after divorce:

**Divorced women shall wait
concerning themselves
for three monthly periods ...**

(SÚRA BAQARA)   Holy Qur'an 2:228

This is in order to see that the marriage conditionally dissolved was likely to result in an issue. Whereas in the case of widowhood an extra period of one month and ten days are prescribed. Very logical everyone will agree, but what is miraculous about all this? Any wise man could have guessed these 3 months period after divorce and 4 months and ten days after the demise of the husband. Muhummed's (pbuh) guess is as good as anybody else's! This is true, but the proof that all this healthy useful teaching is not Muhummed's (pbuh) handiwork is in the verse following the 4 months and ten days period:

**There is no blame on you
if ye make an
offer of betrothal
or hold it in your hearts.**

**God knows that ye cherish
them in your hearts:**

> But do not enter into
> a secret contract with
> them except in terms
> honourable,
>
> Nor resolve on the tie of
> marriage till the term
> prescribed is fulfilled.

(SÚRA BAQARA)   *Holy Qur'an 2:235*

GOD'S FINGERPRINT

"Do not resolve to the tying of the marriage knot till the fixed period of waiting is over." This is not Muhummed's (pbuh) cleverness! This is the Wisdom of the All-Wise God. The Omniscient Creator knows the weaknesses of his creatures. Man in his greed and cupidity will take unfair advantage of the poor distraught widow. She has just lost her backbone and support the breadwinner. She has a number of little mouths to feed and she has also perhaps lost her looks and value in the marriage market has diminished. She is likely to clutch at any straw. In her emotional, unsettled condition when a predator makes the proposal. In her haste and insecurity she might readily accept. The Master Psychologist (not Muhummed pbuh) is fully aware of, all the snares laid by men. Hence the warning — **"NO CONTRACT until the appointed term is fulfilled!"**

The **'iddat'** [1] after a divorce is three months. Here she is given an extra 40 days to regain her equilibrium and equanimity. In the meantime, if suggestions of marriage had come, she would have the opportunity of discussing the matter dispassionately with her friends and relatives. She could avoid the pitfalls of a hasty acceptance with a long drawn out and painful development.

---

1. **'Iddat':** period of waiting after divorce or after bereavement.

Did Muhummed (pbuh) think and work out all these ramifications in the desert fourteen hundred years ago? Alas, you give him too much credit! He is made to repeat again and again that the Qur'anic Wisdom is not of his making, **"It is no less than an inspiration sent down to him**[1] by his Benevolent Creator. If you still doubt his testimony then meet his challenge. He is made to say:

"SAY: IF THE WHOLE OF MANKIND AND JINNS WERE TO GATHER TOGETHER

قُلْ لَّبِنِ اجْتَمَعَتِ الْإِنْسُ وَالْجِنُّ

TO PRODUCE THE LIKE OF THIS QUR'AN,

عَلَى أَن يَأْتُوا بِمِثْلِ هٰذَا الْقُرْآنِ

THEY COULD NOT PRODUCE THE LIKE THEREOF,

لَا يَأْتُونَ بِمِثْلِهِ

EVEN IF THEY BACKED UP EACH OTHER WITH HELP AND SUPPORT."

وَلَوْكَانَ بَعْضُهُمْ لِبَعْضٍ ظَهِيرًا ۝

(SÚRA BANI ISRÁ-ÍL) Holy Qur'an 17:88

The world is challenged to produce a Book like the Holy Qur'an and has not produced one in fourteen centuries. The Arab Christians who boast a population of 15 million today, not to be out done, have produced the Christian gospels in Qur'anic style. They have plagiarised[2] the Holy Qur'an by stealing words and phrases and even the style, not forgetting the ***Bismillah!***[3] Every chapter of their most modern invention begins with the first verse of the Qur'anic Revelation. You have to see it to believe it. Here is a photostat of their new man-made "revelation".

---

1. Holy Qur'an 53:4

2. Plagiarise: To steal and use (the ideas or writings of another) as one's own.

3. The Formula — **"In the name of Allah, Most Gracious, Most Merciful,"** with which each chapter of the Holy Qur'an begins.

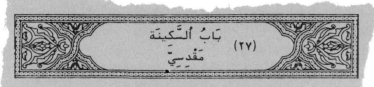

بِسْــــمِ اللَّهِ الرَّحْمَنِ الرَّحِيمِ

(١) قُلْ يَا أَيُّهَا الَّذِينَ آمَنُوا إِنْ كُنْتُمْ تُؤْمِنُونَ بِاللَّهِ حَقًّا

فَآمِنُوا بِيَ وَلَا تَخَافُوا إِنَّ لَكُمْ عِنْدَ اللَّهِ جَنَّاتٍ نُزُلًا (٢)

فَلَأُسْبِقَنَّكُمْ إِلَى اللَّهِ لِأُعِدَّهَا لَكُمْ ثُمَّ لَآتِيَنَّكُمْ نَزْلَةً أُخْرَى (٣)

وَإِنَّكُمْ لَتَعْرِفُونَ السَّبِيلَ إِلَى قِبْلَتِيَ الْعُلْيَا فَقَالَ لَهُ تُومَا

الْحَوَارِيُّ مَوْلَانَا إِنَّا لَا تَمْلِكُ مِنْ ذَلِكَ عِلْمًا (٤) فَقَالَ لَهُ

عِيسَى أَنَا هُوَ الصِّرَاطُ إِلَى اللَّهِ حَقًّا وَمِنْ دُونِي لَا تَسْتَطِيعُونَ

إِلَيْهِ سَبِيلًا (٥) وَمَنْ عَرَفَنِي فَكَأَنَّمَا عَرَفَ اللَّهَ وَهَأَنْتُكُمْ مُنْذُ

Here is another proof, if proof was needed that the Qur'an is inimitable. Try as you might. The challenge still stands. The Holy Qur'an is God's Word revealed to Muhummed (pbuh) **and it is the Miracle of Miracles!**

"AND A MIRACLE INDEED IT IS!"

Rev. Bosworth Smith